images

images

My Life in Film

Ingmar Bergman

Translated from the Swedish by
Marianne Ruuth

Introduction by
Woody Allen

Arcade Publishing • New York

FIRST ENGLISH-LANGUAGE EDITION

Originally published in Sweden by Norstedts Förlag, Stockholm, under the title *Bilder*

Library of Congress Cataloging-in-Publication Data

Bergman, Ingmar, 1918–2007
    [Bilder. English]
    Images : my life in film / Ingmar Bergman ; translated from the Swedish by Marianne Ruuth ; introduction by Woody Allen.
  — 1st English-language ed.
    p.   cm.
   ISBN 978-1-55970-186-0 (hc)
   ISBN 978-1-55970-293-5 (pb)
   1. Bergman, Ingmar, 1918–2007. I. Title.
  PN1998.3.B47A3   1994
  791.43'0233'092 — dc20   93-4759

Published in the United States by Arcade Publishing, Inc., New York
Distributed by Hachette Book Group USA

Visit our Web site at www.arcadepub.com

10 9 8 7 6 5 4 3 2

EB

PRINTED IN THE UNITED STATES OF AMERICA

My play opens with an actor walking down into the audience, where he strangles a critic, then reads aloud from a little black book all the humiliations he has noted therein. Then he throws up on the audience, after which he exits and puts a bullet through his head.

Workbook, July 19, 1964

NOTE

A number of Ingmar Bergman's films were released in the United States and Great Britain under different titles. In this book the first mention lists both titles wherever possible, with the British title appearing between parentheses. Subsequently, either title may be used.

Contents

Introduction

The Man Who Asked Hard Questions by Woody Allen 3

Dreams Dreamers 9

Wild Strawberries 11
Hour of the Wolf 25
Persona 44
Face to Face 66
Cries and Whispers 83
The Silence 104

First Movies 115

Torment (Frenzy) — Port of Call 117
The Devil's Wanton (Prison) 144
Three Strange Loves (Thirst) 154

Jests Jesters 159

The Magician (The Face) 161
The Ritual (The Rite) 173

The Naked Night (Sawdust and Tinsel)   184
The Serpent's Egg   190
From the Life of the Marionettes   209
After the Rehearsal   221

Miscreance Credence   229

The Seventh Seal   231
Through a Glass Darkly   243
Winter Light   257

Other Films   275

To Joy — Monika (Summer with Monika)   277
Shame (The Shame)   298
The Passion of Anna (A Passion)   304
Brink of Life (So Close to Life)   311
Autumn Sonata   326

Farces Frolics   337

The comedies —
Smiles of a Summer Night   339
The Magic Flute   350
Fanny and Alexander   360

Filmography   383

Introduction

THE MAN WHO ASKED HARD QUESTIONS

I GOT THE NEWS IN OVIEDO, a lovely little town in the north of Spain where I was shooting a movie, that Bergman had died. A phone message from a mutual friend was relayed to me on the set. Bergman once told me he didn't want to die on a sunny day, and not having been there, I can only hope he got the flat weather all directors thrive on.

I've said it before to people who have a romanticized view of the artist and hold creation sacred: In the end, your art doesn't save you. No matter what sublime works you fabricate (and Bergman gave us a menu of amazing movie masterpieces) they don't shield you from the fateful knocking at the door that interrupted the knight and his friends at the end of *The Seventh Seal*. And so, on a summer's day in July, Bergman, the great cinematic poet of mortality, couldn't prolong his own inevitable checkmate, and the finest filmmaker of my lifetime was gone.

I have joked about art being the intellectual's Catholicism, that is, a wishful belief in an afterlife. Better than to live on in the hearts and minds of the public is to live on in one's apartment, is how I put it. And certainly Bergman's movies will live on and will be viewed at museums and on TV and sold on DVDs, but knowing him, this was meager compensation, and I am sure he would have been only too glad to barter each one of his films for an additional year of life. This would have given him roughly sixty more birthdays to go on making movies; a remarkable creative output. And there's no doubt in my mind that's how he would have used the extra time, doing the one thing he loved above all else, turning out films.

Bergman enjoyed the process. He cared little about the responses to his films. It pleased him when he was appreciated, but as he told me once, "If they don't like a movie I made, it bothers me — for about thirty seconds." He wasn't interested in box office results, even though producers and distributors called him with the opening weekend figures, which went in one ear and out the other. He said, "By midweek their wildly optimistic prognosticating would come down to nothing." He enjoyed critical acclaim but didn't for a second need it, and while he wanted the audience to enjoy his work, he didn't always make his films easy on them.

Still, those that took some figuring out were well worth the effort. For example, when you grasp that both women in *The Silence* are really only two warring aspects of one woman, the otherwise enigmatic film opens up spellbindingly. Or if you are up on your Danish philosophy before you see *The Seventh Seal* or *The Magician*, it certainly helps, but so amazing were his gifts as a storyteller that he could hold an audience riveted and enthralled with difficult material. I've heard people walk out after certain films of his saying, "I didn't get exactly what I just saw, but I was gripped on the edge of my seat every frame."

Bergman's allegiance was to theatricality, and he was also a great stage director, but his movie work wasn't just informed by theater; it drew on painting, music, literature and philosophy. His work probed the deepest concerns of humanity, often rendering these celluloid poems profound. Mortality, love, art, the silence of God, the difficulty of human relationships, the agony of religious doubt, failed marriage, the inability for people to communicate with one another.

And yet the man was a warm, amusing, joking character, insecure about his immense gifts, beguiled by the ladies. To meet him was not to suddenly enter the creative temple of a formidable, intimidating, dark and brooding genius who intoned complex insights with a Swedish accent about man's dreadful fate in a bleak universe. It was more like this: "Woody, I have this silly dream where I show up on the set to make a film and I can't figure out where to put the camera; the point is, I know I am pretty good at it and I have been doing it for years. You ever have those nervous dreams?" or "You think it will be interesting to make a movie where the camera never moves an inch and the actors just enter and exit frame? Or would people just laugh at me?"

What does one say on the phone to a genius? I didn't think it was a good idea, but in his hands I guess it would have turned out to be something special. After all, the vocabulary he invented to probe the psychological depths of actors also would have sounded preposterous to those who learn filmmaking in the orthodox manner. In film school (I was thrown out of New York University quite rapidly when I was a film major there in the 1950s) the emphasis was always on movement. These are moving pictures, students were taught, and the camera should move. And the teachers were right. But Bergman would put the camera on Liv Ullmann's face or Bibi Andersson's face and leave it there and it wouldn't budge and time passed and more time and an odd and wonderful thing unique to his brilliance would happen. One would get sucked into the character and one was not bored but thrilled.

Bergman, for all his quirks and philosophic and religious obsessions, was a born spinner of tales who couldn't help being entertaining even when all on his mind was dramatizing the ideas of Nietzsche or Kierkegaard. I used to have long phone conversations with him. He would arrange them from the island he lived on. I never accepted his invitations to visit because the plane travel bothered me, and I didn't relish flying on a small aircraft to some speck near Russia for what I envisioned as a lunch of yogurt. We always discussed movies, and of course I let him do most of the talking because I felt privileged hearing his thoughts and ideas. He screened movies for himself every day and never tired of watching them. All kinds, silents and talkies. To go to sleep he'd watch a tape of the kind of movie that didn't make him think and would relax his anxiety, sometimes a James Bond film.

Like all great film stylists, such as Fellini, Antonioni and Buñuel, for example, Bergman has had his critics. But allowing for occasional lapses all these artists' movies have resonated deeply with millions all over the world. Indeed, the people who know film best, the ones who make them — directors, writers, actors, cinematographers, editors — hold Bergman's work in perhaps the greatest awe.

Because I sang his praises so enthusiastically over the decades, when he died many newspapers and magazines called me for comments or interviews. As if I had anything of real value to add to the grim news besides once again simply extolling his greatness. How had he influenced me, they asked? He couldn't have influenced me, I said, he was a genius and I am not a genius and genius cannot be learned or its magic passed on.

When Bergman emerged in the New York art houses as a great filmmaker, I was a young comedy writer and nightclub comic. Can one's work be influenced by Groucho Marx and Ingmar Bergman? But I did manage to absorb one thing from him, a thing not dependent on genius or even talent but something that can actually be learned and developed. I am talking about what is often very loosely called a work ethic but is really plain discipline.

I learned from his example to try to turn out the best work I'm capable of at that given moment, never giving in to the foolish world of hits and flops or succumbing to playing the glitzy role of the film director, but making a movie and moving on to the next one. Bergman made about sixty films in his lifetime, I have made thirty-eight. At least if I can't rise to his quality maybe I can approach his quantity.

WOODY ALLEN

Dreams Dreamers

IN AVAILABLE PHOTOS from the time, the four of us are neatly combed and smiling politely at one another. We are deeply involved in a book project to be called *Bergman on Bergman.* The idea was for three young journalists, armed to the teeth with detailed knowledge, to question me about my movies. The year was 1968, and I had just finished *Shame.*

As I leaf through that book today, I find it to be hypocritical. Hypocritical? That's right, hypocritical. My young interviewers were the bearers of the only true political conviction. They also knew that I had been left behind by the times, demeaned and scorned by the new aesthetics of the younger generation. And yet, I could never claim there was any lack of courtesy or attentiveness on their part. What I did not realize during our sessions was that they were little by little reconstructing a dinosaur piece by piece with the kind assistance of the Monster himself. In that book, I appear less than candid, always on my guard, and quite fearful. Even questions that are only slightly provocative are given short shrift. I take pains to give answers that might arouse sympathy. I plead for an understanding that, in any case, is impossible.

One of the three, Stig Björkman, is something of an exception. Since he was a talented movie director himself, we were able to speak in concrete terms on the basis of our respective professional backgrounds. Björkman was also responsible for what is good in the book: the rich and varied selection, and exquisite montage, of pictures.

I am not saying this curious project failed through any

fault of my interviewers. I had been looking forward to our encounters with childish vanity and excitement. I had imagined that I was going to open up and reveal myself in these pages, taking a well-deserved pride in my life's work. When, too late, I became aware that they were aiming for something quite different, I became unnatural and, as I said, both fearful and worried.

As it turned out, *Shame* (*The Shame* in Great Britain) was to be followed by many more years and many more films, until I decided in 1983 to "hang up" my camera. By then I was able to view my work as a whole and began to realize that I did not mind talking about my past. People were showing genuine interest in my films, not just to be polite or in order to attack me; since I had retired, I was guaranteed harmless.

Now and then my friend Lasse Bergström and I spoke about doing a new *Bergman on Bergman* book — one that would be more truthful, more objective. Bergström would ask the questions, and I would talk, and that would be the only similarity to the earlier book. We kept encouraging each other to do it, and all of a sudden we found ourselves going ahead with it.

What I had not been able to anticipate was that this act of looking back would, at times, turn into a murderous and painful business. *Murderous* and *painful* give a rather violent impression, but those are the best words I can find for it.

For some reason that had never occurred to me before, I have always avoided rescreening my old movies. Whenever I have had to do so or done so out of curiosity, I have been, without exception and no matter which film it was, nervous and upset, and have felt like going out to take a leak, like running to the toilet. I have been overwhelmed with anxiety, felt like crying, been afraid, unhappy, nostalgic, sentimental, and so on. Owing to this unfortunate conjunction of

◁ Wild Strawberries: *"Victor Sjöström's face, his eyes . . ."*

tumultuous feelings, I have, understandably, tended to avoid my movies. Still, I have felt kindly toward them, even the bad ones: I know that I did my best at the time and that each was in its own way truly interesting. (Listen and you will hear how interesting it was at the time!) So I set out to stroll for a while down the pleasantly lighted corridors of memory.

It therefore became necessary to look at my films again, and I thought: All that happened a long time ago. Now I'll be able to handle the emotional challenge. I'll be able to eliminate some of my works immediately. Let Lasse Bergström look at them by himself. After all, he's a film critic. He's seen his share of good and bad without becoming hardened.

Watching forty years of my work over the span of one year turned out to be unexpectedly upsetting, at times unbearable. I suddenly realized that my movies had mostly been conceived in the depths of my soul, in my heart, my brain, my nerves, my sex, and not the least, in my guts. A nameless desire gave them birth. Another desire, which can perhaps be called "the joy of the craftsman," brought them that further step where they were displayed to the world.

I would therefore have to account for their sources, their roots and origins, and remove from their files the blurred X rays of my soul. This process would be plausible with the

△

"The dreams were mainly authentic: the hearse that overturns with the coffin bursting open . . ."

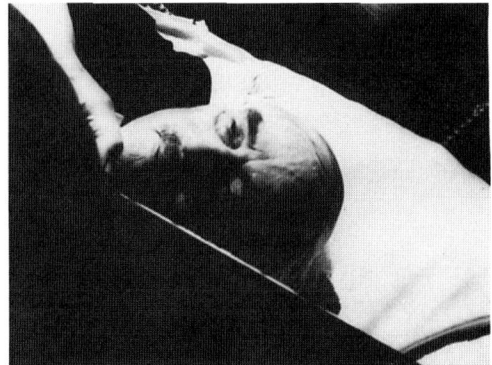

help of my notes and workbooks, as well as those of others; of memories recalled, newspaper articles, and especially with this seventy-year-old man's perceptive, astute, and comprehensive overview of, and objective relations to, a whole host of painful and half-suppressed experiences.

I was going to return to my films and enter their landscapes. It was a hell of a walk.

Wild Strawberries is a good example. With *Wild Strawberries* as a point of departure, I can show how treacherous and tricky my "now-experience" can be. Lasse Bergström and I saw the movie one afternoon in my movie theater on Fårö (Sheep Island). It was an excellent print, and I was deeply moved by Victor Sjöström's face, his eyes, his mouth, the frail nape of his neck with its thinning hair, his hesitant, searching voice. Yes, it was profoundly affecting! The next day we talked about the movie for hours. I reminisced about Victor Sjöström, recalling our mutual difficulties and shortcomings, but also our moments of contact and triumph.

I should add, in this connection, that my workbook for the *Wild Strawberries* screenplay has been lost. (I never save anything, out of superstition. Others have saved things for me.)

When later we read through the transcript of our taped conversations, we discovered that I had not said anything the least bit relevant about the way the film had been made. When I tried to recall the work process, it had totally disappeared. I only remembered — and dimly at that — that I had written the script at the Karolinska Hospital where I had been admitted for general observation and treatment. My friend Sture Helander was chief physician there, and I was given the opportunity to attend his lectures, which dealt with something as new and unusual as psychosomatic troubles. My room was small, and a writing desk had been fitted into it with some difficulty. The window faced north, and from it I could see for miles and miles.

My work year had been rather hectic; during the summer of 1956, we had made *The Seventh Seal.* Then I had directed three plays at the City Theater in Malmö: *Cat on a Hot Tin Roof, Erik XIV,* and *Peer Gynt,* the last of which premiered on March 8, 1957.

After that I spent almost two months in the hospital. The filming of *Wild Strawberries* began during the first part of July and finished on August 27, whereupon I returned immediately to Malmö to begin rehearsals of *The Misanthrope.*

I have only vague memories of that winter of 1956. And if I even try to take a few steps into that confusion, it hurts. A few fragments of a letter emerge suddenly from a lot of other letters of a very different kind. It was written by me as a New Year's greeting and addressed to my friend Helander.

> We begin to rehearse *Peer Gynt* after *Twelfth Night;* if my health were not so poor, it would be a great deal of fun. The whole troupe is in fine fettle and Max [von Sydow] will be magnificent, one can already see that. Mornings are the worst; I never wake up later than four-thirty — then my guts begin churning. At the same time my old anxieties begin, laying things

waste like a blowtorch. Exactly what those anxieties are I can't say. Perhaps I'm simply afraid of not being good enough. On Sundays and Tuesdays (the days when we don't rehearse), I feel a lot better.

And so on. The letter was never mailed. I guess I told myself that I was whining and that my whining was meaningless. I am not overly patient with either my own or other people's whining. The distinct advantage, as well as the disadvantage, of being the director is that you have nobody to blame but yourself. Almost everyone else has something or someone to blame. Not so with directors. They possess the unfathomable possibility of forging their own realities or fates or lives or whatever you want to call it. I have often found solace in that thought, bitter solace, and some vexation.

On closer consideration, and having taken yet another step into the dusky room of *Wild Strawberries*, within the camaraderie and the collective effort I find a negative chaos of human relations. The separation from my third wife was still a source of great pain. It was a strange experience to love someone with whom you could absolutely not live. My life with Bibi Andersson, a life filled with kindness and creativity, was beginning to crumble; why, I don't remember. I was feuding bitterly with my parents. I couldn't talk to my father and didn't even want to. Mother and I tried time and again for a temporary reconciliation, but there were too many skeletons in our closets, too many poisonous misunderstandings. We were making the effort, since we so wanted peace between us, but we kept failing.

I imagine that one of the most impelling forces behind *Wild Strawberries* could be found in that situation. I tried to put myself in my father's place and sought explanations for the bitter quarrels with my mother. I was quite sure I had

"*. . . a calamitous final examination in school, the wife who fornicates in public.*" ▷

been an unwanted child, growing out of a cold womb, one whose birth resulted in a crisis, both physical and psychological. Later, my mother's diary verified this notion of mine: faced with this wretched, almost dying child, she had feelings that were decidedly ambivalent.

In the course of some insignificant media event, I explained that only later had I discovered what the name of the leading character — Isak Borg — really meant. Like most statements made to the media, this is the kind of untruth that fits into the series of more or less clever evasions that create an interview. Isak Borg equals me. *I B* equals *Ice* and *Borg* (the Swedish word for *fortress*). Simple and facile. I had created a figure who, on the outside, looked like my father but *was me, through and through.* I was then thirty-seven, cut off from all human relations. It was I who had done the cutting off, presumably as an act of self-affirmation. I was a loner, a failure, I mean a complete failure. Though successful. And clever. And orderly. And disciplined.

I was looking for my father and my mother, but I could not find them. In the final scene of *Wild Strawberries* there is a strong element of nostalgia and desire: Sara takes Isak Borg by the hand and leads him to a sunlit clearing in the forest. On the other side he can see his parents. They wave to him.

One thread goes through the story in multiple variations: shortcomings, poverty, emptiness, and the absence of grace. I didn't know then, and even today I don't know fully, how through *Wild Strawberries* I was pleading with my parents: see me, understand me, and — if possible — forgive me.

In that earlier book I mentioned, *Bergman on Bergman*, I relate in some detail an early morning trip by car to the city of Uppsala. How, following a sudden impulse, I wanted to visit my grandmother's house at Trädgårdsgatan. How I had stood outside the kitchen door and, for a magical moment,

"Victor Sjöström was an excellent storyteller." ▷

experienced the possibility of plunging back into my childhood. That's a lie. The truth is that I am forever living in my childhood, wandering through darkening apartments, strolling through quiet Uppsala streets, standing in front of the summer cottage and listening to the enormous double-trunk birch tree. I move with dizzying speed. Actually I am living permanently in my dream, from which I make brief forays into reality.

In *Wild Strawberries* I move effortlessly and rather spontaneously between different planes — time-space, dream-reality. I cannot remember that the movement itself caused me any technical difficulties, this movement which later — in *Face to Face* — gave me such insurmountable problems. The dreams were mainly authentic: the hearse that overturns with the coffin bursting open, a calamitous final examination in school, the wife who fornicates in public (a scene which had already appeared in *The Naked Night (Sawdust and Tinsel)*).

The driving force in *Wild Strawberries* is, therefore, a desperate attempt to justify myself to mythologically oversized parents who have turned away, an attempt that was doomed to failure. It wasn't until many years later that my mother and father were transformed into human beings of normal proportions, and the infantile, bitter hatred was dissolved and disappeared. Then we were able to meet in a mood of affection and mutual understanding.

I had thus managed to forget why I made *Wild Strawberries*, and the times when I had to talk about it, I had nothing to say. It was an enigma that was slowly becoming rather interesting, at least to me.

Today I am convinced that if I forgot, if I erased all that, it had to do with Victor Sjöström. When we made the film, the age difference between us was considerable. Later on it was practically nonexistent.

"On the other side he can see his parents. They wave to him." ▷

From the very beginning, the artist Sjöström was overwhelming. He had made the movie that, to me, was the film of all films. I saw it for the first time when I was fifteen; to this day I see it at least once every summer, either alone or in the company of younger people. I clearly see how *The Phantom Carriage* has influenced my own work, right down to minute details. But that is a whole different story.

Victor Sjöström was an excellent storyteller, funny and engaging — especially if some young, beautiful woman happened to be present. We were sitting at the very source of film history, both Swedish and American. What a pity that tape recorders were not available at the time.

All these external facts are easy to recall. What I had not grasped until now was that Victor Sjöström took my text, made it his own, invested it with his own experiences: his pain, his misanthropy, his brutality, sorrow, fear, loneliness, coldness, warmth, harshness, and ennui. Borrowing my father's form, he occupied my soul and made it all his own — *there wasn't even a crumb left over for me!* He did this with the sovereign power and passion of a gargantuan personality. I had nothing to add, not even a sensible or irrational comment. *Wild Strawberries* was no longer my film; it was Victor Sjöström's!

It is probably worth noting that I never for a moment thought of Sjöström when I was writing the screenplay. The suggestion came from the film's producer, Carl Anders Dymling. And as I recall, I thought long and hard before I agreed to let him have the part.

AT FIRST I COULDN'T FIND my workbook for *Hour of the Wolf,*
but then, suddenly, there it was. At times, the demons can
be helpful. But you have to beware. Sometimes they will help
you along to hell.

The notes begin on December 12, 1962. The precise moment when I finished *Winter Light:*

> I am beginning this project in a kind of desperate
> enthusiasm and exhaustion. I was slated to go to Den-
> mark to write a synopsis for a film that would have
> made a million. Three days and three nights of panic,
> with accompanying spiritual and visceral constipation.
> Then I gave up. There are times when self-discipline,
> which is a good thing, becomes self-compulsion, which
> is totally harmful. After having written two pages and
> swallowed a box of laxatives, I gave up.

I have no memory of any of this. I do remember that I
once went to Denmark to write something. It is also possible
that it was a synopsis based on Hjalmar Bergman's novel *The
Boss, Mrs. Ingeborg,* a project Ingrid Bergman was very interested in doing. *

> It felt good to go home. The tension decreased, at
> least temporarily. The excursions into insecurity are

---

*The Swedish novelist Hjalmar Bergman lived from 1863 to 1931.
Hjalmar Bergman, Ingrid Bergman, and Ingmar Bergman were not related.

never very creative. One thing is clear, however. I am going to work on *My Shipwrecked Ones*. I will, without any obligations, find out if we really have something to say to each other or if everything is due to a misunderstanding or ultimately stems from my sole desire to be in pleasant shooting locations. Actually, the whole thing began with my longing to see the ocean. Torö (Thor's Island), to sit on a birch log and look at the waves for all eternity. Then, too, it must have been that long white sandy beach, completely unreal and yet so practical. Flat sand and the rolling ocean waves.

So I had better get to work. I know the following: The luxury liner went down in the middle of the masked ball near some group of deserted islands far out at sea. A number of people managed to swim to shore.

Everything has to be insinuated; nothing must be emphasized, nothing unraveled. The elements restrained, as in the theater. No realism. Everything has to be brilliantly clean, gentle, light, very eighteenth century, unreal, surreal, the colors never realistic.

△

Hour of the Wolf: *arriving at the island. Liv Ullmann and Max von Sydow.*

I am on my way into some kind of comedy:

> I believe that this will inevitably become an ambiguous division between wishes and dreams. Whole series of enigmatic personalities. They enter and disappear in most surprising ways, but this much is clear: He is not master of his characters. He loses them and finds them again.

Then I later wrote to myself:

> Patience, patience, patience, patience, patience, don't panic, take it easy, don't be afraid, don't get tired, don't immediately feel that everything is difficult. The time is long gone when you could dash off a screen-play in three days.

But here it has begun:

> Ah yes, my dear ladies, I saw a large fish, perhaps not a fish, perhaps more of an underwater elephant or perhaps a hippopotamus and a sea serpent that were copulating! I was by the Deep Place in the hollow of the mountainside where I sat, totally relaxed.

Then the Self becomes a bit more specific:

> I was one of the world's most prominent entertain-ment artists. As such, I went on the cruise. They had signed me on for a great deal of money. A time of calm and recovery at sea seemed to me an utterly delightful fantasy. . . .
> But, frankly, I am reaching an age when money is

no longer terribly important. I am alone now, with several marriages behind me. They have cost me a pretty penny. I have many children whom I know only superficially or not at all. My failures as a person are remarkable. Therefore, I put a lot of effort into being an excellent entertainer. I also want to mention that I am not an improvisational artist. I prepare my numbers painstakingly, almost pedantically. During my time on this island, after the shipwreck, I have jotted down several new ideas, which I hope to develop when I return to my studio.

December 27:

How goes my comedy? Oh yes, it has moved forward a little. Still the same old story about my Ghosts, friendly Ghosts, brutal, mean, joyous, stupid, unbelievably stupid, kind, hot, warm, cold, inane, anxious Ghosts. They are conspiring against me more and more, becoming mysterious, ambiguous, weird, and sometimes threatening. That's how it goes. I get a pleasant Companion who gives me different suggestive angles and whimsies. Slowly he begins to change, however. Becomes threatening and cruel.

Hour of the Wolf is seen by some as a regression after *Persona*. It isn't that simple. *Persona* was a breakthrough, a success that gave me the courage to keep on searching along unknown paths. For several reasons that film has become a more open affair than others, more tangible: a woman who is mute, another who speaks; therefore a conflict. *Hour of the Wolf*, on the other hand, is more vague. There is within that film a consciously formal and thematic disintegration. When I see *Hour of the Wolf* today, I understand that it is about a deep-

seated division within me, both hidden and carefully moni-
tored, visible in both my earlier and later work: Aman, in
The Magician (*The Face*); Ester, in *The Silence;* Tomas, in *Face
to Face;* Elisabet, in *Persona;* Ismael, in *Fanny and Alexander.*
To me, *Hour of the Wolf* is important since it is an attempt to
encircle a hard-to-locate set of problems and get inside them.
I dared take a few steps, but I didn't go the whole way.

Had I failed with *Persona*, I would never have dared to
make *Hour of the Wolf*. *Hour of the Wolf* is not a regression
but an unsteady step in the right direction.

In an etching by Axel Fridell, one can see a group of
grotesque cannibals ready to assault a little girl. They are all
waiting for a candle in a darkening room to flicker out. A
frail old man attempts to protect her. A real cannibal, dressed
in a clown's outfit, is waiting in the shadow for the candle to
burn down. Everywhere in the increasing darkness, one
glimpses frightening figures.

> Suggested final scene: I hang myself from a beam in
> the ceiling, something I have actually thought of
> doing for some time in order to become friends with
> my Ghosts. They are waiting for me, right beneath
> my feet. There will be a festive supper — after the
> suicide. The double doors are thrown open. Accom-
> panied by music (a pavane) I step inside, on the lady's
> arm, and proceed to the extravagantly set table.
>
> The Self has a mistress. She lives on the mainland
> but takes care of my household during the summer.
> She is tall and silent and serene. Together we sail
> across to the island; together we walk through the
> house; together we eat supper. During the dinner I
> hand her the housekeeping allowance. Suddenly she
> bursts out laughing. She has lost a tooth. The gap

shows when she laughs, which embarrasses her. I don't want to pretend that she is beautiful, but I like her company and we have lived together for five summers.

Winter Light represents, if you will, a moral victory and a departure. I have always been embarrassed by my need to please. My love for the audience has been rather complicated, with strong elements of my fear of not being liked. In my artistic self-solace has also been included a wish to give solace to my audience. Wait a minute! It isn't as bad as all that! My fear of losing some kind of power over people . . . my legitimate fear of losing my livelihood. The only thing is, sometimes one feels a compelling need to shoot blanks, to leave all the ingratiating stuff behind. At the risk of being forced into double compromises at some later date (the film industry is not especially considerate of its anarchists), it sometimes feels liberating to stand up and, without a gesture of apology or amiability, display an agonizingly human situation. The punishment would certainly be swift and sure. I still have the painful memory of the reception of *Sawdust and Tinsel*, my first attempt in that genre.

The departure is also one of theme. With *Winter Light* I dismiss the religious debate and render an account of the result. Perhaps it is of less importance to the viewers than to me. The film is the tombstone over a traumatic conflict, which ran like an inflamed nerve throughout my conscious life. The images of God are shattered without my perception of Man as the bearer of a holy purpose being obliterated. The surgery has finally been completed.

"The Cannibals" are waiting: Axel Fridell's etching ("The Old Curiosity Shop"/Little Dorrit) *and a scene from* Hour of the Wolf. ▷

These notes were written in 1962, sometime during the Christmas season. Then I heard nothing from my cannibals of *Hour of the Wolf* for almost two years.

When the Royal Dramatic Theater closed for the season on June 15, 1964, I realized I was completely exhausted. By then *The Silence* had opened and the people from whom my wife Käbi and I used to rent a house on Ornö Island did not want us anymore. They were of the opinion that nice tenants should not make obscene films. We had looked forward to a summer on the island — Käbi had worked very hard as well — to our arrival at that quiet, isolated place, which you can only reach by boat. Now we would have to remain in Djursholm the whole summer, and that was not a pleasant prospect. It was a horribly hot summer, and I settled into the guest room, which faced north and was somewhat cooler.

Ivar Lo-Johansson speaks about "the milkmaids' white whip." The white whip for those who manage theaters is to be forever reading plays. If we put on twenty-two plays during a season, that represents perhaps 10 percent of what the theater's managing director reads. To liberate myself from the various projects that endlessly filled my mind and from any thoughts about the upcoming theater season, I set about writing a screenplay, surrounding myself with music and si-

△

From the episode with Johan (Max von Sydow) and the small demon (Mikael Rundquist) in Hour of the Wolf.

lence, which awakened mutual aggressions between Käbi and me, since she was practicing on the grand piano in the living room. It developed into a sophisticated, acoustic terrorism. Sometimes I drove to Dalarö, where I sat on a cliff, gasping, looking out over the bay.

In that mood the writing of *The Cannibals* began:

> Like a dispirited angleworm, I pull myself out of the easy chair and go over to my worktable to try and write. I feel awkward and find the work repugnant. The table shivers and shakes with every damn letter I write. I have to change tables. Perhaps it would be better to stay in my easy chair, with a pillow on my lap. It's better, but it still isn't good. My pen is no damn good either. But the room is reasonably cool. I think I'll stay in the guest room after all. A summary: The story is about Alma. She is twenty-eight years old and has no children.

That's how the story about *The Cannibals* begins. I have turned the perspective around, so that all is seen from Alma's point of view.

If all this ends up being nothing but a game, delineated during a solemn study of one's reflection in a mirror, with a lot of uncalled-for vanity on the one hand, and a vague interest on the other, then it is meaningless. It is perfectly possible that it's meaningless anyway.

It is safe to say that it's no longer a comedy.

Exhaustion does not mean that you simplify but that you complicate; you sink your teeth into something and do too much. Every spare battery is connected and the revolutions are accelerated; the critical judgment is weakened; and the wrong decisions are made, since you are unable to make the right ones.

In *Hour of the Wolf* there is no trace of that exhaustion. And yet the film was made during the strenuous period when I was head of the Royal Dramatic Theater. The dialogue is crisp, a trifle too literary but not overly so.

For a moment I want to go back to the erotic theme; I am referring to a scene I think is well executed, namely, when Johan kills the little demon who has bitten him.

There is only one error: the demon should have been

naked! And to take it one step farther: Johan should have
been naked as well.

I was vaguely aware of this error while we were filming
that scene, but I didn't have the strength or the courage to
suggest it to Max von Sydow, the actor who played Johan.
Had both actors been nude, the scene would have been brutally clear. When the demon clings to Johan's back, trying to
bite him, he is crushed against the mountainside with or-
gasmic force.

Then: Why is Lindhorst* putting makeup on Johan before
Johan goes to the love tryst with Veronica Vogler? From the
beginning it is clear to us that their passion is a passion without emotion, an erotic obsession. We understand that in the
very first scene. Later Alma reads from Johan's diary, from
which one understands that his liaison with Veronica was a
disaster.

Lindhorst's makeup transforms Johan into a mixture of
clown and woman, and then he dresses him in a silk gown,
which makes him even more feminine. The white clowns have

*Archivist Lindhorst (George Rydeberg) is one of the characters Johan
encounters at the castle of Baron von Merken.

The demons in Hour of the Wolf. *Gertrud Fridh with Max von Sydow.
Ulf Johanson in the foreground. Naima Wifstrand. Ingrid Thulin as
Veronica Vogler with Johan (Max von Sydow) in makeup.* ▷

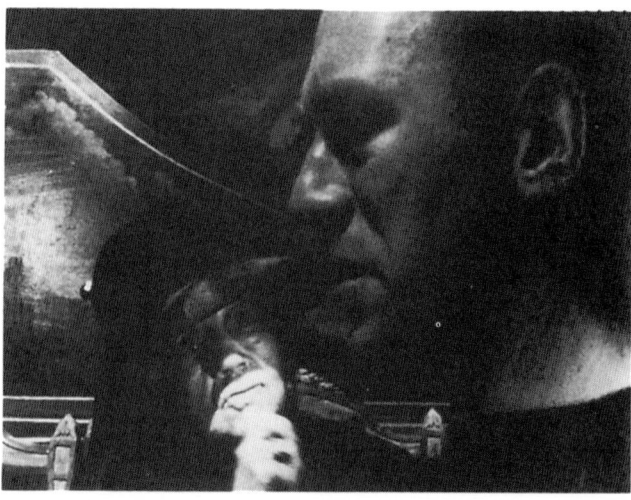

a multiple, ambiguous symbolism: they are beautiful, cruel, dangerous, balancing on the border between death and destructive sexuality.

The pregnant Alma represents that which is living, precisely as Johan describes it: "If I patiently sketched you day after day . . ."

There is no doubt that the demons, in a joking, decisive, and terrible manner, are separating Johan from Alma.

When Johan and Alma walk home from the castle in the windy dawn, she says: "No, I'm not going to run away from you, however afraid I may be. And one thing more: *They want to separate us.* They want to keep you to themselves, but if I'm with you, it will be much more difficult. They are not going to make me run away from you, however hard they try. I'll stay, I will. I'll stay as long as I . . ."

Then the fatal weapon is put between them, and Johan makes his choice. He chooses the dream of the demons instead of the palpable reality of Alma. Here I was setting forth on a problematic path that can ultimately be reached only through poetry or music.

There is no doubt that my upbringing was a fertile ground for the demons of neurosis.

I tried to clarify this point in *The Magic Lantern*.

> Most of our upbringing was based on such concepts as sin, confession, punishment, forgiveness, and grace, concrete factors in relationships between children and parents, between God and ourselves. There was an innate logic in all this, which we accepted and thought we understood.
>
> So punishment was something self-evident, never questioned. It could be swift and simple, a slap in the face or a smack on the bottom, but could also

be utterly sophisticated, refined through generations.

Major crimes reaped exemplary punishment: starting the moment the crime was discovered. The criminal confessed to a lower authority, that is, to the maids or Mother or one of the innumerable female relations living at our parsonage on various occasions.

The immediate consequence of confessing was that you were frozen out. No one spoke or replied to you. As far as I can make out, the idea was to make the criminal long for punishment and forgiveness. After dinner and coffee, the parties were summoned to Father's room, where interrogation and confessions were renewed. After that, the carpet beater was brought in, and you yourself had to declare how many blows you felt you deserved. When the punishment quota had been established, a hard, green cushion was fetched, trousers and underpants pulled down, you prostrated yourself over the cushion, someone held firmly onto your neck, and the blows were administered.

I can't claim that it hurt all that much. The ritual and the humiliation were most painful. My brother got the worst of it. Mother used to sit by his bed, bathing his back where the carpet beater had loosened the skin and streaked his back with bloody weals.

After the blows had been administered, you had to kiss Father's hand, at which point forgiveness was declared and your burden of sin fell away, being replaced by deliverance and grace. Though of course you had to go to bed without supper and evening reading, the relief was nevertheless considerable.

There was also a spontaneous kind of punishment that could be terrifying for a child who was afraid of

the dark: being locked in a special closet for various lengths of time. Alma in the kitchen had told us that in that closet lived a small creature that ate the toes of naughty children. I quite clearly heard something moving in there in the dark, and my terror was total. I don't remember what I did, probably climbed onto shelves or hung from hooks to avoid having my toes thus devoured.

All this comes back in *Fanny and Alexander*. But by then I had reentered the light of day and was able to depict it without a tremor of the hand, without being personally involved.

In *Fanny and Alexander* I could also do it with pleasure. In *Hour of the Wolf* there is neither distance nor objectivity. I simply experimented in a way that may be vital, but the spear was thrown randomly into the darkness. And the path of the spear is imprecise.

Earlier I was quick to downgrade *Hour of the Wolf*, probably because it did touch on so many suppressed aspects of my personality. While *Persona* possesses an intense light, an uninterrupted focus, *Hour of the Wolf* takes place in a land of twilight and also exploits elements that are new to me — romantic irony, ghosts — elements that the film plays with. I still find it funny when the baron without any difficulty rises to the ceiling and says, "Don't pay any attention to this; it's only because I'm jealous." I also feel a quiet joy when the old woman takes off her face and remarks, "Now I can hear the music better." After which she puts her eye into her glass of sherry.

During supper at the castle, the demons look normal, though somewhat incongruous. They stroll in the park; they converse; they put on the marionette theater performance. Everything is rather peaceful.

◁ *With Max von Sydow and Naima Wifstrand in the nighttime forest of* Hour of the Wolf.

But they are living the life of the doomed, in unbearable torment, eternally entangled in one another. They bite each other and eat each other's souls.

Their suffering is eased for a brief period: when *The Magic Flute* is performed in the small marionette theater. The music brings momentary peace and solace.

The camera moves over everyone's face. The rhythm of the text is a code: *Pa*-mi-*na* means *Love*. Does Love still live? *Pamina lebet noch*; Love still lives. The camera on Liv [Ullman]: a double declaration of love. At that time Liv was carrying our daughter, Linn. Linn was born the very day we filmed Tamino's entrance into the palace court.

Johan appears, transformed into a weirdly androgynous creature, and Veronica lies naked and allegedly dead on an autopsy table. He touches her in an endless gesture. She awakens, laughs, and begins to kiss him with small bites. The demons, who have been waiting for this moment, greatly appreciate the scene. One glimpses them in the background; they are sitting and lying on top of one another; a few have climbed up to the window and the ceiling. Then Johan says, "I thank you, the mirror is shattered, but what do the fragments reflect?"

I could not give an answer. Exactly the same words are said by Peter in *From the Life of the Marionettes*. When in his dream he discovers his wife lying murdered, he says, "The mirror is broken, but what do the fragments reflect?"

I still don't have a good answer.

"Their suffering is eased for a brief period: when The Magic Flute *is performed in the small marionette theater."* ▷

I BELIEVE THAT *Persona* is to a great degree connected to my activities as head of the Royal Dramatic Theater. That experience was like a blowtorch, forcing a kind of accelerated ripening and maturing. It clarified and solidified my relation to my profession in a brutal and unequivocal manner.

I had just finished *The Silence*, which lived on its own strength and vitality. The fact that immediately afterward I began shooting *All These Women* (*Now About These Women*) was a mark of my loyalty to the studio, Svensk Filmindustri. It was also further proof of my deplorable inability to hit the brakes when I ought to.

I was named managing director of the Royal Dramatic Theater at Christmas 1962. I should have immediately informed Svensk Filmindustri that we would have to shelve all film plans for the moment. But unfortunately, I felt it wasn't reasonable or possible to postpone making a film that had been so long in preparation.

With my death-defying optimism and incomprehensible love of work, I informed both the minister of education, who had presented me with the offer to head the national theater, and myself: That's fine. I can handle this.

On January 1, 1963, I became the newly appointed head of a theater in an advanced state of disintegration. There was no repertoire, no contracts with the actors for the upcoming season. Organization and administration were sadly lacking. The reconstruction of the theater building itself, which had moved forward in fits and starts, had been stopped altogether owing to lack of money. I found myself in an insoluble and incomprehensibly chaotic situation.

I soon found out that my duties were not limited to raising the artistic pulse and seeing to it that people came to the performances. It was a question of reorganizing the whole company from the bottom up.

No question: the work captivated me. The first year was strangely enjoyable. We had a great deal of luck. The red lights, proclaiming sold-out performances, were switched on, and the attendance figures soared. I was even able to cover the losses of the two superfiascos with which the season ended. The next year, during the same week in June, I opened Harry Martinson's *Three Knives from Wei* at the theater and premiered the film *All These Women*.

I returned to the Royal Dramatic Theater in the fall of 1964, and that year had two solid successes. I directed Ibsen's *Hedda Gabler* with Gertrud Fridh, and Molière's *Don Juan*. But the opposition had grown both inside and outside the theater. Toward the end of the season, the theater ensemble undertook a horrible trip to the inauguration of a new theater in the city of Örebros. People died or fell seriously ill. I myself had a fever of 102, despite which I went on the trip, ending up with double pneumonia and acute penicillin poisoning.

I was exhausted, but I tried to manage the theater anyway. Finally, in April, I was admitted to Sophiahemmet, the royal hospital, for proper care. And I began to write *Persona*, mainly to keep my hand in the creative process.

By that time, *The Cannibals* project had been canceled. Both Svensk Filmindustri and I saw how unrealistic it would be to try to direct such a major production during the summer. That meant there was a hole in the planned production for the year; one film was missing.

That's when I said, "Let's not give up hope. I'll try to make a movie after all. Possibly nothing will come out of it, but at least we can give it a try!"

Thus it was that in April of 1965 I began to take some notes, in the aftermath of my mishandled pneumonia, but this writing was also a result of the stink bomb attacks to which I had been subjected in the executive office of the theater. I was beginning to ask myself: Why am I doing this? Why do I care so much? Is the role of the theater finished? Has the mission of the art been taken over by other forces?

I had good reasons for thinking such thoughts.

It was not a case of developing an aversion to my professional life. Although I am a neurotic person, my relation to my profession has always been astonishingly non-neurotic. I have always had the ability to attach my demons to my chariot. And they have been forced to make themselves useful. At the same time they have still managed to keep on tormenting and embarrassing me in my private life. The owner of the flea circus, as you might be aware, has a habit of letting his artists suck his blood.

So I was convalescing at Sophiahemmet. Slowly I began to realize that my activities as director of Sweden's national theater were hindering my creativity. I had driven all my engines at top speed, and the engines had shaken the old body till it fell apart. So now it was necessary for me to write something that would dissipate the feeling of emptiness, of going nowhere. My emotional state was expressed quite clearly in an essay I wrote when I received the Dutch Erasmus Prize. I entitled it "The Snakeskin" and published it as a preface to *Persona:*

> Artistic creativity in me has always manifested itself as hunger. With quiet satisfaction I have acknowl-

"I have always had the ability to attach my demons to my chariot" (from the filming of The Magic Flute). ▷

edged this need, but I have never in my whole conscious life asked myself where this hunger has come from and why it kept demanding satisfaction. During these last few years, as the hunger begins to abate, I feel a certain urgency to seek out the very reason for my activity.

A very early childhood memory is my strong need to show off whatever I have accomplished; skill in drawing, the art of hitting a ball against a wall, my first strokes when I learned how to swim.

I remember that I had a strong desire to draw the adults' attention to these manifestations of my presence in the world. I felt that my fellow beings never paid enough attention to me. When reality no longer was enough, I began to fantasize, to regale my contemporaries with wild stories about my secret exploits. Those were embarrassing lies, which without fail broke into pieces against the surrounding world's sober skepticism. Finally I pulled out of the fellowship and kept my dream world to myself. A contact-seeking and fantasy-obsessed child had been rather quickly transformed into a wounded and sly daydreamer.

But a daydreamer is not an artist except in his dreams.

It was obvious that cinematography would have to become my means of expression. There I made myself understood through the language that I lacked, through music I had not mastered, and through painting which left me cold. Suddenly I had an opportunity to communicate with the world around me in a language that literally is spoken from soul to soul in expressions that, almost sensuously, escape the restrictive control of the intellect.

With all the pent-up hunger of the child I was, I threw myself at my chosen medium and for twenty years I have tirelessly, and in a kind of frenzy, supplied dreams, sense experiences, fantasies, insane outbursts, neuroses, cramped faith, and pure unadulterated lies. My hunger has endlessly renewed itself. Money, fame, and success have been surprising, but basically indifferent, consequences of my rampage. Having said that, I am in no way downgrading or negating what I have possibly accomplished. Art as self-satisfaction obviously has its value, especially to the artist.

So if I want to be completely honest, art (not just the art of the cinema) is for me unimportant.

Literature, painting, music, film, and theater give birth to and feed upon themselves. New mutations, new combinations occur and are destroyed; viewed from the outside the movement seems feverishly vital, nourished by the artists' unbridled eagerness to project to themselves and to a more and more distracted audience a world that has ceased to ask what they think. There are a few isolated places where the artists are punished, the arts themselves are considered risky and deserving of being suffocated or guided. Generally speaking, however, art is free, shameless, irresponsible, and as I said: its constant movement is intense, almost feverish; it resembles, in my opinion, a snake's skin full of ants. The snake is long since dead, emptied, deprived of its poison, but the skin moves, full of bustling life.

I hope and believe that others have a more balanced and allegedly objective opinion. If I raise all these tedious matters and if despite all I've said I claim I still want to create art, there is a very simple reason

(putting aside all the purely material motivations).

The reason is curiosity. A limitless, never satisfied, ever renewed, unbearable curiosity, drives me forward, never leaves me in peace; it has completely replaced my hunger for contact and fellowship of earlier times.

I feel like a prisoner who, after a long detention, suddenly stumbles out into the hurly-burly of life. I am in the grip of an uncontrollable curiosity. I note, I observe, I look everywhere; everything is unreal, fantastic, frightening, or ridiculous. I catch a speck of dust floating in the air; maybe it's the germ of a film — what does it matter? It doesn't matter, but I find it interesting, therefore I insist that it is a film. I come and go with this object that belongs to me, and I care for it with joy or sorrow. I push and am pushed by other ants; we are doing a colossal piece of work. The snakeskin moves. This, and only this, is *my* truth. I don't ask that it be true for anybody else, and as solace for eternity it's obviously rather slim pickings, but as a foundation for artistic activity for a few more years it is in fact enough, at least for me.

To be an artist for one's own sake is not always pleasant. But it has one enormous advantage: the artist shares his condition with every other living being who also exists solely for his own sake. When all is said and done, we doubtless constitute a fairly large brotherhood, which thus exists within a selfish community on our warm and dirty earth, beneath a cold and empty sky.

"The Snakeskin" was written in direct connection with the work on *Persona*. This can be illustrated by a note from April 29 in the workbook:

◁ Persona: *Elisabet Vogler (Liv Ullmann) and her nurse, Alma (Bibi Andersson).*

I will attempt to keep the following commands:

Breakfast at half past seven with the other patients.

Thereafter *immediately get up* and take *a morning walk.*

No *newspapers* or *magazines* during the aforementioned time.

No *contact* with the theater.

Refuse to receive *letters, telegrams, or telephone calls.*

Visits to home allowed during the evening.

I feel that the final battle is fast approaching. I must not postpone it further. I must arrive at some form of clarity. Otherwise Bergman will definitely go to hell.

It is clear from this passage that the crisis runs deep. I laid down for myself the same commandments when, later, I was trying to get back on my feet following the whole affair about my taxes.* Punctiliousness then became my way of surviving. From this crisis, *Persona* was born and grew:

*In January 1976, while Bergman was in the midst of a rehearsal, the Swedish police took him into custody for questioning about alleged tax irregularities. Charges were brought and subsequently dropped, but the incident had a shattering effect upon him. Three months later, he left Sweden for West Germany. "I can no longer live in a land where my honor is impugned," he declared. After nearly six years of self-imposed exile in West Germany, where he made three films, Bergman returned home to Sweden to make *Fanny and Alexander.*

With Sven Nykvist. ▷

So she has been an actress — one may give her that? Then she fell silent. Nothing remarkable about that.

I'll have to start with a scene in which the doctor tells nurse Alma what has taken place. That first scene is all-important. The patient and the person caring for her grow close together, like nerves and flesh. The only thing is, she refuses to speak. In fact, she doesn't want to lie.

This is one of the first notes in my workbook, dated April 12. Something else is also written there, something I did not act upon but which still has to do with *Persona*, especially with the title. "When nurse Alma's fiancé visits her, she *hears* for the first time how he speaks. She notes how he touches her. She becomes frightened, since she sees that he behaves as if he were acting a part."

When you bleed, you feel bad, and then you don't act.

It was an extremely difficult period of my life. I had a feeling that a threat was hanging over my head:

Could one make this into an inner happening? I mean, suggest that it is a composition for different voices in the same soul's concerto grosso? Anyhow, the time and space factors must be of secondary significance. One second must be able to stretch itself out over a long period of time and contain a handful of lines strewn without any apparent connection.

This problem is evident in the completed film. The actors move in and out of rooms without transfer distances. Whenever suitable, an occurrence is prolonged or shortened. The conception of time is suspended.

Then a note follows that goes far back into my childhood:

> I imagine a white, washed-out strip of film. It runs
> through the projector and gradually there are words
> on the sound tape (which perhaps runs beside the
> film strip itself). Gradually the precise word I'm look-
> ing for comes into focus. Then a face you can barely
> make out dissolves in all that whiteness. That's Alma's
> face. Mrs. Vogler's face.

When I was a boy, there was a toy store where you could buy
used film. It cost five öre [about one penny] a yard. I put
thirty or forty yards of the film into a strong soda solution
and let the pieces soak for half an hour. The emulsion dissolved and the layer of images disappeared. The strips of
film became white, innocent, transparent. Pictureless.

With different colored india inks I could now draw new
pictures. When Norman McLaren's directly drawn films appeared after the war, it was no news to me. The strip of film
that rushes through the projector and explodes in pictures
and brief sequences was something I had carried around with
me for a long time.

Throughout most of the month of May I still had attacks
of fever:

> All this weird fever and all these solitary reflections.
> I have never had it so good, and so bad. I believe
> that if I really tried, I might perhaps attain some-
> thing unique, something I had been unable to reach
> earlier. A transformation of the themes. Something
> simply happens and without anyone asking how it
> happens.

56

Alma is learning to know herself. Through Mrs. Vogler, nurse Alma is off in search of herself.

Alma tells a long, totally banal story about her life and her great love for a married man, about her abortion and about Karl Henrik whom she really doesn't love, and who was a disappointment in bed. Then she drinks some wine, lets herself go, starts crying, and sobs in Mrs. Vogler's arms.

Mrs. Vogler is full of sympathy. The scene goes on from morning to noon, from evening to night, and on to morning. And Alma is becoming increasingly attached to Mrs. Vogler.

I think it's a good thing that at this point different documents exist, for instance, the letter from Mrs. Vogler to Dr. Lindkvist. Which is filled with light-hearted banter but also contains, on a humorous note, a funny but harsh portrait of nurse Alma's character.

I pretend that I'm an adult. I am constantly astonished that people take me seriously. I say: I want this and I would like that. . . . They listen respectfully to my points of view, and often they do what I tell them. Or even praise me for being right. As for me, I never think that all these people are children who *act* at being adults. The only difference is that they have forgotten or never think about the fact that they are actually children.

My parents spoke of *piety*, of *love*, and of *humility*. I have really tried hard. But as long as there was a God in my world, I couldn't even get close to my goals. My humility was not humble enough. My love remained nonetheless far less than the love of Christ or

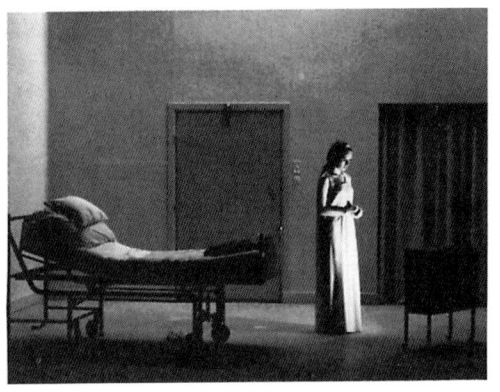

of the saints or even my own mother's love. And my piety was forever poisoned by grave doubts. Now that God is gone, I feel that *all this* is mine; *piety* toward life, *humility* before my meaningless fate, and *love* for the other children who are afraid, who are ill, who are cruel.

The following was written on Ornö in May. I am getting close to the gist and core of both *Persona* and "The Snakeskin":

> Mrs. Vogler desires the truth. She has looked for it everywhere, and sometimes she seems to have found something to hold on to, something lasting, but then suddenly the ground has given way under her feet. The truth had dissolved and disappeared or had, in the worst case, turned into a lie.
>
> My art cannot melt, transform, or forget: the boy in the photo with his hands in the air or the man who set himself on fire to bear witness to his faith.
>
> I am unable to grasp the large catastrophes. They

△
The outer world intrudes on Elisabet Vogler in her sickroom.

leave my heart untouched. At most I can read about such atrocities with a kind of greed — a pornography of horror. But I shall never rid myself of those images. Images that turn my art into a bag of tricks, into something indifferent, meaningless. The question is whether art has any possibility of surviving except as an alternative to other leisure activities: these inflections, these circus tricks, all this nonsense, this puffed-up self-satisfaction. If in spite of this I continue my work as an artist, I will no longer do it as an escape or as an adult game but in the full awareness that I am working within an accepted convention that, on a few rare occasions, can give me and my fellow beings a few seconds of solace or reflection. The main task of my profession is, when all is said and done, to support me, and, as long as nobody seriously questions this fact, I shall continue, by a pure survival instinct, to keep working.

"Then I felt that every inflection of my voice, every word in my mouth, was a lie, a play whose sole purpose was to cover emptiness and boredom. There was only

60

one way I could avoid a state of despair and a breakdown. To be silent. And to reach behind the silence
for clarity or at least try to collect the resources that
might still be available to me."

Here, in the diary of Mrs. Vogler, lies the foundation
of *Persona*. These were new thoughts to me. I had never
foreseen that my activities had a direct relation to society
or to the world. *The Magician* — with another silent Vogler
in the center — is a playful approach to the question, nothing
more.

On the final pages in the workbook appears the decisive
variation:

After the major confrontation, it is evening, then
night. When Alma falls asleep or is on the verge of
falling asleep, it is as if someone were moving in the
room, as if the fog had entered and made her numb,
as if some cosmic anxiety had overwhelmed her, and
she drags herself out of bed to vomit, but can't, and
she goes back to bed. Then she sees that the door to
Mrs. Vogler's bedroom is partly open. She enters
and finds Mrs. Vogler unconscious or seemingly dead.
She is frightened and grabs the telephone, but there
is no dial tone. She returns to the dead woman,
glancing slyly at her, and suddenly they *exchange per-
sonalities*. This way, exactly how I don't know, she
experiences, with a fragmentary sharpness, the condition of the other woman's soul, to the point of ab-
surdity. She meets Mrs. Vogler, who now is Alma and
who speaks with her voice. They sit across from each
other, they speak to each other with inflections of
voice and gestures, they insult, they torment, they

hurt one another, they laugh and play. It is a *mirror scene*.

The confrontation is a monologue that has been doubled. The monologue comes, so to speak, from two directions, first from Elisabet Vogler, then from nurse Alma.

Sven Nykvist and I had originally planned a conventional type of lighting on Liv Ullmann and Bibi Andersson. But it didn't work. We then agreed to keep half of their faces in complete darkness — there wouldn't even be any leveling light.

From there on it was a natural evolution, in the final part of the monologue, to combine the two illuminated halves of their faces, to let them float together to become *one* face.

In most people one side of the face is more attractive than the other, their so-called good side. The half-illuminated images of Liv's and Bibi's faces that we combined into one showed their respective bad sides.

When I received the double-copied film from the laboratory, I asked Liv and Bibi to come to the editing room.

Bibi exclaims in surprise: "But Liv, you look so strange!" And Liv says: "No, it's you, Bibi, you look very strange!" Spontaneously they denied their own less-than-good facial half.

The screenplay for *Persona* does not look like a regular scenario.

When you write a scenario, you are anticipating the technical challenges as well. You are, so to speak, writing the score. Then all you have to do is put the music on the stands and let the orchestra play.

I cannot arrive at the soundstage or the exterior location and assume that "things will fall into place one way or

"From there on it was a natural evolution, in the final part of the monologue, to combine the two illuminated halves of their faces, to let them float together to become one *face."* ▷

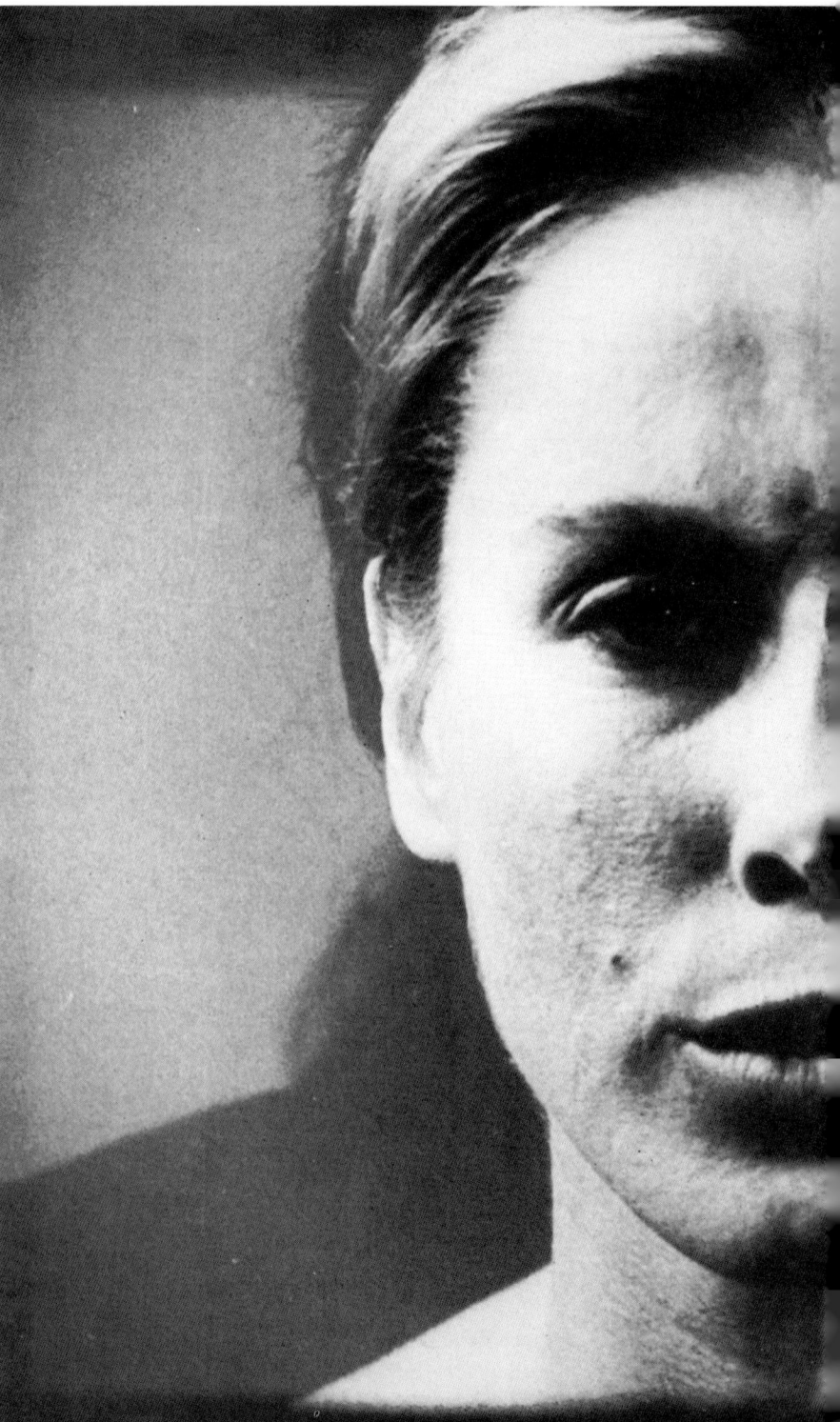

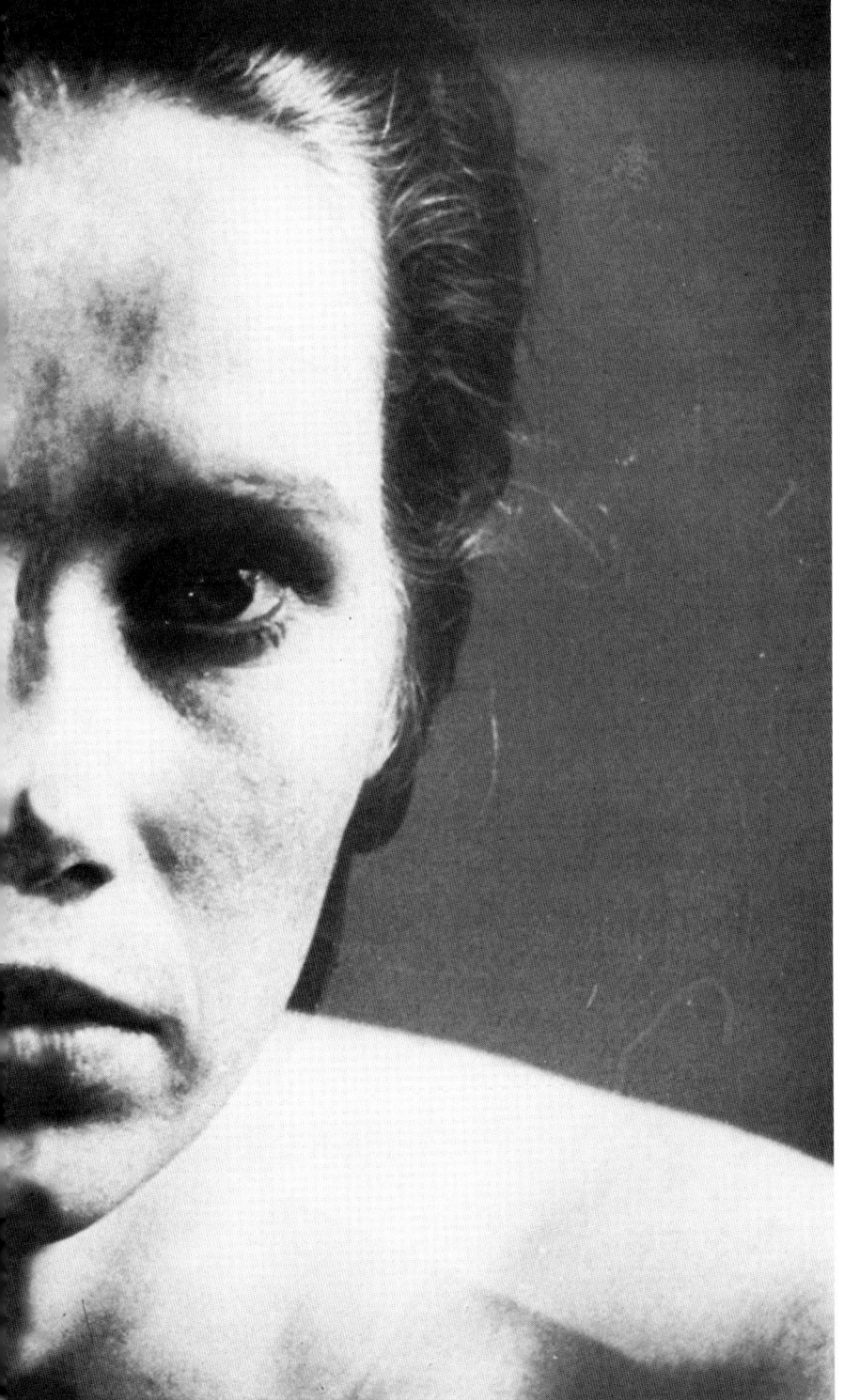

another." You cannot improvise on an improvisation. I dare to improvise only if I know that I will be able to go back to a carefully constructed plan. I cannot trust that inspiration will strike when I get to the set.

When you read the script of *Persona*, it may look like an improvisation, but it is painstakingly planned. Nonetheless I have never shot as many retakes during the making of any other film. When I say retakes I do not mean repeated takes of the same scene the same day. I mean retakes that are a consequence of my seeing the previous day's rushes and not being satisfied with what I saw.

We began filming in Stockholm and got off to a bad start.

But, slowly and squeakingly, we cranked it out. Suddenly I enjoyed saying: "No, let's do it better, let's do it this way or that, and here we could do it a bit differently." Nobody ever became upset. Half the battle is won when nobody starts feeling guilty. The movie also naturally profited from the strong personal feelings that emerged during the filming. It was in short a happy set. In spite of the grueling work, I had a feeling that I was working with complete freedom both with the camera and with my collaborators, who followed my every twist and turn.

When I returned to the Royal Dramatic Theater in the fall, it was like going back to the slave galley. What a difference between the meaningless, stressful administrative work at the theater and the freedom I had experienced filming *Persona!* At some time or other, I said that *Persona* saved my life — that is no exaggeration. If I had not found the strength to make that film, I would probably have been all washed up. One significant point: for the first time I did not care in the least whether the result would be a commercial success. The gospel according to which one must be comprehensible at all costs, one that had been dinned into me ever since I worked as the lowliest manuscript slave at Svensk Filmindustri, could finally go to hell (which is where it belongs!).

Today I feel that in *Persona* — and later in *Cries and Whispers* — I had gone as far as I could go. And that in these two instances, when working in total freedom, I touched wordless secrets that only the cinema can discover.

I WRITE IN *The Magic Lantern:*

> *Face to Face* was intended as a film about dreams and
> reality. The dreams were to become tangible reality.
> Reality would dissolve and become dream. I have oc-
> casionally managed to move unhindered between
> dream and reality: *Wild Strawberries, Persona, The Si-
> lence, Cries and Whispers*. This time it was more difficult.
> My intentions required an inspiration which failed
> me. The dream sequences became synthetic, the real-
> ity blurred. There are a few solid scenes here and
> there, and Liv Ullmann struggled like a lioness. Her
> strength and talent held the film together. But even
> she could not save the culmination, the primal scream,
> which amounted to an enthusiastic but ill-digested
> fruit of my reading. Artistic license sneered through
> the thinly woven fabric.

But the case of *Face to Face* is more complicated than that.
In *The Magic Lantern*, I dismiss it briefly and lightly. Earlier
on I simply dismissed it or declared it an idiot. That in itself
is slightly suspicious.

Now I see it like this: From the beginning and up to the
main character's attempted suicide, *Face to Face* is perfectly
acceptable. The story is clearly told, though rather compressed. There are no real weaknesses in the material itself.
If the second part had maintained the same level as the first,
the film would have been saved.

My workbook, dated April 13, 1974:

> So now I have completed *The Merry Widow*. It was with great relief that I dismissed the troublesome lady (Streisand). I have also said good-bye to the film about Jesus. Too long, too many togas, too many quotations. What I long for now is to walk along my own path. At the theater I always follow others' paths; when it comes to my films I want to be myself.
>
> This is a feeling that grows stronger and stronger. As is the desire to force my way into the secrets beyond the walls of reality. To find a maximum expression with a minimum of external gestures. And yet, on this subject I have to say something that I must tell myself is extremely important: I do not want to follow beaten paths. I still maintain that in the context of that technique *Cries and Whispers* goes as far as one can go.

I also write that I look forward to the filming of *The Magic Flute*, which is imminent. "Let's see if I feel the same way in July."

> Technically speaking, there is the pleasant notion of constructing a single, strange room in the studio at Dämba and thus, through varying transformations of the human beings who are moving within it, depict the past. And there is also the secret person behind the tapestry in the other room. The person who affects what happens as well as what does not happen. The one who is there and yet is not!

That thought had haunted me for a long time: Behind the wall or the tapestry would be a powerful, hermaphroditic creature, controlling whatever was happening in the magic room.

At that time the small soundstage at Dämba, where we had filmed *Scenes from a Marriage*, still existed. It was pleasant and practical. We lived and worked on Fårö Island. The process of minimizing, of simplifying, has always been stimulating to me. So I imagined that we would shape the film within the very limited confines of the soundstage.

After that, nothing is written in my workbook until July 1:

> So now the filming of *The Magic Flute* is finished. It has been a remarkable period of my life. This joy, this proximity to the music every day! All the affection and tenderness I encountered.
>
> It was almost so that I did not notice how heavy and complicated it had become: except for the fact that I kept getting colds, yes, it has become a real neurosis. It has cast a shadow over my existence, and there were times when I thought I wasn't completely sane.

Back at Fårö I began cautiously to outline *Face to Face:*

> She has sent the children abroad. The husband is on a business trip. The house they live in is being re-modeled. So she moves into her parents' apartment on Strandvägen, beyond the Djurgårds Bridge, near the Oscar Church. She thinks she'll be here for some time and get a lot of work done. Our heroine is especially looking forward to being by herself in the summer city and to thinking about herself and her own work without distraction.
>
> The danger of not feeling loved, the fear that comes with the insight that one is not loved, the pain in not

being loved, the attempt to forget that one is not loved.

Then some time goes by. This is written more or less in mid-August:

> What if one turned the picture upside down? The dreams are reality, the reality of the days' events the unreal: the silence of a summer day in the streets around Karla Square. Sunday, with its desolate ringing of church bells, the twilight hours, filled with morbid longings, slightly feverish. And then the light in the large, empty apartment.

Here it begins to come together:

> Seven dreams with small islands of reality! The distance between body and soul, the body being something alien. Keeping body and emotions separate. The dream of humility, the erotic dream, the melancholy dream, the horror dream, the funny dream, the annihilation dream, the dream of the mother.

Then I suddenly imagine the whole thing as a masquerade. On September 25 I write:

> Hesitation and confusion greater than ever — or have I simply forgotten how it usually is? A lot of irrelevant viewpoints obviously mingle with my reasoning, views that I don't even want to think about since I find them so embarrassing.

Slowly I begin to understand that thanks to this film, and a screenplay that offers me stubborn resistance, I am trying to reach certain complications within myself. My reluctance when it comes to *Face to Face* probably stems, at least superficially, from the fact that I am touching on a number of my own inner conflicts without reaching or unmasking them. But at the same time I have sold out something important and have failed. Painfully, I was moving in on it. I have made a gigantic effort to bring something complicated into the light of day. It's one thing to work on a screenplay. It takes place between yourself, your pen, your piece of paper, and a span of time. It's an entirely different matter when you stand there in front of the whole immense machinery.

Suddenly the film *as it ought to have been* emerges from my workbook:

> She sits on the floor in her grandmother's apartment, and the statue moves in the sunshine. On the stairs she meets a large dog that bares its teeth. Then her husband arrives. He is dressed as a woman. She goes looking for a doctor. She is a psychiatrist herself and says that "she doesn't understand this particular dream in spite of having understood everything that has happened to her over these last thirty years." Then the old lady raises herself from her enormous, dirty bed and looks at her with her one, ailing eye. But grandmother and grandfather hug each other, and grandmother caresses grandfather's cheeks and whispers tender words to him in spite of his not being able to utter more than a few isolated syllables.
>
> But behind all this, behind the drapes, a whispered conversation is carried on about what ought to be done with her sexually, perhaps a widening of her anal opening. And at the same moment She appears, the Other, who takes such things lightly and caresses

Liv Ullmann and Erland Josephson in Face to Face. ▷

her in all sorts of ways. It is unexpectedly pleasant. But now somebody arrives and asks for her help, really pleads with her, somebody in a desperate situation. She throws a tantrum, followed by an anxiety attack, because the tension is not lessening. But, in spite of everything, it's a relief to plan and carry out that murder of Maria she has been thinking about for so long. Although afterward it will be even more difficult to find someone who will care for me and tell me not to be afraid. And if I change my clothes completely and go to a party, everybody must see and understand that I am innocent and cast their suspicions on somebody else.

But in the room with the candelabras everybody is masked, and suddenly they begin to dance a dance she doesn't know, a pavane.

Somebody says that several of those who are dancing are dead and have come to honor the festivities with their presence. The tabletop is black and shiny. She leans her breasts against the top of the table and sinks slowly downward as somebody licks her whole body, especially between her legs. It doesn't distress her but on the contrary fills her with a feeling of pleasure. She laughs, and a dark-haired girl with large red hands lies down on top of her. Beautiful music from a piano that's out of tune. Just then the door opens, the wide, old-fashioned double door, and her husband enters, along with several policemen, and accuses her of murdering Maria. Then she speaks passionately in her own defense, sitting naked on the floor in the oblong, drafty room. The one-eyed woman raises her hand and places a finger to her lips in a commanding gesture that calls for silence.

That's how *Face to Face* should have been made.

If I had had the experience I have today and the strength I had then, I would have translated this material into practically feasible solutions and not hesitated for a moment.

It would have been a sacrosanct cinematographic piece of poetry.

To me, this is not a continuation of the line from *Cries and Whispers*. It goes far beyond *Cries and Whispers*. Here, finally, all forms of storytelling are dissolved.

Instead the daily grind of the screenplay goes on, and the story takes shape. The first half is falling nicely into place. The only thing left is the woman with the blind eye.

October 5:
> Could lament forever and ever about pleasure and displeasure, about difficulties and adversities and about boredom, but I will not. I think that I have never been more disinclined and hesitant than I am now! Perhaps I am in touch with a sorrow that wants to appear. Where does it come from? What is it made up of? Is there anyone in the world who has it as good as I do?

My repulsion and my unwillingness, needless to say, stem from the fact that I have betrayed my idea, and I keep jumping from one treacherous ice floe to another.

Sunday, October 13:
> Great discouragement, which changes into determination. I feel as if, at the end of this, which is slavery, the real film is hiding. If I push and pull and bluff my way through, perhaps I will haul it out of the darkness, and then it will have been worth the trouble.

There is no doubt that there exists a huge shout trying to find its voice. Then the question is whether I have the ability to release the shout, to set it free.

And this, too, dated October 20:

Will I be able to get close to the point where my own despair is hiding, where my own suicide lies in wait? I don't know.

This is the true birth: hold me, help me, be kind to me, hold me tight, hold me tight, why isn't there anybody who cares about me? Why is nobody holding my head? It is far too big. Please, I am freezing, I can't go on like this. Kill me again, I don't want to live, it can't be true, look how long my arms are, and emptiness is everywhere.

The person crying out isn't Jenny!

On November 1, I write: "Today I finished writing the whole script for the first time. Came right through it and out on the other side." Then I begin all over again, rereading, correcting, rewriting.

November 24:

Today we are going to Stockholm. So begins the second act, the one focused on the outside world; I can't say that I'm looking forward to it with great impatience. I am going to meet with Erland [Josephson] and see what he has to say. I hope he'll be candid. If he thinks I should abandon this project, I will. It's pointless to throw myself into some big, expensive project when my desire is zero. I am also worried about *Twelfth Night*. This time I'm getting into something I have never tried before, and it feels difficult,

◁ *The primal scream. Liv Ullmann.*

if not impossible. I wonder if it's not simply that my body and soul are saying "no" after a long period of intense activity; that may well be. Everything is fluid; everything is diffuse. As for me, I am filled with malaise. At the same time I am well aware that a large percentage of this malaise stems from my difficulty in getting started, my fear of people, fear that it won't be any good, fear of life, of moving at all.

Then came the period when I was working on *Twelfth Night* at the Royal Dramatic Theater.

March 1, 1975:
Returned to Fårö Friday. The premiere of *Twelfth Night* went very well, and the reviews were for the most part tremendous. Rehearsals went exceedingly quickly. It was like a real party. Made a point of not dealing with *Face to Face* during this whole time except when it was absolutely necessary. I'm going to concentrate on rewriting the dreams.

Monday, April 21:
Today is the last day at Fårö. Tomorrow we leave for Stockholm, and the following Monday we start filming. It actually feels good, apart from my usual anguish. I even have the impression it's going to be fun, a kind of challenge. In other words, desire. That terrible depression that followed the writing of the screenplay has disappeared altogether. It was almost

like an illness. The trip to the United States was also stimulating. And good for our finances. We can look to the future with confidence.

July 1:

Have just returned to Fårö after having finished shooting. Actually it went terribly fast. All of a sudden we were halfway through, all of a sudden there were only five days left, and then all of a sudden it was finished, and we all met at the Stallmästaregården Restaurant to celebrate, complete with speeches and cigars and nostalgia and confused feelings. I don't really know how it went. With *The Magic Flute*, we all knew it was good. Here I know nothing. Toward the end I felt completely exhausted. Anyhow, now it's over. Liv asked me what I thought. I said, I think it's fine.

When we were in the United States, Dino De Laurentiis asked me: "Are you doing anything I could have?" I heard myself answer, "I'm making a psychological thriller about the breakdown of a human being and her dreams." "It sounds great," he said. So we signed a contract.

This should have been a happy period of my life. I had *The Magic Flute* behind me, as well as *Scenes from a Marriage* and *Cries and Whispers*. I was successful at the theater. Our little company was producing the films of other directors, and the money was flowing in. It was precisely the right time to tackle a difficult task. My artistic self-confidence was as high as it's ever been. I could do whatever I wanted, and anyone and everyone was willing to finance my efforts.

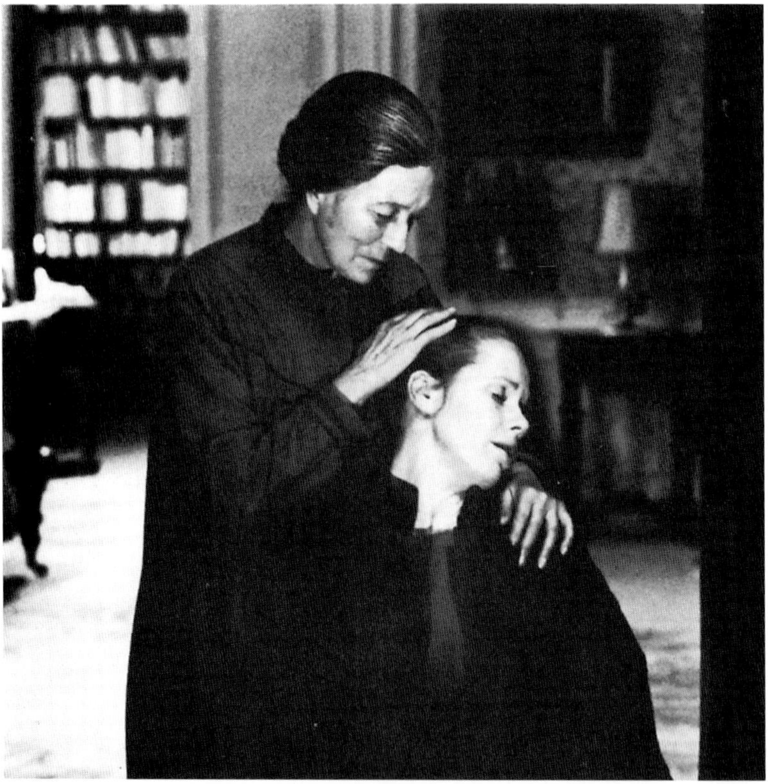

During the filming of *Face to Face* everybody was very enthusiastic, and that of course is all-important. Nobody seemed to care that I kept remaking the dreams incessantly, changing them and moving them around. I even stuck in my old Fridell etching with snow on the furniture and the little girl who stands there holding the candle that illuminates the terrible clown.

Two short dream sequences strike me as acceptable. One is when the lady with one eye comes over to Jenny and strokes her hair. The other one, which at least is honestly thought out, is Jenny's brief encounter with her parents after the automobile accident. From the viewpoint of direction, it's a rather good scene. They crawl behind the Dutch-tiled stove and start to cry when Jenny hits them. But in one way the scene is poorly directed: Jenny should have remained completely calm rather than acting in the same way as her parents do. I did not understand that at the time. Still, a concrete dream atmosphere does exist at this point.

All the rest is forced. I am roving erratically in exactly what I warn against in my foreword to the screenplay: a landscape of clichés.

Deep inside a yellow cardboard box, I am hiding a terrible little short story. I wrote it during the 1940s. A boy is in his grandmother's apartment; it is night, and he can't seem to fall asleep; two tiny people emerge and run across the floor. He catches one and crushes it with his hand. It's a little girl. The story is about childish sexuality and childish cruelty. My sister insists with emphatic stubbornness that my dark closet originated in Uppsala. It was Grandma's special method of punishment, not that of my parents. If ever I was locked into a closet at home, it was the one where I kept my toys and the flashlight with a red-and-green light that I could use to

◁ *"Two short dream sequences strike me as acceptable." The brief encounter with the parents. The woman with one eye and Jenny.*

play cinema with. So it was actually quite nice and didn't frighten me at all.

To sit locked in a closet in my grandmother's old-fashioned apartment must have been far worse. The only thing is, I have completely suppressed that memory. To me, Grandma was and remained a figure of light.

Here I let her appear in Jenny's primal ode, but I cannot give shape and form to my memory. The memory arises so suddenly, and is so sharply painful, that I immediately exile it back to darkness. My artistic impotence is total.

But in the point of departure lies a truth. Grandmother *could have had* two faces.

From my early childhood I remember a conversation full of hate between my maternal grandmother and my father, which I overheard from an adjacent room. They were sitting at the table, drinking tea, and suddenly Grandma spoke in a tone of voice I had never heard her use before. I remember that it frightened me: Grandma had another voice!

That is what I dimly remembered! Jenny's grandmother should suddenly appear in a frightening light, and then, when Jenny returns home, her grandmother is a sad little old lady.

Dino De Laurentiis was delighted with the film, which received rave reviews in America. Perhaps it did present something new that had never been tried before. Now when I see *Face to Face*, I remember an old farce with Bob Hope, Bing Crosby, and Dorothy Lamour. It's called *The Road to Morocco*. They have been shipwrecked and come floating on a raft in front of a projected New York in the background. In the final scene, Bob Hope throws himself to the ground and begins to scream and foam at the mouth. The others stare at him in astonishment and ask what in the world he is doing.

" 'This is how you have to do it if you want to win an Oscar.' " Bob Hope with Bing Crosby and Dorothy Lamour in The Road to Morocco *(Paramount).* ▷

He immediately calms down and says, "This is how you have to do it if you want to win an Oscar."

When I see *Face to Face* and Liv Ullmann's incredibly loyal effort on my behalf, I still can't help thinking of *The Road to Morocco*.

THE FIRST IMAGE kept coming back, over and over: the room draped all in red with women clad in white. That's the way it is: Images obstinately resurface without my knowing what they want with me; then they disappear only to come back, looking exactly the same.

Four women dressed in white in a big red room. They came and went, whispered to one another, and were utterly secretive. At the time my mind was on other matters, but since the images kept coming back so insistently I understood that they wanted something from me.

I also point this out in my introduction to the published screenplay of *Cries and Whispers*:

> The scene I just described has haunted me for a full year. In the beginning, of course, I didn't know what the women's names were or why they came and went in the gray light of dawn in a red room. Time and time again, I rejected this image and refused to base a film (or whatever it is) on it. But the image has persisted and reluctantly I have identified it: three women who are waiting for the fourth one to die. They take turns sitting with her.

At first my workbook is mostly about *The Touch*. Under the entry date July 5, 1970, I write:

I've finished the screenplay, although not without a fair amount of inner resistance. I baptized it *The Touch*. As good a name as any other.

Now I'm going to take time off until August 3, when we begin the preparations in earnest. I feel depressed and ill at ease. I'd be happy to drop this film.

The Touch was supposed to make a lot of money for its author. I have probably resisted the temptation to make money more often than I have yielded to it. But there were times when I did yield completely, and I have inevitably lived to regret it.

The intention was to shoot *The Touch* in both English and Swedish. In an original version that doesn't seem to exist anymore, English was spoken by those who were English-speaking and Swedish by those who were Swedes. I believe that it just possibly was slightly less unbearable than the totally English-language version, which was made at the request of the Americans.

The story I bungled so badly was based on something extremely personal to me: the secret life of someone who loves becomes gradually the only real life and the real life becomes an illusion.

Bibi Andersson felt instinctively that this part did not suit her. I convinced her to do it anyhow, since I felt I needed a loyal friend in this foreign production. Besides, Bibi had a good command of English. The fact that she became pregnant after having accepted the part threw a terrible monkey wrench into what seemed, on the surface at least, a matter-of-fact, methodical production set.

Cries and Whispers began to make its way forward during this depressing period.

◁ Cries and Whispers: *the white-clad women in the park.*

At the same time, I was also working on an idea that was new and seductive: *the motionless camera*. I decided I would place the camera in one particular position in the room, and it would only be allowed to take one step forward or one step back. It would be the characters who would have to move in relation to the lens. All the camera would do was film without ever getting excited or taking part. Behind this idea was my conviction that the more violent the action, the less the camera should participate. It should remain coldly objective even when the action was moving toward emotional highs.

Sven Nykvist and I thought long and hard about how this camera should behave. We arrived at different solutions, but the whole thing became too complicated and we finally gave up on it.

Very little of this experimentation can be found in *Cries and Whispers*. When you discover that you are working on something that translates into such enormous technical complications that it begins to have a negative effect on the result, that it becomes a hindrance rather than a source of inspiration, then it's high time to cut your losses.

My workbook, July 10, 1970:

> It's good to be free; for then you can sleep and let desire and malaise follow each other without caring what happens. I'm going to become completely rusty. Only a few notations about *Cries and Whispers*, to see where I'm at.

(The title is actually borrowed from a music critic who wrote in a review of a Mozart quartet that it was like "cries and whispers.")

Bibi Andersson with Elliott Gould in The Touch. ▷

88

I'm going to have Liv, and then there should be Ingrid
[Thulin], and I would very much like to have Harriet
[Andersson], too, since she belongs to this breed of
enigmatic women. And then I want Mia Farrow; let's
see if that works out. It probably will; why shouldn't
it? And then some heavy, resigned femininity; is it
possibly Gunnel [Lindblom]?

July 26:
Agnes (homage to Strindberg) is the eyes that see and
the consciousness that registers. It's a little facile, but
it will do.

There is Amalia, Aunt Amalia, seated on the toilet
eating a liver pâté sandwich, who keeps up an exces-
sively detailed monologue about her digestion, her
intestines, and her stools. And she also must always
have the door open. In a room, at the far end (and
we hear her screams now and then), there is Beata,
who is big and round and always nude and lusty and
furious and not allowed to go out. In this house, in
these rooms, time has ceased to exist (but in any event
it's Grandmother's apartment).

I think we should not even try to look for any kind
of explanation. The person who has come to pay a
visit is there, and that suffices.

I wonder if Agnes should not be welcomed by one
of her sisters who is pale, small, and full of wisdom.
A sister who will accompany her and who grows fond
of her.

The only thing is, she will offer weird explanations
and will never explain what Agnes wants to know. She
will wear glasses and have a harsh little laugh but be

endowed with great tenderness and friendliness, and then she'll have some slight defect — trouble swallowing, I suspect, or something similar.

It must not be done academically, so that Agnes meets first one sister, then another, and then the third; that will be boring.

The farther she goes into this house, the more she will get in touch with herself. She will evolve in these dark-red rooms, which I am going to describe in detail, and, naturally, she will have an air of constant astonishment; no, she won't be astonished at all — everything will seem perfectly natural to her.

August 15:

There is going to be a theme and different movements. For instance, the first movement will be about "this tangle of lies." It will probably turn out that each of these women will represent one movement, and the first movement will be a variation on this theme: "This tangle of lies" will go on for twenty minutes without interruption. The words will ultimately become meaningless, and the behavior will be out of sync; illogical forces that one cannot account for will come into play. It's possible to take away all the explanatory parts, all unnecessary and supportive lines and positions. "This tangle of lies."

First movement.

August 21:

Everything is red. As an additional slightly odd bonus, the man in charge of publicity in America for *The*

Touch sent me a big book about a woman painter, Leonor Fini, and in her studies of women one finds both Agnes von Krusenstjerna and some notion of my description of *Cries and Whispers*. A strange coincidence. But overall, I felt that her painting was mostly a perfumed warning example.

All my films can be thought in black and white, except for *Cries and Whispers*. In the screenplay, I say that I have thought of the color red as the interior of the soul. When I was a child, I saw the soul as a shadowy dragon, blue as smoke, hovering like an enormous winged creature, half bird, half fish. But inside the dragon everything was red.

Six months are to pass before I return to *Cries and Whispers*.

March 21, 1971:
Have read through what I have written about *Whispering Cries*. On some points things are somewhat clearer, but by and large the concept is unchanged since the last time. Anyway, the theme attracts me as strongly as before.

The scenes must be wedged into each other in a totally self-evident manner. What is actually happening is probably the following: Afternoon, silence. The picture moves from room to room. Large, red rooms filled with furniture, clocks, things. In the distance somebody is disengaged. That is Sofia who moves around, far away and with great difficulty. Calls out for Anna. The bedroom door. Sofia is put to bed to rest. She is afraid of lying down. Afraid of everything around her.

Sofia is frightened and puts up a heartbreaking

battle against death. She has enormous spiritual strength. Nobody is stronger than she.

Kristina is a widow whose marriage had not been easy. Was she really? And if so, why? Is that really interesting? I think I'm off on the wrong path. More important things are at stake. Find out instead what makes this film so necessary.

Brief impressions:

Maria and Kristina are sitting across from each other; they have both been crying; both are expressing despair and profound affection. They are holding hands, their faces touch.

Evening. Lena walks into the room of the person who is dying, takes care of her, lies down beside her, and offers her breast.

Kristina: "Everything is just a tangle of lies." Before going to the bedroom where her husband is waiting for her, she crushes a glass, which she inserts in her vagina, as much to be hurt as to hurt.

Maria, in love with herself, completely absorbed by her own beauty and her body's matchless perfection, spends hours in front of her mirror. Her little cough. Her tentative politeness. Her nearsightedness, and her gentleness.

(A consoling film, a film offering solace. If only I could achieve something of that sort, it would be a tremendous load off my chest. Otherwise, it's hardly worth making this film.)

March 30:

What if Agnes were the one who is dying, and her sisters come to see her. And the only one who takes care of her is Lena. Agnes's lucidity, her fear of

From the filming of Cries and Whispers. *With Ingrid Thulin. Harriet Andersson, Liv Ullmann, and Sven Nykvist. Ingrid Thulin and Liv Ullmann. The three sisters.* ▷

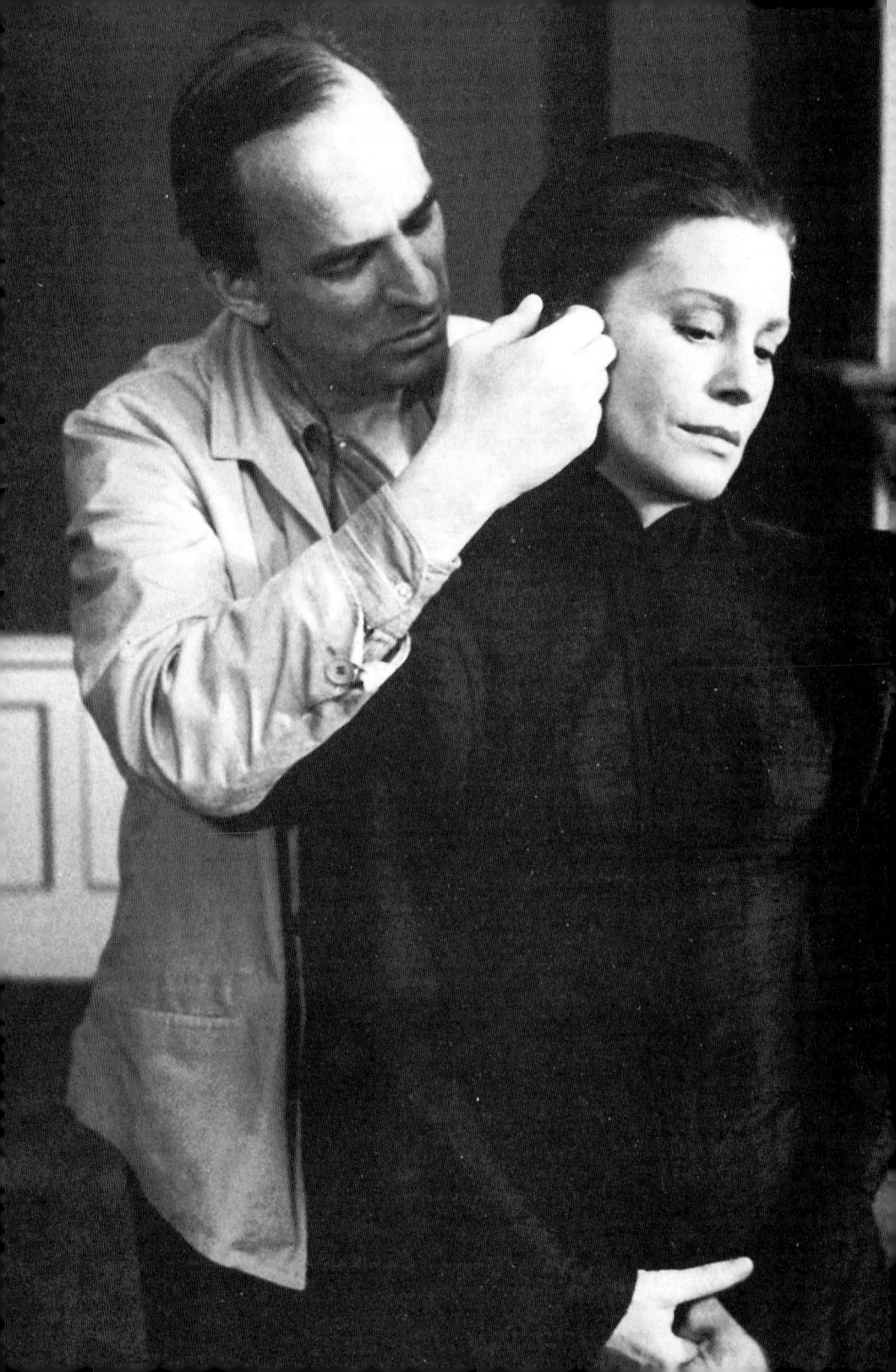

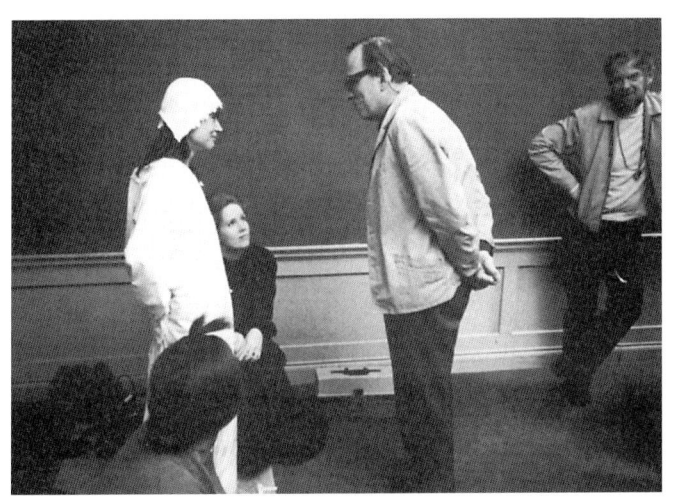

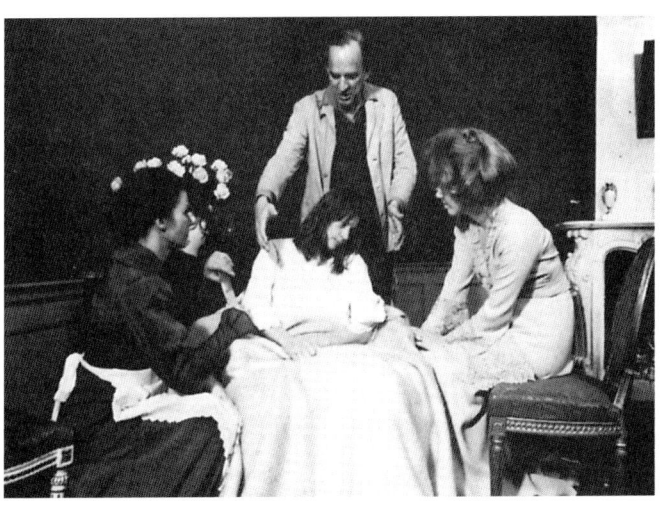

death — her readiness and her humble spirit — her fragility and strength.

I wrote *Cries and Whispers* from the end of March until the beginning of June 1971, during an almost hermetic isolation on Fårö Island. At the same time, the drama surrounding Ingrid von Rosen's breakup of her eighteen-year marriage was taking place. In September we began shooting the film. In November, when the film was finished, Ingrid and I were married.

April 20:
I cannot allow myself to get so upset because Ingrid tells me about some new phase of our personal drama. I have to do my best to keep my screenplay and my thoughts together. Damn it, I have to remind myself that something will always be happening. I have to keep on working in spite of it. The days are long; big clear days. Substantial, like cows, a kind of damn large animal.

AGNES	the dying one
MARIA	the most beautiful one
KARIN	the strongest one
ANNA	the serving one

No emotions regarding Death. Let it appear, reveal it in all its ugliness, give it its voice, its majesty.

With the mourners and Anders Ek at the deathbed. ▷

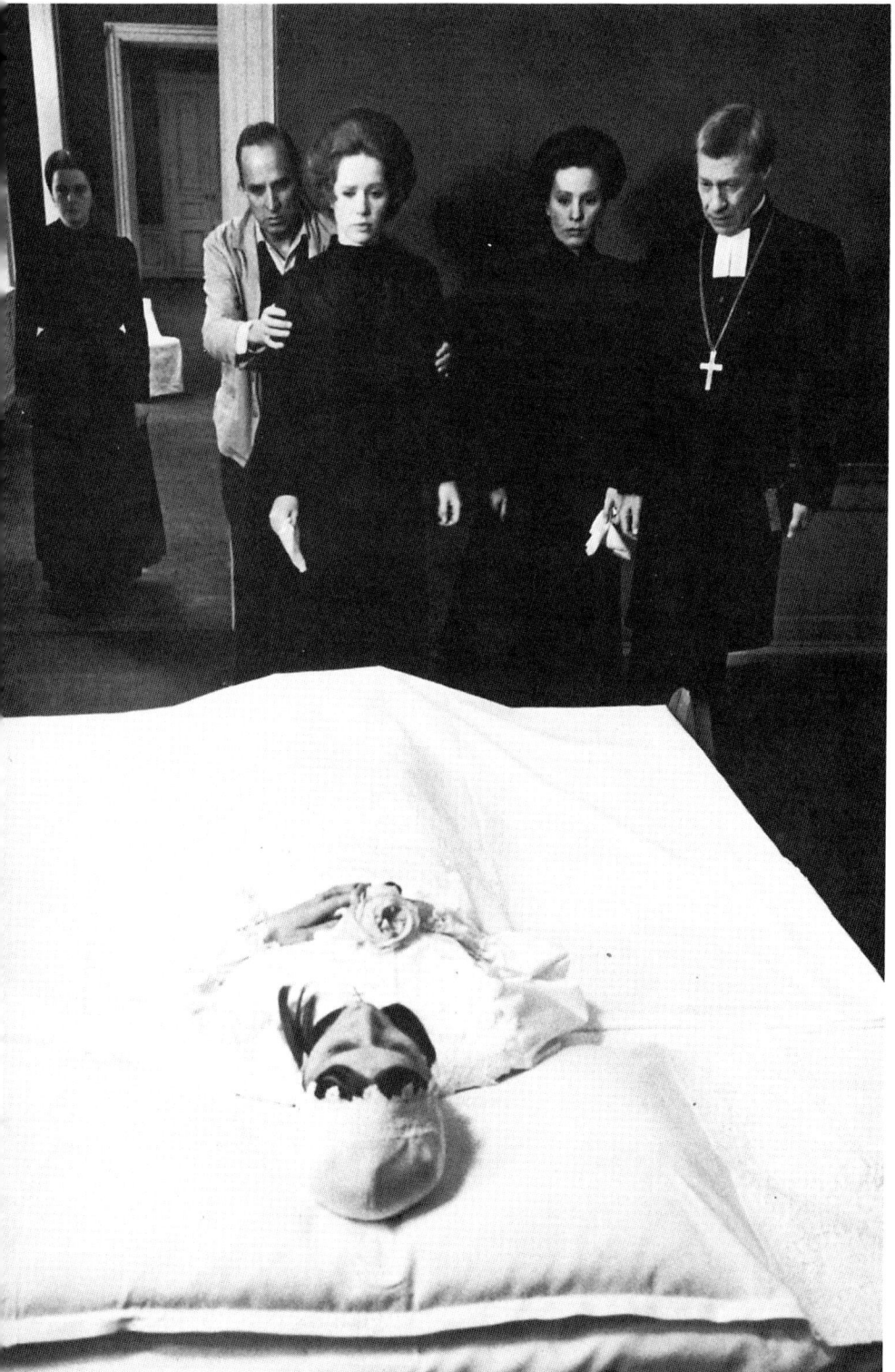

Now comes THE STEP that has to be taken. Agnes dies at the beginning of the drama. Yet she is not dead. She is lying in the room, in her bed; she calls out to the others, the tears streaming down her cheeks. Take me, keep me warm! Stay with me! Don't abandon me. The only one who pays any attention to her cries and offers her tenderness is Anna, who tries to warm her with her own body.

The two sisters are standing motionless, turned toward the dawn; they listen, terrified, to the lament of the one who is dead.

But now it is quiet in the room. They look at each other, but they can hardly see each other's faces in the pale light of dawn.

I am going to cry now.

No, you are not going to cry.

Maria turns toward the mirror with her hand extended, and it is as if her hand is a stranger. She cries out: My hand has become a stranger to me; I can't feel it anymore.

Karin is the abandoned one. She is the one who is deeply wounded but also has trouble between her legs, like paralysis that begins in her womb and rises to her breasts. Sudden disgust.

Maria is slightly enigmatic. I can see her clearly, but she moves away all the time.

Agnes has always been alone since she has always been ill. But in her there is no bitterness, no cynicism, no disgust.

Here, in my solitude, I have the feeling that I contain too much humanity. It oozes out of me like a broken tube of toothpaste; it doesn't want to stay within the confines of my body. A strange feeling of weight and volume. Soul volume perhaps, which rises like clouds of smoke and envelops my body.

April 22:

I believe that the film — or whatever it is — consists of this poem: a human being dies but, as in a nightmare, gets stuck halfway through and pleads for tenderness, mercy, deliverance, something. Two other human beings are there, and their actions, their thoughts are in relation to the dead, not-dead, dead. The third person saves her by gently rocking, so she can find peace, by going with her part of the way.

I believe this is the poem or the invention, or whatever you want to call it. It requires both rigor and a keen ear. Which means that I can't take anything lightly but also that I don't suddenly tie myself up in knots.

April 23:

Today, during my regular daily walk, these women acquired the power of speech and they stated clearly that they also wanted to talk. That they really wanted to have the proper opportunity to make themselves heard and if they didn't, then we'd never reach the goal we were aiming for.

One scene I envision is when the sisters, with infinite care, take their sick little sister out to the park to look at the autumn, to revisit the old swing where they used to sit together when they were children.

One scene I envision is the dinner the two sisters are eating together: they are silent, dignified, dressed

in black. Anna is there, too, silently waiting on the table.

One scene I envision is when the sisters, in a state of despair, touch each other's faces and hands, unable to speak.

April 26:

I ought to dedicate this film to Agnes von Krusenstjerna. I believe that when I reread her novels I received the strangest, most palpable impulses.

April 28:

Is it beginning to open up a little now, or is it still standing with its back to me, refusing to speak to me? (Remember, Bergman, you are going to work with four women who know the score! And who will also be capable of portraying everything!)

April 30:

Perhaps I should write a line or two, even today, in spite of this headache, this equanimity, and this small measure of disappointment and boredom. But my morning walk was good. Now I don't think about *The Touch* anymore. It bores me to death.

Sometimes I have the vague idea of producing a unity, flowing without interruptions, without "scenes," if only I could get to that point!

Everything unnecessary is wrong. The only thing necessary is what is unique, unshakable.

The prologue with the four women in the red room, dressed in white.

Agnes dead, with all the necessary sharpness of details.

◁ *Harriet Andersson as Agnes.*

Agnes is not dead.

What happens when Agnes is not dead but calls for help?

Anna's sacrifice.

The two women outside the door. Agnes's lament ceases. Her altered limbs, stiffening.

The epilogue: The four women come and go in the room; now they are dressed in black. Agnes is dead; she stands in the middle of the room, holding her face in her hands.

(All right now, it's been decided once and for all; the die is cast. Either that or nothing. I *can't* abandon an image that has haunted me so long and so stubbornly. It just can't be wrong. Even if my common sense, or whatever kind of second-rate mechanism, keeps advising me to drop the whole project . . .)

That's the way it is.

May 12:

Writing a screenplay is like a long, affectionate message to the actors and the technicians. I think that's fine. To comment throughout on what is seen, on what is happening. To toss overboard all verbiage. To keep in close contact always with those who are going to make the film.

May 23:

I believe I'm off on the wrong track. From the concrete, fluid dream that was unfolding, I have been derailed into some kind of boring, psychologizing, elaborate description, without any substance or excite-

In the park of Taxinge castle. ▷

ment. That must not happen, and that explains to some extent my malaise and my feeling that I'm working in vain.

May 26:
The doctor pays a call. He is heavy, pale, friendly, frigid. He cures Anna's little girl. Maria's daughter sleeps quietly in a nicely decorated nursery. Seduction. The doctor and Maria in front of the mirror; by the way, he calls her "Marie" the whole time. The husband threatens to shoot himself. He is fully aware that she is unfaithful to him, etc., etc.

On that subject, today I weigh five tons and a few hundred kilos more.

When the filming began in the fall of 1971, we had found an ideal location, Taxinge castle, outside of Mariefred. Inside it was totally dilapidated, but there was ample space for everything we needed: dining room, storage area, technical spaces, location sites, and administration offices. We stayed at the hotel in Mariefred. We didn't show the dailies in a movie theater but at the editing table that had been adjusted and arranged for that purpose.

The color had been carefully tested. When Sven Nykvist and I began to shoot in color, we had tested everything that possibly could be tested; not only the makeup, the hair, the costumes, but every object, wallcovering, the upholstery, every inch of carpeting. Everything had been controlled down to the last detail. Everything we planned to use for exterior shots had also been tested. The same was true for the makeup for the exteriors. There was not one detail that, in the course of our preparations, had not been presented to the camera.

When four extraordinary actresses are brought together, fatal emotional collisions can easily result. But the women were good, loyal, and helpful. Besides, most important, they were all incredibly talented. I have absolutely no reason to complain. And I'm happy to report that I did not.

THE SILENCE WAS ORIGINALLY called *Timoka*. That was pure coincidence. I saw the title of an Estonian book without knowing what the word meant. I thought it was a good name for a foreign city. In fact, the word means "belonging to the executioner."

A note in my workbook, dated September 12, 1961:

> On my way to Rättvik and Siljansborg to scout out locations for *Winter Light*. Evening. Nykvist and I discuss lighting. The whole complex of sensations that occurs when our car meets an oncoming car or passes another car. It brings to my mind the unwilled dream, the dream without beginning or end, which leads nowhere and refuses to let itself be revealed. Four strong young women are pushing a wheelchair. In it an old male skeleton, old as the hills, is sitting, a ghost. The old man has had a stroke, is deaf and almost blind. The young women push him in the sunshine, laughing and talking. In the sunshine beneath the flowering fruit trees. One of the women trips and falls beside the wheelchair. The others laugh uncontrollably.

In the following notation is hidden the first outline of *The Silence:*

> The old man walks through Siljansborg Hotel. He is going to take communion; he stands for a moment in the open door between the dark room and the light

room with the golden wallpaper. Strong sunlight on
his head, and his cheek, blue from the cold. A red
flower is resplendent on a rococo dresser. Over it
hangs a portrait of Queen Victoria. The old hospital
with its treatment rooms and equipment. The flat-
footed Frida, the sunlamps, the baths. The dead body
topples out of the toy closet in the nursery.

My brother and I had a tall closet in our room, painted
white. I often dreamed that I opened the doors. Out would
fall an incredibly old man, a corpse.

The pornographic book with the red cover, the funeral chapel with its yellow light through hazy windows. The smell of faded flowers, embalming fluids,
and tears on mourning veils, damp handkerchiefs.
The one who is dying is speaking about food, of pig's
throat and excrements. He can still move his fingers.

While the notes progress, a boy makes his way into the
story. The old man and a very young boy are traveling:

I and my friend, the aging poet, are on our way home
to Sweden after a long trip abroad. Suddenly he suffers a hemorrhage and loses consciousness. We therefore have to stop in the nearest city. A doctor explains
through a translator that my friend needs immediate
surgery and therefore has to be admitted to a hospital.
That is what happened. I took a room at a nearby
hotel and visited him every day. During this time he
was forever writing poems. I spent the days sight-
seeing in this gray, dusty, dreary city. Sirens that
scream for no apparent reason from the roofs of the

With Jörgen Lindström in the hotel corridor. ▷

buildings, the bells ringing, the variety theater with its pornographic stage show. The poet has begun to learn the incomprehensible language of the country.

It could also be a husband and wife with a child on a journey, and the husband takes ill. The wife visits the city, and the boy has his experiences in the hotel room all alone or spies on his mother in the corridors.

The foreign city is a motif that has stalked me for a long time. Before *The Silence* I wrote the outline for a film that was never made. It dealt with a couple of acrobats who have lost their partner and are caught in some German city, Hanover or Duisburg. The time is toward the end of the Second World War. During the course of repeated bombings, their relationship begins to fall apart.

Within this outline is concealed not only *The Silence* but *The Serpent's Egg* as well. And the idea of the lost partner also reappears in *The Ritual* (*The Rite*).

If I dig deep enough, I believe that the root of the city theme comes from a short story by Sigfrid Siwertz. *The Circle,* published in 1907, includes a couple of stories that take place in Berlin. One of them, entitled "The Dark Goddess of Victory," must have hit me like a bullet straight into my young consciousness.

This story became the basis for a recurring dream: I am in an enormous, foreign city. I am on my way toward the forbidden part of town. It is not even some dubious area of ill repute with its steaming flesh pots, but something much worse. There the laws of reality and the rules of society cease to exist. Anything can happen and everything does. I dreamed this dream over and over again. The irritating thing was, I was always on my way toward the forbidden part of the city, but I never actually reached it. Either I happened to wake up, or it changed into another dream.

Early in the 1950s, I wrote a radio play that I called *The City*. There the mood is of a war that is imminent or just over, but the atmosphere is quite different from that of *The Silence*. The city is built on land that has been mined and is crisscrossed with underground galleries. Houses cave in; abysses open up; streets rupture. The play is about a man who comes to this foreign but strangely familiar city. The play has a lot to do with my life situation at the time. I had just left my wife and children, and, both on the personal and the artistic level, my life was marked by one failure after the other.

If I probe further to seek the origins of the foreign city, I reach my first experiences in Stockholm. At the age of ten I began my life as a vagabond. Often the goal of my wandering was Birger Jarl's arcade, which to me was a magical place with its peep shows and its little movie theater, the Maxim. For seventy-five öre [about 15 cents], one could sneak into that time's R-rated movies or, better yet, climb up into the projection room manned by the aging homosexual. In the store windows there were corsets and douches, prostheses and mildly pornographic printed material.

When you see *The Silence* today, you have to admit that it suffers from a severe literary list (as a ship with an unbalanced load) in two or three sequences.

First and foremost, that is true in the confrontations between the two sisters. The tentative dialogue between Anna and Ester with which the film ends is also unnecessary.

Other than that, I have no objections. I can see details we could have improved upon if we had had more time and more money; a few street scenes, the scene in the variety theater, and so on. But we did what we could to make the

Gunnel Lindblom and Birger Malmsten. ▷

scenes comprehensible. Sometimes it's actually an advantage not to have too much money.

The pictorial style of *Through a Glass Darkly* and *Winter Light* had been restrained, even chaste. An American distributor asked, despair in his voice: "Ingmar, why don't you move your camera anymore?"

In *The Silence*, Sven and I had decided to be uninhibitedly unchaste. It contains a cinematic sensuality that I still experience with delight. To put it simply: we had an enormous amount of fun making *The Silence*. Furthermore, the actresses were talented, disciplined, and almost always in a good mood.

That *The Silence* in some ways became their undoing is another story. The film made them all internationally known. And other countries chose, as usual, to misunderstand the uniqueness of their respective talents.

The sisters in The Silence: *Gunnel Lindblom and Ingrid Thulin.* ▷

First Movies

THE SUMMER OF 1941 I TURNED twenty-three and fled to
Grandma's house in Dalecarlia. My private life was chaotic.
What's more, I had also been drafted into the military at
different times and as a result developed an ulcer and an
exemption.

My mother lived alone at Varoms. I had earlier written
sporadically about this period, but only for the bottom
drawer. Yet that stay in Dalecarlia, far from all my complications, meant relative relaxation. And for the first time in
my life I began to write uninterruptedly. The result was
twelve stage plays and one opera libretto.

I brought one of the plays to Stockholm and gave it to
Claes Hoogland, who was the head of the Student Theater.
The title of the play was *Kasper's Death*. I was given the chance
to direct it in the fall of 1941. It turned out to be a modest
success.

As a result I was summoned to Stina Bergman at Svensk
Filmindustri. She had happened to see one of the play's performances and thought she detected a dramatic talent that
ought to be developed. She offered me a paying contract
with Svensk Filmindustri's script department.

Stina Bergman was the widow of the novelist and playwright Hjalmar Bergman, and head of the studio's script
department. When Victor Sjöström had moved to Hollywood
in 1923, the Bergmans had followed. For Hjalmar Bergman
the American adventure was a catastrophe, but Stina studied
the mechanics of Hollywood and learned things quickly. In
her, Svensk Filmindustri acquired a screenplay executive

117

with extensive knowledge of American film drama technique.

This technique was extremely obvious, almost rigid; the audience must never have the slightest doubt where they were in a story. Nor could there be any doubt about who was who, and the transitions between various points of the story were to be treated with care. High points should be allotted and placed at specific places in the script, and the culmination had to be saved for the end. Dialogue had to be kept short. Literary terms were forbidden.

My first task was to head for the Sigtuna Foundation to rework a well-known author's disastrous screenplay. Svensk Filmindustri footed the bill. After three weeks I returned with a version that created a certain amount of enthusiasm. The film was never shot, but I became a regular employee as scriptwriter with a monthly salary, a desk, a telephone, and my own office high up under the eaves of Number 30 Kungsgatan.

It turned out that I had landed on a slaveship where Stina Bergman was in full charge. Already working there was Rune Lindström, whose *Himlaspelet* (*Heaven's Game*) had been a considerable success. There was also Gardar Sahlberg, who had a doctor's degree in philosophy. Ensconced in a somewhat more elegant office was director Gustaf Molander's constant co-worker Gösta Stevens. At full strength, the galley contained half a dozen slaves. From nine in the morning to five in the afternoon we sat at our desks, trying to make screenplays out of the novels, short stories, or synopses that we were given. Stina Bergman's regime was friendly but firm.

I was newly married and lived with my wife Else Fisher in a two-room apartment in Abrahamsberg. She was a choreographer, which in those days wasn't a particularly profitable occupation either. We never had enough money. To remedy this situation, I tried to write my own stories alongside those forced upon me on the slaveship.

I recalled that I had written a short story in a blue notebook the summer after my baccalaureate exam, and that it dealt with my last year as a student.

I brought the short story with me to the Sigtuna Foundation, where Svensk Filmindustri had sent me to doctor another script. I did the slave job during the first part of the day and during the afternoons I worked on *Torment* (*Frenzy*). When I returned to Number 30 Kungsgatan, I was able to deliver two screenplays.

My dual submission was followed by a long and resounding silence. Nothing happened until Gustaf Molander happened to read *Torment*. He wrote to Carl Anders Dymling (who had become head of Svensk Filmindustri in 1942) that this story contained much that was objectionable and unpleasant but also a considerable amount of joy and truth. According to Molander, *Torment* ought to be filmed.

Stina Bergman showed me his comments, at the same time rebuking me mildly for my penchant for darkness and terrible things. "Sometimes you are just like Hjalmar!" I received these words as a message from a Higher Power, though trembling inwardly with modest pride. Hjalmar Bergman was my idol.

It so happened that Svensk Filmindustri had decided upon a special anniversary celebration — the studio was twenty-five years old. The anniversary fell during the 1944–45 season, and to mark the occasion the studio was going to make six films of quality. Among the directors who had been hired was Alf Sjöberg. Only they did not have a suitable script for him. It was then that Stina Bergman remembered *Torment*.

Before I knew what was happening, I was sitting with

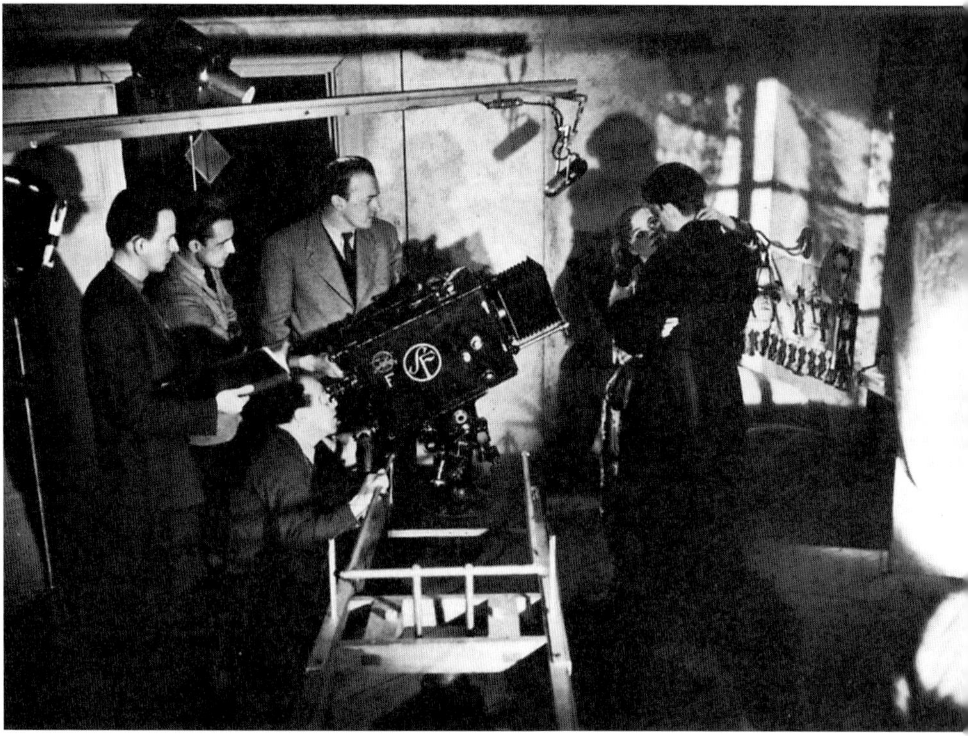

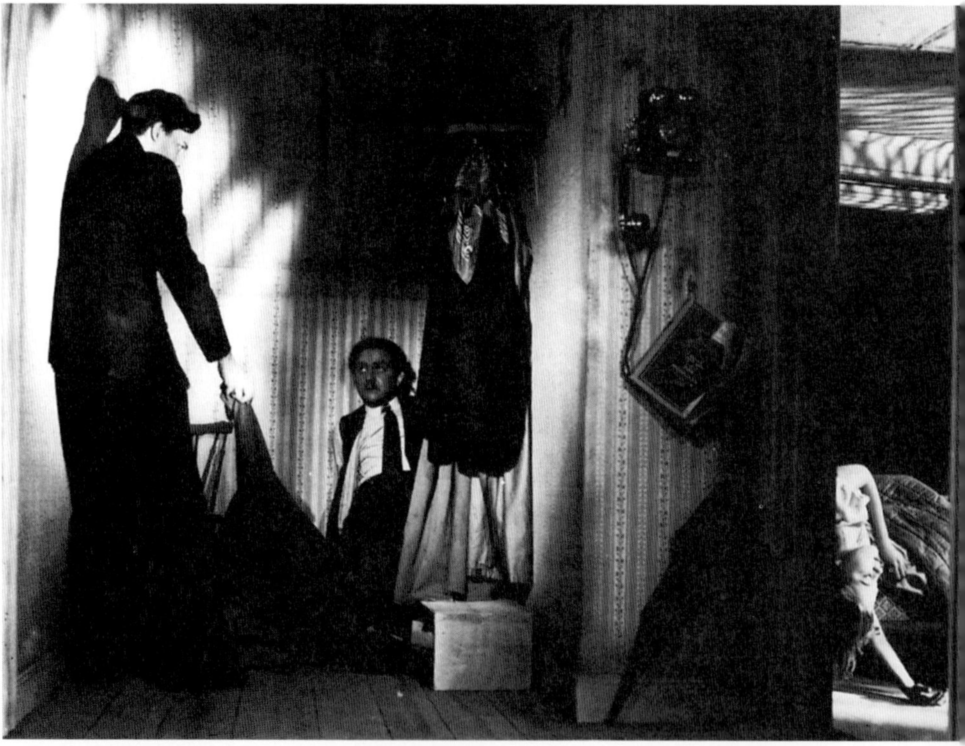

Alf Sjöberg in his little house, a cultural monument, on Djurgården, quickly seduced by his blunt charm, his knowledge, and his enthusiasm. He was amiable and generous, and I was suddenly brought into a world that I ardently desired. For too long I had been forced to make my nest on the periphery.

Alf Sjöberg allowed me, albeit with considerable hesitation, to be present during the filming, as "scriptgirl." In that capacity I was a near catastrophe. In spite of that, Alf Sjöberg manifested an unbelievable professional patience with me, and I adored him.

To me, *Torment* was an obsessive, anger-filled story about the torments of school and youth. Alf Sjöberg saw other things in it. Through various artistic devices he transformed it into a nightmare. Moreover, he made Caligula, the Latin master, into a crypto-Nazi and brought home the point that the actor Stig Järrel should be blond and insignificant. Not black and diabolic with expansive gestures and expressions. Alf Sjöberg and Järrel gave the character an inner pressure, which in the end became decisive for the whole movie.

When the filming was nearly finished, the then drama critic Herbert Grevenius called me and asked if I wanted to head the municipal theater in Helsingborg. I had to go to Alf Sjöberg and negotiate a day's leave in order to travel down to Helsingborg and sign a contract with the theater's board of directors. Sjöberg laughed, hugged me, and said: "You're crazy."

When the film was virtually done, I made my debut as a movie director. Originally, *Torment* ends after all the students have passed their final exam, except for one, played by Alf Kjellin, who walks out through a backdoor into the rain. Caligula stands in the window, waving good-bye. Everybody felt that this ending was too dark. I had to write an additional

◁ *With Alf Sjöberg during a take for* Torment. *In front of Martin Bodin's camera: Alf Kjellin and Mai Zetterling. Stig Järrel's Caligula is unmasked.*

scene in the dead girl's apartment where the principal of the school has a heart-to-heart talk with Kjellin while Caligula, the scared loser, is screaming on the stairs below. The new final scene shows Kjellin in the light of dawn. Walking toward the awakening city.

I was told to shoot these last exteriors, since Sjöberg was otherwise engaged. They were my first professionally filmed images. I was more excited than I can describe. The small film crew threatened to walk off the set and go home. I screamed and swore so loudly that people woke up and looked out their windows. It was four o'clock in the morning.

Of the six anniversary productions, *Torment* ended up being the only success. In addition, my first season in Helsingborg also turned out to be remarkably successful. I directed six plays, and the audience figures rose rapidly. The drama critics began to come down from Stockholm. In short, we were doing very well.

Even before the filming of *Torment*, I had bombarded Carl Anders Dymling with pleas asking to be allowed to make my own film but had been turned down. Then one day he sent me a Danish play. Its title was *Moderdyret* (*The Maternal Instinct*), its author Leck Fischer. Dymling promised me that I

△
Final shots from Torment. *"I made my debut as a movie director."*

would be allowed to direct the film if I could manage to wring a good script from this grandiose drivel.

Wildly happy, I spent my nights writing the scenario, at breakneck speed. After presenting it, I was forced to do two or three rewrites before it was decided that I could make the film during the summer of 1945. Inspired by the success of *Torment*, I christened it *Crisis*.

It turned out to be an apt title.

I still recall the first day of shooting as a complete and unadulterated horror.

The first day of shooting any film is always especially tense. That is how it has been for me, up to and including *Fanny and Alexander*. But this first shooting day was the first one in my cinematic life. I had made meticulous preparations. Every scene was carefully thought out, every camera angle prepared. In theory I knew exactly what I wanted to do. In reality, everything went straight to hell.

There is a classic Spanish play about a couple of lovers who are kept apart by every means possible. When finally they are allowed to spend their first night together as lovers, they enter the bedroom through separate doors and drop dead.

That is exactly what happened to me.

The day was hotter than hell, and we were working in a studio with a glass roof. Gösta Roosling, the cinematographer, was not used to the complicated lighting and heavy cameras of the time. He had earned his considerable professional reputation by working with a light camera for the exteriors and in royal solitude. His assistant was inexperienced, and the sound technician a walking catastrophe. The female lead, Dagny Lind, had hardly ever appeared in front of a movie camera before, and she was paralyzed with fright.

Generally speaking, back then one was supposed to do eight camera angle shots per day, which corresponded to one every hour. This first day we managed to do two. Later, when we viewed that day's rushes, everything was out of focus. What's more, the microphone was visible at the edge of the picture. Dagny Lind spoke as one does on stage. The scenes were the kind you see in the theater. In short, a veritable catastrophe.

In *The Magic Lantern* I relate the difficulties of shooting this film:

> I realized at once that I had landed myself in an apparatus I had by no means mastered, and I also realized that Dagny Lind, whom I had insisted had to play the title role, was not a film actress and was sorely lacking in experience. I saw with icy clarity that everyone realized I was incompetent. To confront their mistrust, all I could come up with were insults and outbursts of rage.

At an early stage, when the studio executives wanted to abort the filming, Dymling intervened, having seen three weeks of dailies. He suggested that we start all over again from the beginning. I was deeply grateful to him.

My next guardian angel was Victor Sjöström, who occupied an ill-defined role as artistic adviser to the studio:

As if by chance, Victor Sjöström, began to turn up wherever I was. He grasped me firmly by the nape of my neck and walked me like that back and forth across the asphalted area outside the studio, mostly in silence, but suddenly he would say things that were simple and comprehensible: "You make your scenes too complicated. Neither you nor Roosling can cope with those complications. Film the actors from the front; they like that and it's the best way. Don't keep arguing with everyone. They simply get angry and do a less good job. Don't turn everything into major issues; it'll suffocate the audience. A minor detail should be treated like a minor detail without necessarily having to look like one." We walked round and round, back and forth across the asphalt, he holding onto the back of my neck and being down-to-earth, factual, and not angry with me, although I was being so unpleasant.

But the catastrophic events accelerated. Nothing did what I wanted it to do. We went on location to Hedemora and stayed at the city hotel. It was the rainiest summer in recorded history, and during three weeks we managed to shoot four scenes out of the twenty we had anticipated. We played cards and drank and suffered from melancholy. Finally we were called back.

The rest of the exteriors were shot at Djurgården. The

Crisis: *with Gösta Roosling on the roof and Inga Landgré in the bus. Marianne Löfgren in the beauty salon.* ▷

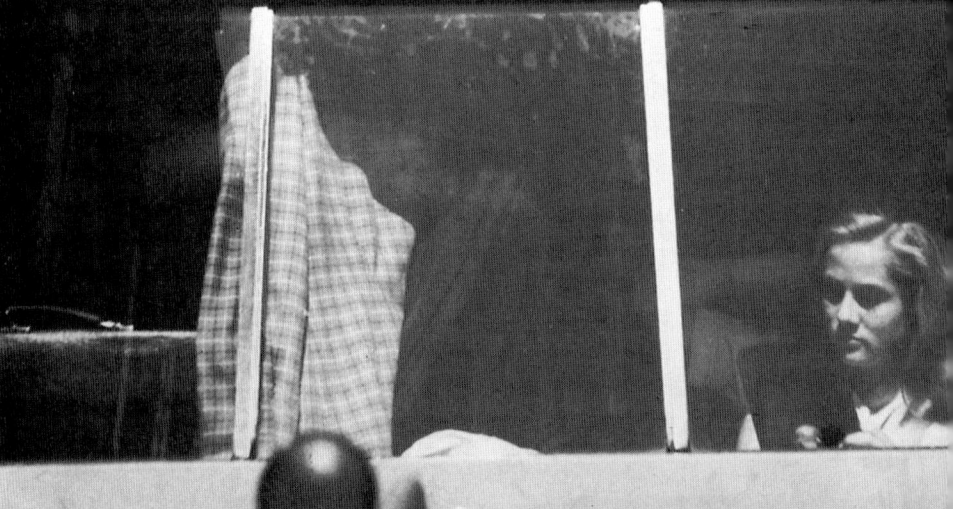

expensive safari to Hedemora had been perfectly meaningless.

Another catastrophe followed shortly thereafter. There is a scene in *Crisis* where the gigolo, Jack (Stig Olin), shoots himself on the street outside the beauty parlor where his lover and her daughter both work. Next to the beauty parlor is a music hall.

In vain I had looked all over Stockholm for a suitable location. Suddenly the architect came to me and announced that the construction crew was going to build my street at the studio. "It'll be exactly the way you want it." All of a sudden I imagined that the management liked my film despite everything that had happened and believed it would be a success. The street was my reward.

What I had not grasped was that I was being used as a pawn in the ongoing dirty dealings between the studio in Råsunda and the head office in Stockholm. About twenty movies were produced annually at the studio. There were several hundred employees. It was a large, independent operation under the guidance of Harald Molander, an outstanding intriguer who hated Carl Anders Dymling and his staff at the head office.

Those in the studio reasoned as follows: Ingmar Bergman is Dymling's protégé. We are going to see to it that the film is a total fiasco. From the start we have maintained that Bergman's *Crisis* is a mad undertaking. Now we can add the costs for the complicated building of a street for a film that is already way over budget. That will guarantee that *Crisis* will become an economic disaster, Bergman will be out, and Dymling's position weakened. Their logic was not without merit.

So the street was built and also a summer studio beyond the façades of the houses. Even this latter construction was charged to my film. The street was paved with cobblestones, and everybody was happy.

Finally we were ready to shoot the scene outside the beauty parlor where Jack was going to shoot himself underneath a flickering theater sign. The high brick wall was in place; it was raining; and the ambulance was in position. The asphalt glistened. I was drunk with the happiness only arrogance and false power can bring.

As is often the case during night filming, the electricians and grips were slightly drunk. I had positioned the camera high up on a scaffolding to get a full shot. When they were about to lower the camera, one of the grips fell headlong to the ground, and the heavy camera came crashing down on top of him. The ambulance, which, as I said, was on the spot, carted him off to the hospital. The crew insisted on quitting work and going home, but I refused to interrupt the filming. Then the sullen Swedish silence entered the picture. They did what they were told — but unwillingly. When I went home later that night, I was ready to give up.

The grip survived the accident. The filming of *Crisis* dragged on, but the increasing hostility between me and the crew grew greater with each passing day. There were arguments and disputes over everything. How would I ever learn this profession?

In addition to the friendly Victor Sjöström, who insisted on treating me as a fellow director, I gained one ally after the long shooting was ended, the film's editor, Oscar Rosander.

When I went to his house after the shooting was completed, and I was disappointed, bleeding, and furious, he treated me with abrupt and friendly objectivity. Mercilessly he pointed out what was bad, terrible, or unacceptable in my film. But he praised me for what he liked. He also initiated me into the secrets of editing — among other things, a basic truth: that editing occurs during the filming itself, the rhythm is created in the script. I know that many directors hold the opposite view. For me, Oscar Rosander's teaching has been fundamental.

Crisis opened in February of 1946 and was a bona fide fiasco. By then I was back at the theater in Helsingborg. From the Company, not a peep was heard. The studio head, Harald Molander, had publicly stated that if Bergman returned to the studio, he would resign. The defeat was total.

Then Lorens Marmstedt came into the picture. I had met him a few times with Alf Sjöberg. At one time or another, he had said, "I nibble with pleasure on talented people. You are going to come to me and make movies." That was after the success of *Torment.*

A few days after the premiere of *Crisis*, the telephone rang. It was Lorens, saying: "Dear Ingmar. That was an *awful* film! Hard to imagine anything worse! I suppose your phone is ringing off the hook with offers."

Lorens Marmstedt was an independent producer with a small but well-regarded production company, Terrafilm. He had just been asked by Karl Kilbom, of Sweden's Folkbio-grafer Company,* to produce two films. The first project was a Norwegian play called *Good People* by Oscar Braathen. Herbert Grevenius had written a screenplay that Lorens wanted me to read.

Herbert Grevenius was the foremost theater critic of the

---

*"People's Movie Houses," involved in production as well as distribution and exhibition.

Lorens Marmstedt with Mauritz Stiller on the wall. Stina Bergman with Hjalmar. ▷

1940s, and we were good friends. He was the driving force behind the decision to make me the head of Helsingborg's City Theater. He was also the one who, in 1946, through his connections with Torsten Hammarén, opened the doors for me to Gothenburg's City Theater.

I read Herbert's screenplay and found it rather tedious. Lorens Marmstedt agreed and asked me how much time it would take me to rewrite it. I promised to do it over the weekend if I was provided with a secretary.

During the next thirty-six hours I was sitting with a rather spunky beauty, dictating a new screenplay. Perhaps it wasn't any better, but at least the everyday pepper-and-salt tone was broken, which might have been an advantage.

For Lorens, it wasn't a great gamble this time. My apprenticeship would be paid for by Sweden's Folkbiografer. Three weeks after the script was approved, we were already shooting. The actors had been hired by Marmstedt, and the time schedule was set: the filming had to be completed in four weeks.

Lorens was a harsh teacher. He was ruthlessly critical and forced me to reshoot scenes he found poor. He could say: "I've been speaking with Hasse Ekman, who has seen the rushes, and I've spoken to Kilbom. I must keep things open! It may well be that you won't even be allowed to finish shooting. Bear in mind that Birger Malmsten is no Jean Gabin and *most of all* that you're no Marcel Carné."

Lamely I tried to defend myself by pointing out some scenes I thought were pretty good. Then Lorens looked at me with his icy light-blue eyes and said: "I don't understand how you can wallow in this simmering self-satisfaction!"

I raged; I was desperate and humiliated; but I had to admit he was right. Every day he took the trouble to sit through the rushes. Even though he criticized and insulted me in front

It Rains on Our Love. *The bad one and the good one: Ludde Gentzel with Barbro Kollberg and Gösta Cederlund with Birger Malmsten.* ▷ *Barbro Kollberg and Birger Malmsten.* ▷▷

of the staff, I had to take it, since he was participating passionately in the birth and development of the film. I cannot remember that he praised me even once during *It Rains on Our Love* for anything I had done.

What he did do was give me a lesson. He said: "When you and your pals see the dailies, you're in a state of emotional chaos. No matter what, you want everything to be good. That's the reason you have a natural tendency to make excuses for your failures and overestimate what you're seeing. All of you are supporting one another. This is normal, but it's also dangerous. Submit yourself to a psychological exercise. Don't be enthusiastic. Don't be critical either. Put yourself at point zero. Don't let your emotions get involved in what you're seeing. Then you'll see everything."

This piece of advice has been invaluable to me throughout my professional life.

The movie opened that same year, in November 1946, and was a modest critical success. Those who had totally lambasted *Crisis* now adopted a more positive wait-and-see attitude, and Lorens Marmstedt came back with another project, again for Sweden's Folkbiografer: a play by the Finnish-Swedish author Martin Söderhjelm, *A Ship Bound for India*.

The author had written his own screenplay, but it was unusable. Lorens suggested that he and I go to Cannes. I would write the screenplay, and he would play roulette. In between we could eat and drink well and meet ladies suitable to the purpose.

We had a good time. I lived in a small room on the top floor of the Hotel Majestic with a view of the railway and two fire walls and wrote like one obsessed. In less than two weeks the screenplay was finished. There were not many words left of Martin Söderhjelm's play.

Before we had time to reflect, we were in production. This time I had, against Marmstedt's wishes, insisted that Gertrud Fridh play the female lead. She was highly talented but not a conventional beauty by any means. Lorens became alarmed when he saw her screen test and demanded that her makeup be redone. The result was that she looked like a cheap whore in some French melodrama.

Just as in *Crisis*, there are some parts that show strength and vitality. The camera stands where it should stand; the people behave as they ought to behave. For a few brief moments I am really making a film.

When I had finished *A Ship Bound for India*, I was swimming in euphoria. I was great. I thought I was terrific, just as good as the French directors who were my idols. At first Lorens Marmstedt was rather positive. But then he went to the Cannes Film Festival to present the movie. He called me in a panic and urged me to cut more than a thousand feet, to avoid a complete fiasco. In high dudgeon, despite a somewhat faltering egomania, I informed him that I had no intention of cutting even one foot from this masterpiece.

The Swedish premiere turned out to be a bizarre event. The print had not been checked, owing to lack of time. It was transported directly from the laboratory to the projectionist's booth at the Royal Theater. At the time no preview screenings for critics were held, so they were there en masse for the opening. I was also present, along with the actors Gertrud Fridh and Birger Malmsten. Quickly we became aware that there had been an accident involving the sound track of the print. You could not hear the dialogue. I called up to the projectionist and told him to turn up the volume. The result: you could hear even less. As if this wasn't enough, the third and fourth acts had been mixed up when they packed the reels. So the fourth act went first. When the

mix-up of the acts became evident, I hammered on the door of the projectionist's booth, but that man had locked himself in. After lengthy negotiations through the closed iron door, I managed to convince him to stop the film in the middle of the fourth act and to start over the third.

Party afterward at the Gondolen Restaurant. It is the only time in my life when I got so drunk I passed out.

I woke up in the staircase of an apartment building on Artillerigatan. That same morning I was supposed to take a plane to Gothenburg to get ready for the dress rehearsal at the City Theater. Somehow I got myself to Bromma airport in what I can only describe as a lamentable condition. In the waiting room sat Hasse Ekman, fresh and sweet-smelling with an unbelievably gorgeous Eva Henning at his side. He was reading the reviews of my film.

He consoled me as best he could, quoting his father, the famous actor Gösta Ekman, who used to say after one of his many fiascos: "There will be other newspapers tomorrow!"

A Ship Bound for India was a major disaster. What had happened to the print at the premiere nonetheless served as a useful lesson to me. When I returned to Svensk Filmindustri to make *Port of Call*, I occupied the sound department and the laboratory every free moment I had and learned everything I could about sound, film developing, and copying. I learned also about the camera and the various camera lenses. No technician would ever walk all over me again. I began to learn how I wanted things to be done.

In spite of all that had happened, Lorens Marmstedt did not throw me out. With great diplomacy he pointed out that now would be the perfect time for at least one modest audience success. Otherwise my days as a movie director might be numbered.

A Ship Bound for India as well as *It Rains on Our Love* had

◁ A Ship Bound for India: *Gertrud Fridh with Birger Malmsten and Holger Löwenadler.*

been made for Sweden's Folkbiografer. Now Marmstedt suggested that I make a film for his own company, Terrafilm. It must be noted that Lorens was a passionate gambler, able to put his money on the same number a whole evening.

He had bought the movie rights to a novel by Dagmar Edqvist called *Music in Darkness*, which told the story of a blind musician. For the time being I would have to stuff my demons into an old sack. Here I was not going to have any use for them.

I read the novel; I hated it and decided to tell Lorens how I felt. He declared that he had no intention of coming up with any other offer. Finally we agreed that we would go and see Dagmar Edqvist together. She turned out to be an adorable woman, funny, warm, and intelligent. Also very feminine and pretty. I caved in. She and I would write the screenplay together.

The film was shot during the fall of 1947. My only memory of the filming is that I kept thinking: Make sure there are no tedious parts. Keep it entertaining. That was my only ambition.

Music in Darkness (known in the United States as *Night Is My Future*) became a respectable product in the style of director Gustaf Molander. It was generally well received and was a modest box-office success to boot.

Lorens Marmstedt had bet on the right number. I thanked him by leaving for Svensk Filmindustri, where Gustaf Molander had meanwhile made a film out of my original screenplay, *Woman without a Face*, which became a considerable success. Furthermore, the studio executives had figured out how much *Music in Darkness* had brought in at the box office. So my summons to return home was not exactly an unselfish gesture.

"For the time being I would have to stuff my demons into an old sack."
Mai Zetterling and Birger Malmsten in Music in Darkness. ▷

Lorens, however, showed no bitterness and would, before long, be back in my professional life.

Port of Call [Bergman's next film] was not a remarkable story. To me, it was a question of piecing together a suitable movie out of Olle Länsberg's voluminous material. Before we knew what hit us, we were already shooting the film.

Strongly influenced by Rossellini and the Italian neorealists, I tried to include as many exteriors as possible. What went wrong was that, in spite of my good intentions, too much of the film was shot in the studio for people to say that I had made a clean break with the Swedish film tradition of shooting films in the studio.

◁ *Neorealism and the studio in* Port of Call.

PORT OF CALL OPENED in October 1948 and was a relative success. At about the same time Ellen, my wife then, and I went to the summer cottage in Dalecarlia where I had spent my childhood. There I wrote the screenplay for *The Devil's Wanton* (*Prison*).

It was late autumn, and we were in great spirits. We burned fires in the tiled stoves in the two main rooms as well as in the kitchen stove. Ellen occupied the living room, working on her choreography, while I reigned in the bedroom, where I wrote what would be the first film of my own. There was peace and good feelings between us. When not working, we went for long walks. The success of *Port of Call* was beneficial. It was an altogether good time.

During the previous summer I had written the story of Birgitta Carolina as a long short story with the title "True Story," alluding to a very popular genre in weekly magazines at the time that was called "true stories from life." I wanted my story to be that way: with inhibited swings between unabashed sentimentality and genuine feelings. I was extremely pleased with the title of the film, finding it suitably ironic.

But my producer Lorens Marmstedt, who knew everything there was to know about Swedish movie audiences, said that people didn't understand irony; they'd just get mad as hell. He asked me to find another title. First I came up with *The Prison* and then simply *Prison*, which was typical for the 1940s and, actually, a much worse title than *True Story*.

I hesitated when I handed the screenplay to Lorens Marmstedt and said something like, "You don't have to bother with this. But if you have the time and inclination at some point, take a look at it." I did not even give Svensk Filmindustri a chance to consider it, fully realizing that it would be futile.

Two days later Lorens called me and said in his roundabout way, "Very touching . . . I don't know . . . perhaps . . . after all. Touching but not moving! One can't tell. Possibly? How fast can you work?"

"Eighteen days. Not less than eighteen days," I said. Then we discussed actors, and he called around and told each one, "Don't count on getting your regular salary because this is an *artistic* film and one has to sacrifice something for Art!" I myself did not receive a penny, just 10 percent of the profit. There never was any profit!

Prison came to be seen, through no fault of its own, as a film typifying the 1940s. This had to do not only with the title but with the fact that because Tomas, played by Birger Malmsten, is a journalist and author, he is presumed to be active in the literary circles of that decade. But this inference is a superficial one. I had no contact whatsoever with Sweden's literary culture, and its authors had no contact with me. If they thought of me at all, they might have expressed themselves in somewhat the same way as Gunnar Ollén did when, as the person responsible for selecting plays for the Swedish Radio, he rejected my play *To My Terror:* "Unfortunately you will probably never become a real writer, Ingmar, but keep going! And good luck!"

In the end, the conditions for getting *Prison* made were that it would be a low-budget movie. Lorens Marmstedt gave me free rein as long as I promised to keep the costs far below normal. We also had to deal with the rationing of film stock: eight thousand meters — twenty-five thousand feet — and no more! The problems stimulated me, and I wrote an article that reported on the economical and practical prerequisites for making a low-budget film:

> Make a cheap film, make the cheapest film that has ever been made in a Swedish studio, and you will be given great freedom to create according to your own conscience and as you think best.
>
> For this reason I set out to cut every cost across the line in my budgetary calculations. The regimen went as follows: Cut down the number of shooting days. Limit the building of sets. No extras. No music (or only sparingly used). Ban overtime. Limit use of raw film. Film exteriors without sound or lighting. Conduct all rehearsals outside of the actual shooting time. Begin early in the morning. See to it that the shooting of excessive material is stopped. Trim the screenplay meticulously.
>
> The procedure does not sound remarkable. You do long scenes, but you do long scenes where the length is not noticeable.
>
> Through this arrangement, the director gains time, continuity, and concentration. However, he loses opportunities to cut out something that doesn't work, decrease a pause, or cheat on the rhythm. The editing is already taking place mainly in the camera.

Of course the whole idea of long takes was dangerous in the extreme. I was far from being technically mature enough for such adventures, but it was, in all probability, the only way *Prison* could have been made.

We had to save on absolutely everything. We managed to borrow one set for free from another movie. The scenes in the attic and the passage up the attic stairs were shot in Novilla in Djurgården. But most of the film was shot in the studio at Gärdet. We kept using three walls that had their wallpaper changed over and over. Doors and windows swapped places.

One important scene that exists both in the prose version and in the final screenplay did not find its way into the finished film. I made a strong effort to incorporate it but somehow failed. Birgitta Carolina meets a painter at the boardinghouse, and in the original story, the episode is described as follows:

> Mrs. Bolin's salon was filled with old-fashioned furniture. There were thick carpets on the floor, many paintings with Italian motifs on the walls, small statuettes, a tall tiled stove that stood sleeping in a corner, enormous sofas and armchairs, a crystal chandelier on the ceiling, and three windows, framed by heavily draped curtains and facing a street edged with linden trees. On one wall a black clock was ticking majestically; on a big-bellied chest of drawers stood a small ornamental French clock with quick, tinkling pulse beats; and on the tiled stove ledge were mementos, shells, and photographs of Mrs. Bolin's relatives from the past hundred years artfully arranged.
>
> "In a little while the sun will rise and then I'm going to show you something remarkable," Andreas said gravely. "Something that has never ceased to astonish me and fill me with a fear-tinged reverence for this old room and all other old rooms where people have lived together for a long time. But wait. Right now the sun is rising at the end of the street, and now it sneaks in here. Look, look! Do you see?"
>
> He pointed excitedly toward the wall.

Prison: *Doris Svedlund on the staircase with Irma Christenson. Curt Masreliez and Stig Olin. Making a film within a film, with Hasse Ekman as the director.* ▷

"Don't you see it there on the wall? There! And there! And there!"

"No," said Birgitta Carolina, "I see nothing."

He brought her closer to the wall where the first ray of sun glowed.

"Do you see it now?" he asked, and his voice trembled a little. "Look here! And here . . . and here!"

She had already noticed the unusual pattern of the wallpaper, but now she discovered all of a sudden that it changed when the sun caressed it, and that a myriad of faces became visible in the trembling ray of light.

"I see," Birgitta Carolina whispered.

"Yes, it's remarkable indeed," Andreas said.

Then he didn't dare say more so as not to disturb the enigmatic play on the wall. After a few minutes, not only were faces revealed where the sun's rays hit, but the whole wall was full of them; there were hundreds, perhaps thousands, of faces.

And in the silence Birgitta Carolina could hear a chorus of whispering voices. They were faint, distant, but she could discern each of them quite distinctly. Everybody was speaking at the same time; a few were laughing, others crying; some sounded friendly, others hard and indifferent. There were old voices, childish voices, the voices of young women, and the whiny high-pitched sounds made by old men; the thundering baritones of executives mingled with the good-humored neighing laughter of nice uncles. It sounded like abstract music of some kind, and it rose and descended like the swell of an endless sea breaking upon the shore.

"It's as if that wall with its covering were a photographic plate," Andreas said. "And this room a magic camera. Every person who has ever been inside this room has been photographed. Look here!" he said and pulled her along, pointing toward an open-mouthed, half-averted face that was his own.

Suddenly all the clocks struck five-thirty, and a huge garbage truck clattered by in the street, the sunlight turned off, the faces disappeared, the voices died off, and the room regained its appearance of a middle-class drawing room from a helplessly sunken time.

Grandmother's dining room in Uppsala had a wallpaper-covered door. When Grandpa died, she had divided the large apartment in half. The wallpapered door in the dining room was the closed-up passage to the other apartment. Or perhaps it led simply to a closet? I never opened it. I didn't dare.

If I keep in mind that the break between several realities has shaped my life from its beginning all the way to the present, I see that my creative results are relatively meager. Only a few times have I managed to force fluid borders. In *Prison* I definitely did not succeed. The wallpaper vision ended up in the wastebasket.

For a long time after filming I felt no connection whatsoever to *Prison*, which is noticeable when I speak about it in *Bergman on Bergman*.

But as I am now able to view my work as a whole, the film seems to take on a certain lucidity. It encompasses a cinematic joyousness that, in spite of my lack of experience, is reasonably controlled.

Prison was well cast. In that area, Lorens Marmstedt was generous and invaluable. He convinced Hasse Ekman, who was important and busy, to participate as well as Ekman's wife at the time, Eva Henning, who had just enjoyed great

success in Ekman's *The Banquet*. Hasse Ekman was unswervingly loyal and helpful.

Eva Henning brought a totally unexpected tone of pure sorrow to the film. She has a brief scene with the director in which she says, "Is it so that we as children collect something that we later, when we are adults, waste: something that's called — spirit?" Eva Henning does the scene absolutely beautifully with her austerity, her warmth, and her sense of humor.

Doris Svedlund as Birgitta Carolina was also lovely. It was important to me that she not look like the typical Swedish movie whore. *Prison* is, after all, a story about a soul, and she is the soul. Doris shone with her own enigmatic light.

The farce that Thomas and Birgitta Carolina present in the little toy projector in the attic is one that I made up as a child. It is about a man who is locked up in a mystical room where all kinds of atrocities happen to him: A spider descends from the ceiling; a villain appears with a long knife ready to kill him; the devil jumps out of a chest; and Death, a skull, jiggles in front of a window with wide-slatted blinds.

We filmed the farce quickly and efficiently. The acting trio in it consisted of three Italians, the Brothers Bragazzi. They

△

"We filmed the farce quickly and efficiently. The acting trio in it consisted of three Italians, the Brothers Bragazzi."

had performed at the China Variety Theater and had remained in Sweden for the duration of the war.

They arrived at the studio early in the morning. We picked out some clothing from Sandrew's costume department. Göran Strindberg set up four open lamps with straight light and installed grease-proof paper so there wouldn't be any shadows. I told the story, and the Bragazzis began playing like children.

We filmed all of it before lunch. The material was sent to the lab immediately. The next morning it was developed and copied. Then Lennart Wallén and I put the little farce together in the editing room of Terrafilm, whereupon we summoned Lorens Marmstedt and held our world premiere.

Lorens laughed till he cried. Then he treated us to champagne.

THIRST IS A COLLECTION of short stories by Birgit Tengroth that caused quite a sensation when it was first published. Svensk Filmindustri bought the movie rights, and Herbert Grevenius wrote a good screenplay in which he tied the different stories together into one coherent script with parallel plots and flashbacks.

My instincts told me correctly that Birgit Tengroth should play Viola. I felt intensely that I needed her cooperation on several levels. In her discreet, tactful way she helped me shape the lesbian episode. This was, at that time, inflammatory stuff, and, of course, the film censors cut a substantial piece of the dramatic scene between Birgit Tengroth and Mimi Nelson, a cut that renders the end of the sequence incomprehensible.

Birgit Tengroth also made a directorial contribution that I will not forget; it taught me something new and decisive.

The two women are sitting together in the summer twilight, sharing a bottle of wine. Birgit is rather drunk and gets a cigarette from Mimi, who also lights it for her. Then Mimi slowly brings the burning match toward her own face and holds it for a moment by her right eye before it goes out.

This was Birgit Tengroth's idea. I remember it clearly since I had never done anything like that. To build the plot with small, almost imperceptible, suggestive details became a special component in my future filmmaking.

A large part of the film takes place during a train journey

Birgit Tengroth's directorial contribution in Thirst *(with* Mimi Nelson*); later put to good use in* Hour of the Wolf *with Liv Ullmann and Max von Sydow.* ▷

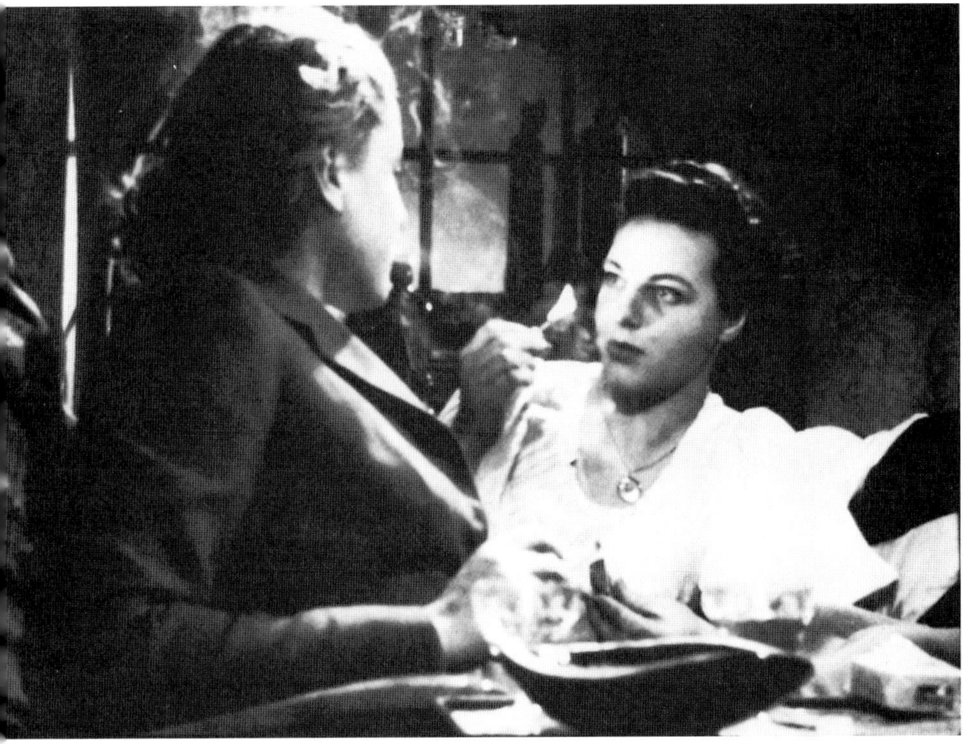

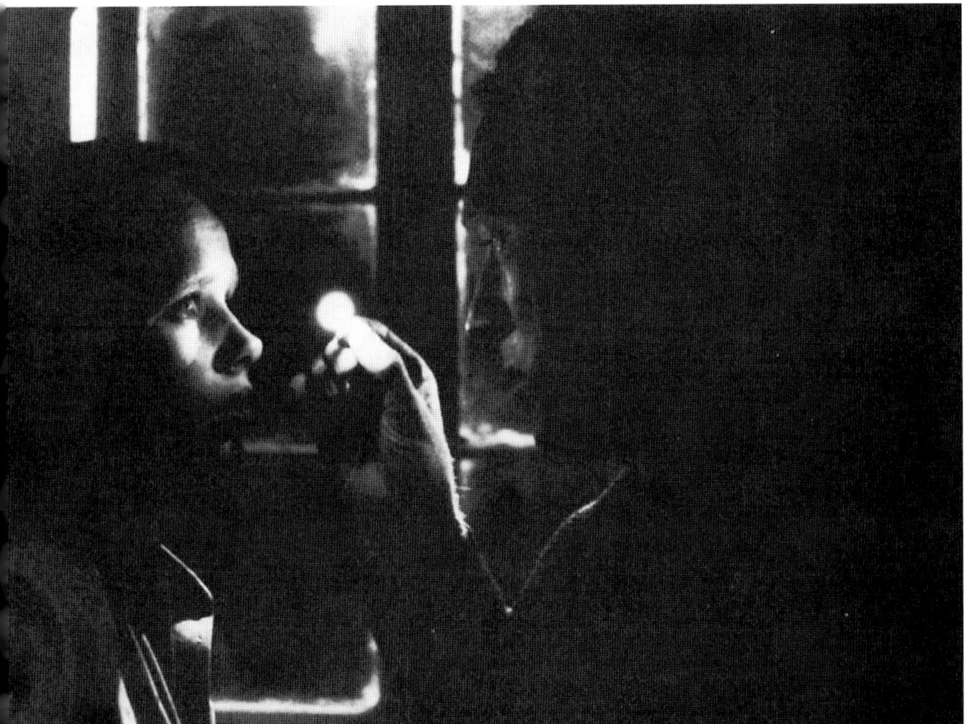

through war-torn Germany.* In *Prison* I had begun to experiment with longer takes. In order to develop that technique, we had to build a monstrous train car, one that could be taken apart in different sections. The clumsy camera used at the time could then roam around freely in compartments, corridors, and other spaces.

The long scenes in *Prison* had come about for economical reasons. Here I was striving for another simplification: for the complicated camera movements to go undetected.

The studio train was far from perfect: you can see the seams if you look closely. Furthermore, I had wanted the ruins of buildings, seen through the train window, to be actually filmed in Germany, but that couldn't be done for reasons of economy. The homemade result was a less than convincing compromise.

Other than that, *Thirst* (known as *Three Strange Loves* in the United States) does show a respectable cinematographic vitality. I was developing my own way of making movies. I made myself master the ungainly machinery, and it functioned by and large as I wanted it to function. That was always a triumph.

*That is, Germany after World War II.

◁ *The train in* Thirst: *interior with Eva Henning and Birger Malmsten; exterior with extras.*

Jests Jesters

I DIRECTED STAGE PLAYS at the Malmö City Theater from 1952 to the beginning of 1959. Consequently, *The Magician* (*The Face*), born during the summer of 1958, mirrors the experiences from that period.

Those were work-saturated and bohemian years. Bibi Andersson and I lived in a small, crowded apartment, two and a half tiny rooms, in a part of town called the Star Houses on Limhamnsvägen. Malmö City Theater had, with exemplary wisdom, acquired a number of apartments when these houses were built. They were on the same side of town as the theater, and one could quickly and easily reach the latter by car or public transportation.

We lived at the theater except on Tuesday nights, when there were no performances and theatrical plays were replaced by symphony concerts. This was our time to be together. I bought my first 16 mm sound projector and began to collect films seriously. We arranged movie evenings at home.

The intensive work collaboration made for a closeness, the likes of which I have not experienced before or after. We all still speak of this time as the best in our lives. A furious work pace and good professional collaboration can construct a fine corset against the onset of neuroses, threatening breakdowns, and disintegration.

There is, in other words, a connection between *The Face* and our existence then. In comparison, we had remarkably pale relations with the city's inhabitants and very little contact with outsiders.

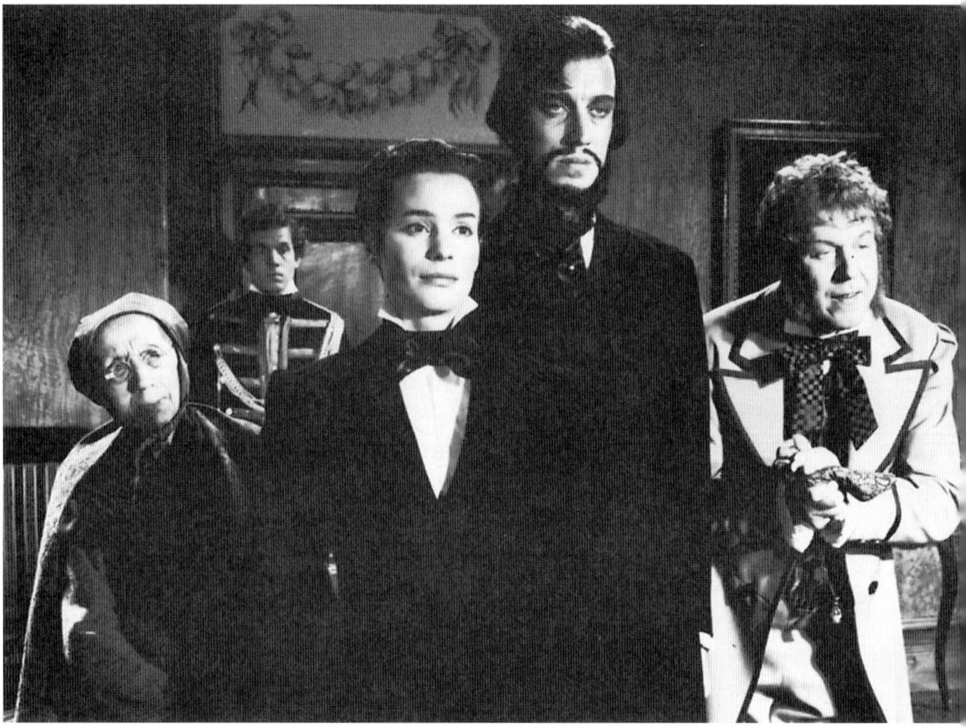

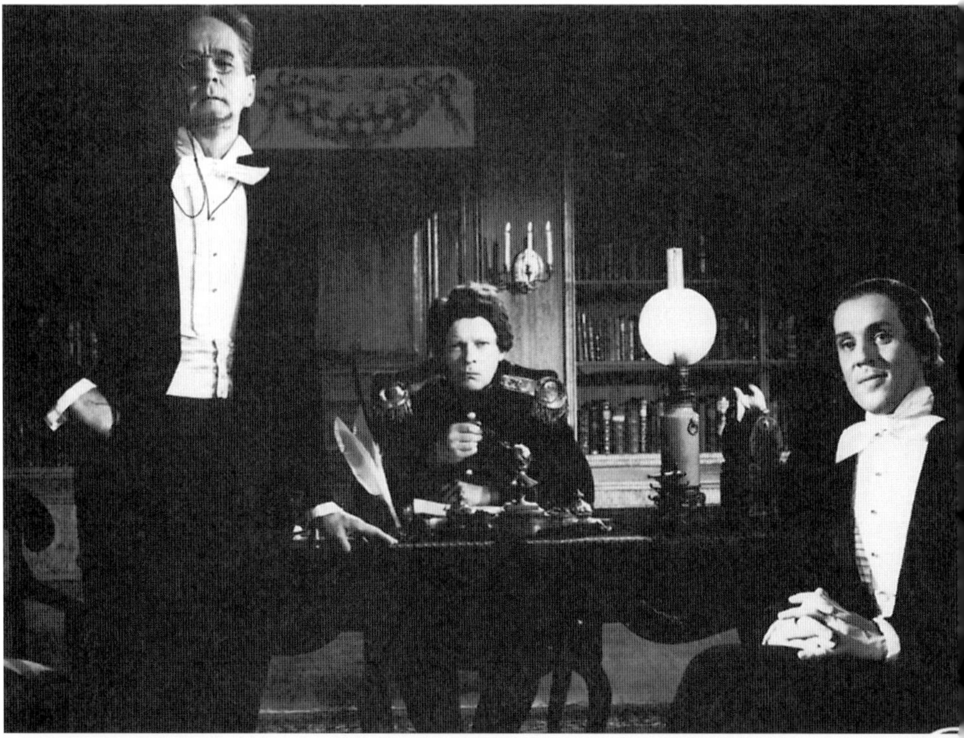

When I was managing director for the theater in Helsingborg, things were completely different. The people in Helsingborg thought it was great fun to have actors in town. Every Saturday we were invited to Fahlman's pastry shop where we ingested free cakes and hot chocolate with whipped cream. We were frequently invited to the homes of people in the community, where we ate more than our fill. A grocery store across the street had a fine assortment of food as well as its own kitchen; there we could buy a substantial dinner any day of the week for one krona [about 20 cents]. We were also lucky enough to rent a couple of apartments in an old house from the eighteenth century for next to nothing. And though the maitre d' at the exclusive Grand Hotel didn't want us in the main dining room, we were welcome to frequent the smaller restaurant in the back where, after evening performances, we were served hash, schnapps, and beer for 1.75 kronor [about 35 cents]. If we didn't have any money, which happened often, our credit could be extended to dizzying heights. We were invited to castles and mansions if we in turn would sing, read, or act. We felt enmeshed and fully involved in the life of the city. The hospitality and ambiance were great.

Malmö, however, was a different kind of city. Credit at the restaurants and bars was niggardly, often nonexistent. Yes, we were given a good table at Kramer Restaurant, and people displayed a friendly interest in what we were doing, but we kept mostly to ourselves.

The audience to whom we played but with whom we spent no time is represented in *The Face* by the consul Egerman's family. The consul is an amiable, dogged enthusiast who wants to keep his distance and formulate rules, and who, for understandable reasons, panics when he discovers that his wife has become involved with the rabble.

◁ *The jesters and the bourgeoisie in* The Face.

In the theater profession we often suffer from the delusion that we are attractive as long as we are masked. The public believes that it loves us when it sees us in light of our work and our public persona. But if we are seen without our masks (or, even worse, if we are asking for money), we are instantly transformed into less than nothing. I am fond of saying that we in the theater fulfill our 100 percent capacity only when we appear on stage. When we step off the stage, we are reduced to less than 35 percent. We try to convince ourselves and most of all each other that we remain at 100 percent. That is a fundamental mistake. We become victims of our own illusion. We subject ourselves to passion and marry each other and forget that our starting point is our profession and not how we appear out in the street after the last curtain.

As I remember it, the police chief in *The Face* is a consciously calculated target. He represents my critics. It was a rather good-natured jest with everyone who wanted to keep me in line and master me. The drama critics back then saw it as their duty to keep urging me to do this and not that. They probably enjoyed giving me a spanking publicly.

The character of the health official also had a real-life counterpart.

Over the years I have not intentionally created a multitude of malicious portraits of people I know. The quarreling marital couple, Stig Ahlgren and Birgit Tengroth in *Wild Strawberries*, is a sad exception, one which I regret. The health official Vergérus in *The Face* is a much more amusing caricature. He was born out of an irresistible desire to take a small revenge on Harry Schein.

Schein was the movie critic at Bonnier's *Literary Magazine*, which at the time was a heavyweight cultural organ. Schein is intelligent and arrogant, and what he wrote was echoed in the inner circles. I felt that he treated me in an exceedingly

"The character of the health official also had a real-life counterpart." With Harry Schein in the studio. Vergérus examines Vogler (Gunnar Björnstrand and Max von Sydow). ▷

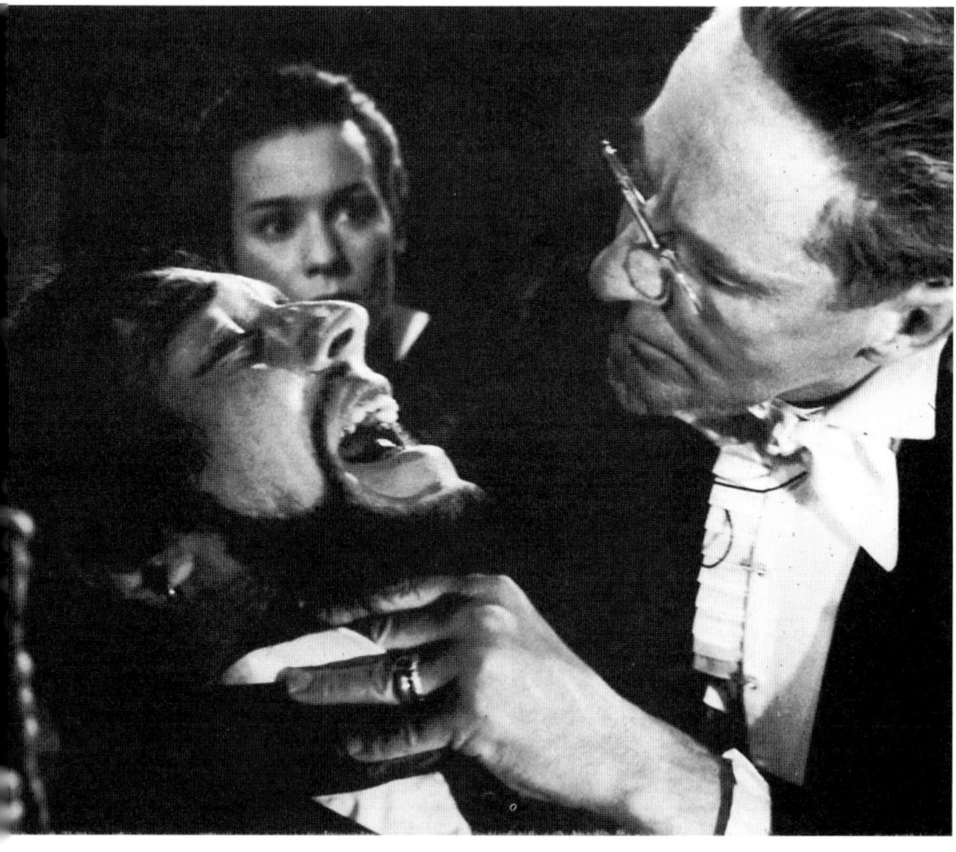

humiliating manner, which he later insisted that he did not do.

Furthermore, Harry Schein was married to Ingrid Thulin. On several occasions he expressed the opinion that she ought to give up film and theater. He encouraged her to involve herself instead in arts and crafts.

I figured out a sophisticated way, in my opinion, to thwart Harry Schein's intent. I knew that Ingrid Thulin did not want anything in the world more passionately than to continue her career as an actress, and therefore I talked her into joining the ensemble at Malmö City Theater. I wanted to prove to Harry Schein that he was wrong. He has never liked to be wrong.

In the end, in order to see his wife, Harry had to commute regularly between Malmö and Stockholm.

It was natural that Bibi and I, somewhat cautiously, began to see Ingrid and Harry socially. I did not feel completely comfortable doing this. Deep inside I imagined that there was an insurmountable gap between his kind and mine, that he wanted to get at me, and that, at the bottom of the superficial graciousness we displayed toward each other, there existed a hard-to-define animosity. It must be emphasized that all this is long since gone. Harry is now one of my few close friends.

But at the time I decided to model the health official Vergérus on Harry Schein.

Vergérus says to Manda Vogler:

> "I feel I can trust you with a secret. This entire evening I have been fighting a hard battle against an unexplainable sympathy for you and your esteemed husband, the magician.
>
> "Immediately when you entered the room, I was

strongly drawn to your faces, your silence, your natural dignity. It is indeed unfortunate, and I would not tell you this if I wasn't a bit intoxicated."

Manda replies, "If that's how you feel, you ought to leave us alone." Vergérus answers, "I can't do that." Manda: "Why?" Vergérus: "Because you represent what I hate most of all: that which cannot be explained."

But the actual focal point of the story is, of course, the androgynous Aman/Manda. It is around her and her enigmatic personality that everything rotates.

Manda represents the belief in the holiness of human beings. Vogler, on the other hand, has given up. He is involved in the cheapest kind of theater, and she knows it.

Manda is very open in her talk with Vergérus. The miracle happened once, and she herself carries it. She loves Vogler in spite of being fully aware that he has lost his faith.

If Vogler is a magician, who, even though he is tired to death, keeps repeating his by now meaningless hocus-pocus, then Tubal is the exploiter, the salesman of art. Tubal is Bergman, the director, trying to convince Dymling, the head of the studio, of the usefulness and quality of his latest film.

In front of extremely skeptical studio executives, I managed to sell *The Face* as a hell of an erotic comedy.

In all fairness, even the studio management could no longer deny that I was successful. They had denied it as long as they possibly could. It had become a standing ritual for the head accountant, Juberg, at the start of every one of my films, to step into the executive office with his accounting ledgers and show what serious losses my latest movies had inflicted upon the company.

But now there was *Smiles of a Summer Night*, which everyone had originally greeted with feelings of despair. This film, as

Naima Wifstrand — "She is two hundred years old and a witch." The actor Johan Spegel (played by Bengt Ekerot) with Volger (Max von Sydow). ▷

well as *Wild Strawberries*, was an unexpected colossal success both in Sweden and in other countries. The studio had begun to sell Bergman movies to other interested countries, and it was a situation so new that the studio began to behave not unlike an old maid who suddenly finds herself being courted by the most exotic suitors. The studio had no experience when it came to foreign sales. Oh yes, a small export department existed, but I am not even sure that those who worked there spoke any foreign languages. There was total confusion, which often resulted in my films falling into the hands of robbers. In time, the United States became the exception; two young men started a distribution company called Janusfilm. They suffered from a combination of idealism and poverty and worked hard to bring out and popularize my films.

In the cast of *The Face* there is an old grandmother whom Naima Wifstrand portrays with inimitable wisdom. She is two hundred years old and a witch, who can make candleholders topple over and glasses explode. She is an authentic old sorceress with roots in ancient traditions; at the same time she is the smartest one in the troupe. She sells concocted love potions and saves the money that she earns from her sorcery, planning to retire and become harmless.

The other central character is Johan Spegel, the actor. He dies twice. Just like Agnes in *Cries and Whispers*, he dies but gets stuck on the way. Here, Spegel is dead and yet not dead:

> I didn't die. But I have already begun to haunt the place. Actually I come off better as a ghost than as a human being. I have become convincing. I was never convincing as an actor.

He is the one who immediately sees through Vogler's disguise: "An impostor who needs to hide his real face?"

The night before Vogler's big magic séance, Spegel and Vogler meet for the second time: "They meet behind the screen where the shadows are at their deepest, next to the drape with its pictures of stars and secret signs." Spegel's face is turned toward the darkness.

> I have prayed *one* prayer all my life. Deploy me. Make use of me. But God never realized what a strong and devoted slave I had become. So I was left unused. No, that's a lie, too. You go step by step by step into the darkness. Movement itself is the only truth.

This is the same Spegel who said earlier:

> I always longed for a knife. An edge that would bare my entrails. Remove my brain, my heart. Relieve me of my contents. Cut away my tongue and my sex. A sharp knife-edge to scrape out all impurity. Then the so-called spirit could rise up out of this meaningless cadaver.

This might sound obscure, but it contains a central point. The words mirrored my longing for *pure artistry*. I had an idea that one day I would have the courage to be incorruptible, perhaps even leave my intentions behind.

It stands in natural opposition to all the rest that exists in *The Face*: the whoring, for instance!

I had often felt that I was involved in a continuous, rather joyous prostitution. My job was to beguile the audience. It was show business from morning till night. It was good fun, no question about it. But underneath it all prevailed a violent yearning, which I let Spegel express.

The screenplay for *The Face* is dated June 4, 1958, and on June 30 we began filming. We continued throughout the summer, or until August 27, when the summer vacation was over and it was time to return to the theater.

The Face was created in an atmosphere of high spirits despite the black components in the tale we were spinning. Most certainly this had to do with the feeling of camaraderie in our troupe of jesters, for such we were during our Malmö period. Later, when I repeated themes from *The Face* in *The Ritual*, they took on a totally different and much more rancid note.

THE FIRST OUTLINE FOR *The Ritual* (*The Rite*) is a dialogue I wrote on February 27, 1967, in the middle of my work on *Shame*:

"Well, Mr. Artist, please be so kind as to describe what you did and how you did it."

"Should I do that, Your Grace? (Laughter.) It will only result in your being horribly angry."

"I will not be angry."

"Oh yes, you will, because you are here in order to make it difficult for me and for yourself, and if you don't let yourself be angry, you won't have the strength to do it. You can't stand people like us; isn't that right? Look into my eyes, Mr. Judge. (Mildly.) That's how things are."

"No, young Mr. Faggot. It is far from being that simple."

"I know that it's not that simple, and therefore I will voluntarily show you what we did, my friend and I. We call it . . ." (Stops himself, hesitating.)

"What do you call your escapade?"

"We call it 'intercessional prayer.' "

" 'Intercessional prayer.' For whom?"

"I don't know, Mr. Judge. We had this sudden desire to celebrate a ritual, an incantation, a formula, a vanity, a cloud, the shadow of a cloud. Your Grace must have felt weakness at some time, perhaps as a child. No, we weren't going to speak of Your Grace."

"Get to the point, Mister!"

"Oh yes, my friend has created a frightful mask, which he wears in a number we do together at the theater. It is a mother-in-law number; perhaps I should mention that I myself portray the poor husband."

He shows a frightful mask depicting an old hag with green hair and movable eyes and a terribly twisted mouth surrounded by warts and a beard.

"When you were caught, in other words."

"I was dressed in women's clothing, calm, collected, and perfumed, and my friend was naked except for a false breast. It was, so to speak, very private, and it took place at twilight. I was standing by the window, and between my hands I held a . . . a . . . (cries quietly) a chamber vessel, a drinking vessel I'd like to say, filled with red wine. So I was standing there in the twilight, and the trees were soughing, and it was raining, I believe, but not a heavy downpour, just a mild rain. So there I was standing by the window (turns to Markus); dear Markus, stand behind me where you did stand, and let the judge see. Take the mask in your left hand and put your right hand over your heart."

"Well, what are you going to do?"

"Excuse me, Your Grace, but I'm so upset, it's so — (cries) — painful to repeat our little game, or whatever it was, here in front of you. I mean, one false intonation and everything could be lost."

"Hurry up, do what has to be done. I don't have all the time in the world."

"Well, I beheld the dark, shiny wine deep down in the bottom of the vessel, and then I whispered, 'Show thyself, O God.' Then Markus raised the mask behind my shoulder so that the old hag's face, illuminated by the meager light from the window, was reflected in the wine *like this*, and I whispered: 'Thank you, O God, for letting me receive you,' and then I bent over the reflection and drank the wine, like this. But then Markus laughed, and the solemnity disappeared, and I broke wind. He called that a really fitting closing hymn. And then we were caught in the act."

This is the genesis of *The Ritual*. Two homosexual men are standing by a window, more or less undressed, and not paying much attention, or else they would have realized that they are standing by a window. Outside the window is a park and a street, and somebody has seen them and reported them. They have been involved in a game. Markus, who is a sculptor, has created a horrid mask that depicts the nameless man's mother-in-law, and then they are suddenly playing the ancient elevation rite, once performed by the ancient Greeks.

The original idea, in other words, is cruder, more easily understood, and much more unpleasant than the finished film.

I read about the elevation rite in connection with my study of the Bacchants and then spoke with Lars Levi Laestadius about a performance on the theater's large stage of Euripides' *Bacchae* with Gertrud Fridh as Dionysus and Max von Sydow as Pentheus. We began to plan and prepare for the play but still had some misgivings. Malmö City Theater really had only one mission: to get people into the theater. So we weighed the advantages against the disadvantages and canceled the project without further sentiment. The theater was fighting for its life, and this project was both too large and too small.

In ancient Greece, theater was inextricably tied to religious rituals. The audience arrived long before sunrise. At dawn the masked priests appeared. When the sun rose over the mountains, it illuminated the center of the stage, where a small altar was erected. The blood of a sacrificial animal was collected in a large vessel. One of the priests hid behind the others. He wore a golden mask, like that of a god. When the sun had risen even higher, two priests elevated the vessel at a precise moment, so that the audience could see the godly mask reflected in the blood. An orchestra of drums and pan flutes played, and the priests sang. After a few minutes the officiant lowered the vessel and drank the blood.

My first thought was to film *The Ritual* simultaneously with *Shame.* The latter consisted of almost 100 percent exteriors, but we built a house for the filming that could double as a studio. On rainy days we stayed indoors and played with the camera, which is why I call *The Ritual* "an exercise for camera and four actors."

I wrote *The Ritual* quickly and without pretensions. For various reasons it was not filmed at the same time as *Shame* as I had originally planned, but I wouldn't let go of it. I managed to interest Ingrid Thulin, Gunnar Björnstrand, Erik Hell, and Anders Ek in a quick production. We would rehearse for a week and then film for nine days.

There is not much lighting in *The Ritual.* The film is markedly aggressive and received startled reactions, both within the television's theater department and from the critics.

When I ended my tenure as head of the Royal Dramatic Theater, I could barely contain a heavy fury: We had completely revitalized a theater that had been like Sleeping Beauty's castle and had, as the Swedes say, "put the church in the middle of the village," meaning that we had put the chief thing in the chief place. We had reorganized the house from top to bottom and had begun to play timely dramas. We offered children's theater on the large stage there and we also rented the China Variety Theater, which was close by, where we put on plays for various schools. We toured. We kept up an accelerated production tempo, doing more than twenty plays per season. In short, we utilized the resources of the theater to the maximum degree. For this, we (I) kept being reprimanded.

My fury had to be channeled — it broke out in *The Ritual*.

More or less consciously I divided myself into three characters in the film.

Sebastian Fischer (Anders Ek) is irresponsible, lecherous, unpredictable, infantile, emotionally disturbed, and always on the verge of a nervous breakdown, but he is also creative, deeply anarchistic, epicurean, lazy, amiable, soft, and brutal.

Hans Winkelmann (Gunnar Björnstrand), on the other hand, is orderly, strictly disciplined with a deep sense of responsibility, socially aware, good-humored, and patient.

The woman, Thea (Ingrid Thulin), is, I believe, a half-conscious attempt to depict my own intuition. She is faceless, doesn't recognize her maturity, submissive, and has a need to please. She has sudden impulses, speaks with God, angels, and demons, believes herself to be a saint. She tries to accomplish stigmatization, is unbearably sensitive — cannot even stand to wear clothes at times. She is neither constructive nor destructive. She is a kind of satellite dish for secret signals from extraterrestrial radio stations.

These three characters are inextricably entwined; they cannot get away from each other and cannot function in pairs. Only in the tension between the three points of the triangle can anything be accomplished. It was an ambitious effort to divide myself and depict how I really function, what forces keep my machine going.

Thea has sister characters from other films: Karin in *Through a Glass Darkly* goes through the wallpaper and speaks

The four actors in The Ritual: *Anders Ek with Gunnar Björnstrand and with Ingrid Thulin. Erik Hell.* ▷

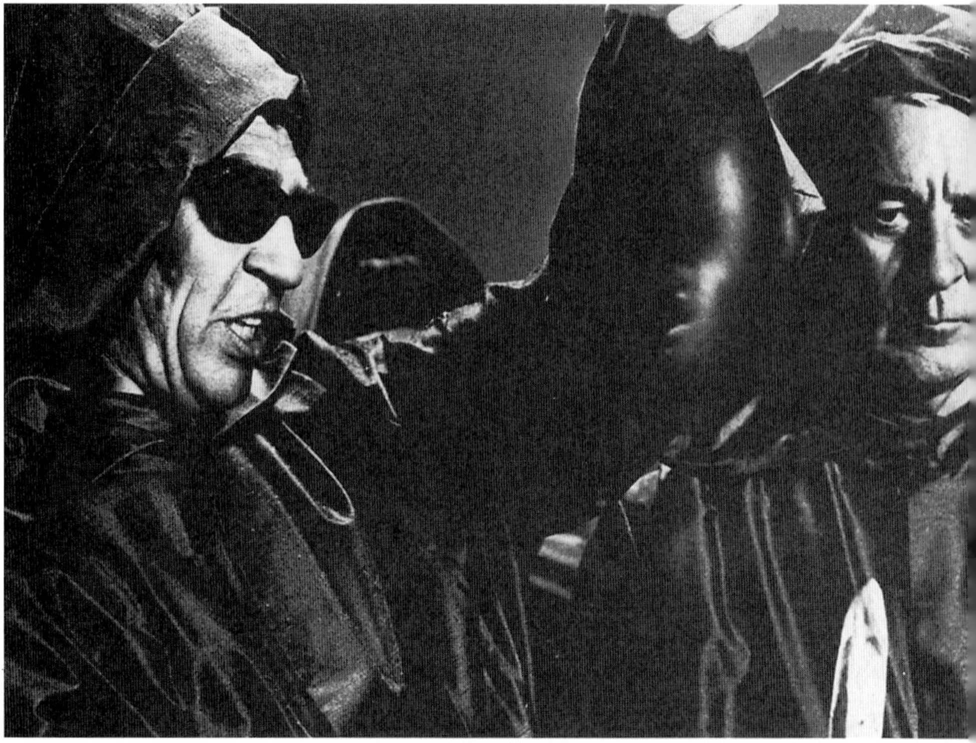

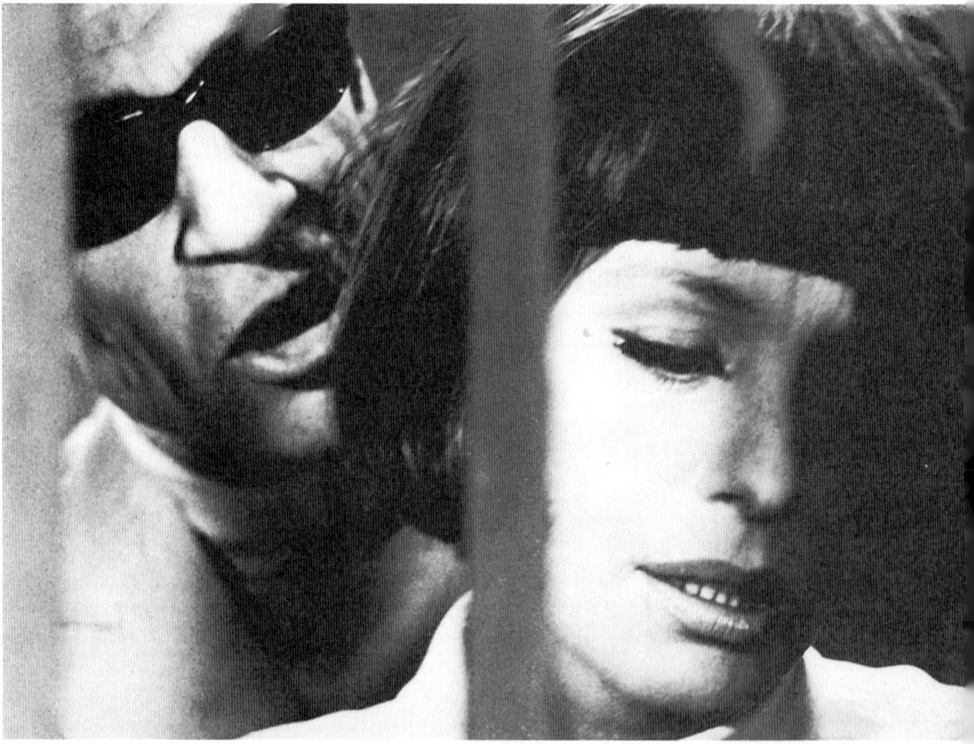

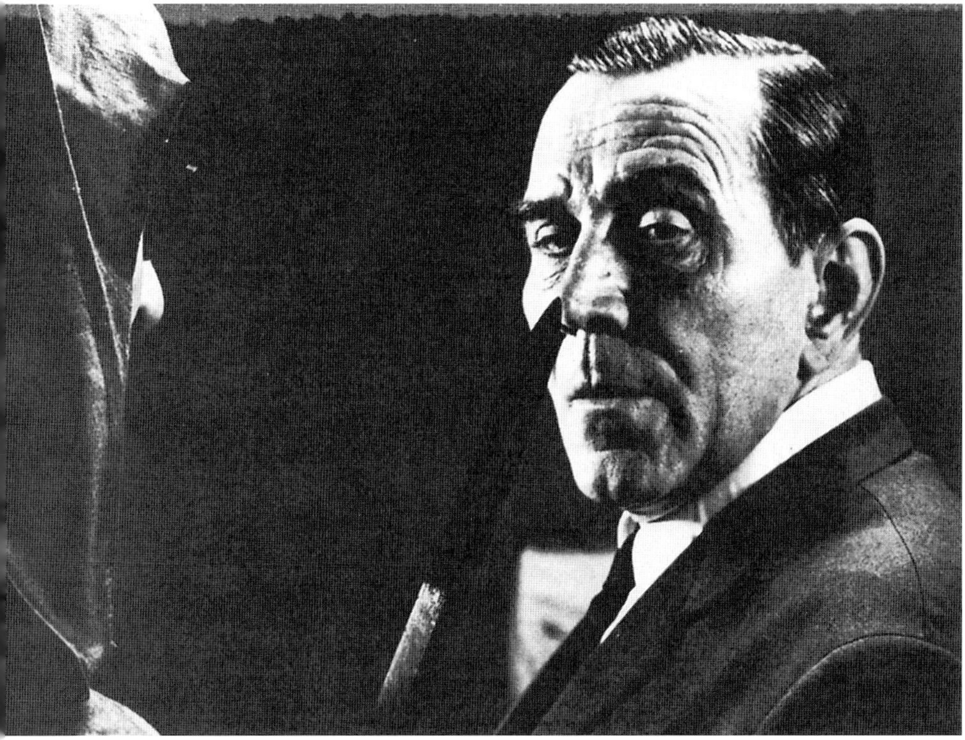

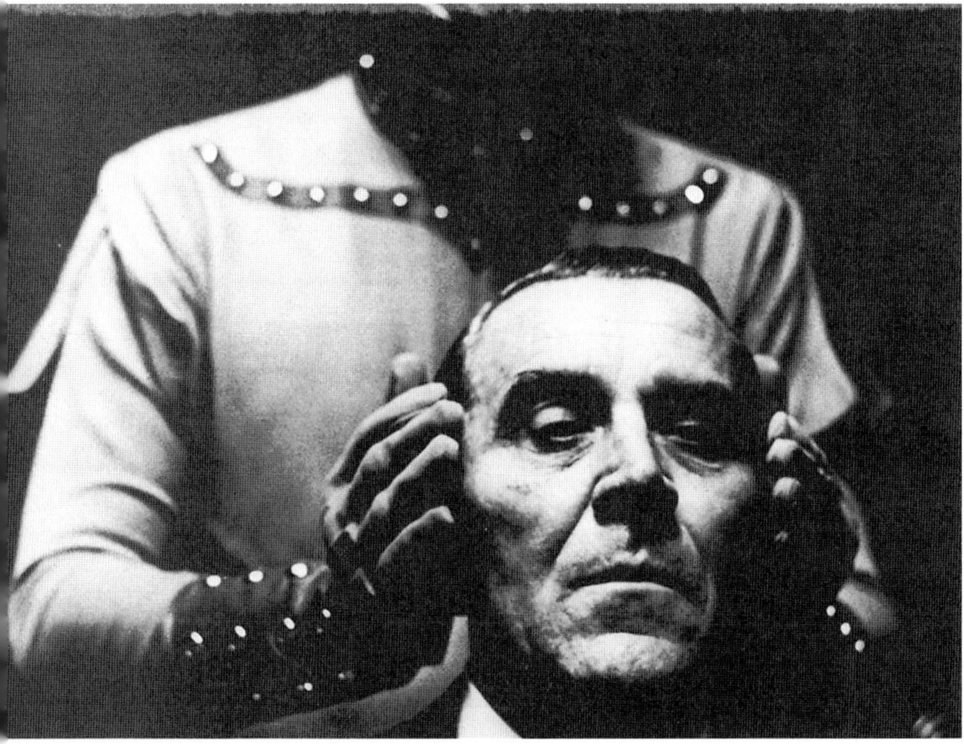

with a spider-god; Agnes in *Cries and Whispers* gets stuck on
the road between life and death; Aman/Manda in *The Face*
has an ever-shifting sexual identity. Thea also has cousins
such as Ismael in *Fanny and Alexander*, who has to be kept in
a locked room.

From this trinitarian perspective, the years at the Royal
Dramatic Theater were not good ones. Neither Sebastian nor
Thea has any room to speak of in which to live and move.
The orderly Hans Winkelmann has the floor. The other two
fall silent, weaken, and withdraw.

Through this interpretation, Thea's attempts to account
for herself become understandable:

> I pretend I am a saint or a martyr. That's why I'm
> calling myself Thea. I can sit for hours at the big table
> in the hallway, gazing at the palms of my hands. Once
> a blush appeared in my left palm. But there was never
> any blood. I pretend I am sacrificing myself in order
> to save Hans or Sebastian. I pretend ecstasy and con-
> versations with the Holy Virgin, faith and disbelief,
> defiance and doubt: I am a poor sinner with an in-
> supportable burden of guilt. So then I reject my faith
> and forgive myself. It's all a game. Within the game
> I am the same all the time, sometimes utterly tragic,
> sometimes boundlessly exhilarated. All marked by the
> same insignificant effort. It's like incessantly running
> water.
>
> I complained to a doctor. (How many doctors I have
> seen!) He told me that my traveling life was harmful
> to my psyche. He prescribed home, husband, chil-
> dren. Security, order, everyday life. Facticities, he
> called it. He maintained that one must not screen
> oneself off from reality, as I had done. I asked him

With Anders Ek and Gunnar Björnstrand. ▷

then if reality was the majority's idea of the journey
of life or if there could possibly be different kinds of
realities, each as real as another. He answered me that
one had to live the best one could. I said that I was
absolutely not unhappy, and then he shrugged and
wrote out a prescription.

I had hoped that a sympathetic light would fall on the poor
judge (Erik Hell), but I realize that I was not particularly
successful.

The judge pleads with the three artists to try to see him
as a human being. But it is too late. He has committed the
rape, and he is going to die. It is a condemned man who
appeals to them even as the headsman's ax is lowered.

Today when I watch *The Ritual* or read the screenplay, I
see how I could have made the film differently. Although it
is tightly constructed and even somewhat entertaining in
parts, *The Ritual* is hard to understand in some places, for
instance, the scene with Sebastian's outburst in front of the
judge:

I lack a declaration of faith and do not belong to any
church. I have never needed any god or salvation or
eternal life. I am my own god; I supply my own angels
and demons. I exist on a stony beach, which lowers
itself in waves toward a protective ocean. A dog barks;
a child cries; the day sinks and becomes night. *You
can never scare me.* No human being will be able to
scare me ever again. I have a prayer that I repeat to
myself in absolute stillness: May a wind come to stir

up the ocean and the stifling twilight. May a bird come from the water out there and explode the silence with its call.

Twelve years later Sebastian is scared out of his mind. We'll talk about that a bit later.

I DON'T HAVE MUCH to say about *The Naked Night* (*Sawdust and Tinsel*). One could insist that the film is a pandemonium — but a well-organized pandemonium. I wrote it in a small hotel on Mosebacke Square, in the same building where the South Theater is situated. The room was narrow, with a panoramic view of the city and the bay. A winding secret staircase connected the theater with the hotel. In the evenings I could hear music from the revue being performed below. At night, the actors and their strange guests partied in the hotel's dining room. In this setting, *Sawdust and Tinsel* was born in less than three weeks. I remember that the demons, the demons of retrospective jealousy, were bridled and made to pull a loaded wagon; they were forced into productive activity. I wrote the film straight through from beginning to end, without stopping to think or add or fill in.

The drama had its origin in a dream. I depicted the dream in the flashback about Frost and Alma. It's rather easy to interpret. A few years earlier I had been madly in love. Pretending professional interest, I enticed my beloved to tell me in detail about her multifaceted erotic experiences. The peculiar excitement of a fresh jealousy over her long-past actions scratched and tore at my innards and my genitals. The most primitive rituals of shame became a permanent alloy in my jealousy. Jealousy became a kind of dynamite that nearly exploded out of me, its creator. To express it in musical terms, one could say that the main theme is the episode with Frost and Alma. There follows, within an undivided time frame, a number of thematic variations of erotics and humiliation in ever-changing combinations.

Sawdust and Tinsel is relatively honest and shamelessly personal. Albert Johansson, the circus owner, loves both Anne and his chaotic life in the circus. And yet, he is strongly drawn toward the bourgeois security he had in life with his now-abandoned wife. To put it briefly: he is a walking chaos of conflicting emotions. The fact that Åke Grönberg played Albert, and that the part was expressly written for him, has nothing to do with any influence from Dupont's film *Variety* with Emil Jannings. It's much simpler than that: if a scrawny director aims for a self-portrait, of course he chooses a fat actor to play himself.

Åke Grönberg was first and foremost a comedy actor with an, allegedly, affable chubbiness. As Albert, he liberated other forces within himself. During the shooting, he was mostly wild and raging since he had moved on to what, to him, was insecure and foreign ground. When in one of his lighter moods, however, he would sing to us. Folk songs and favorite old pop tunes and obscene ditties. I loved and hated him. I imagine that he had similar feelings toward me.

From that tension a creation sprang into existence.

If *Sawdust and Tinsel* is influenced by any film, it is not Dupont's *Variety*. *Variety* is set similarly but stands thematically in exact opposition to *Sawdust and Tinsel*. In *Variety*, Jannings kills the lover. Here, Albert transcends his jealousy and humiliations because of an irresistible need to like people.

We were on location for quite a long time, filming outdoors in all types of weather. Gradually, we entered into a higher (strongly aromatic!) symbiosis with the circus people and the animals. Whichever way you look at it, it was a crazy time. And as I said in the beginning: I don't have a hell of a lot to say about *Sawdust and Tinsel*.

Sawdust and Tinsel: *the flashback with Frost and Alma (Anders Ek and Gudrun Brost). Hasse Ekman and Harriet Andersson. Åke Grönberg with Anders Ek.* ▷

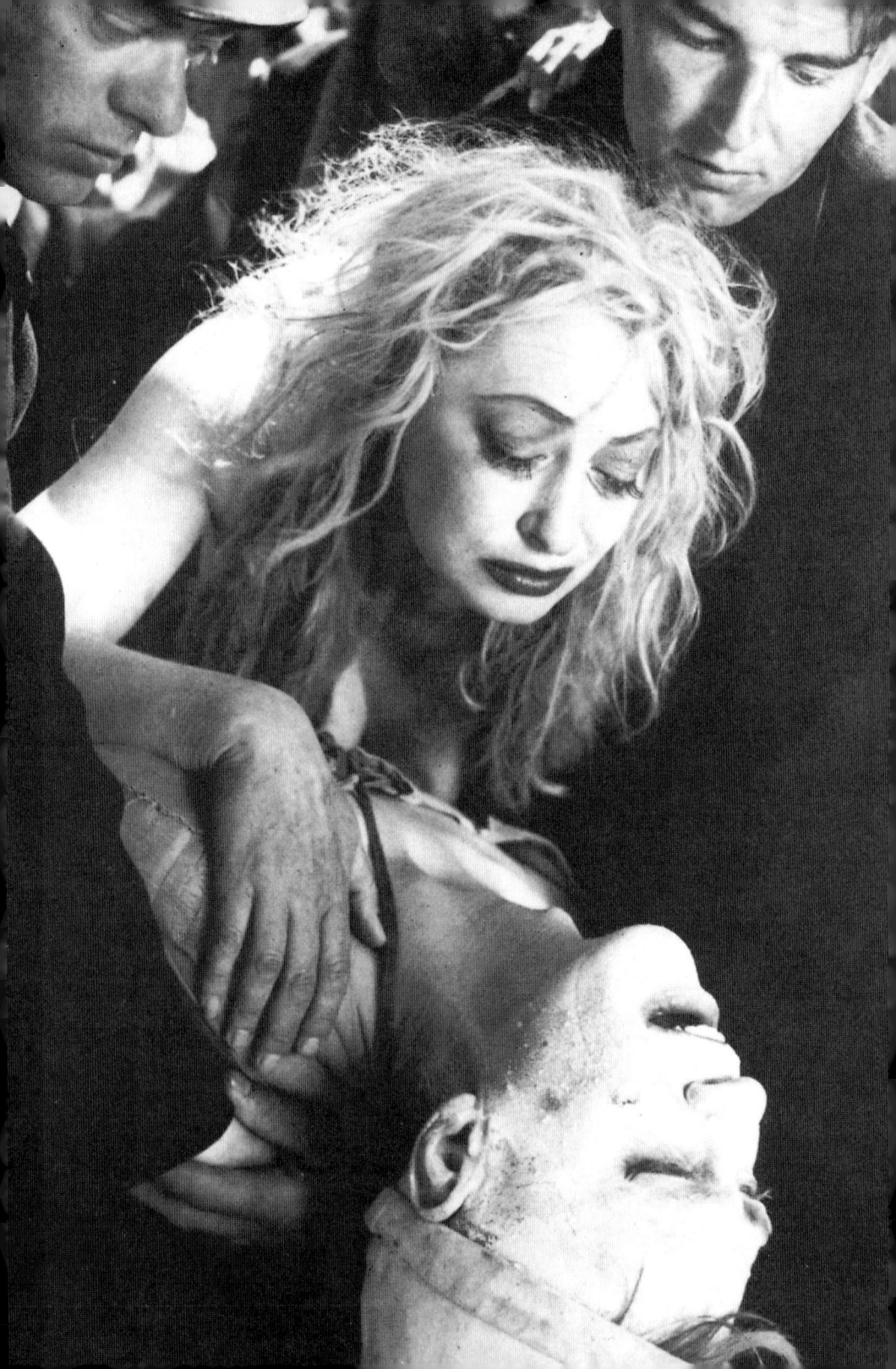

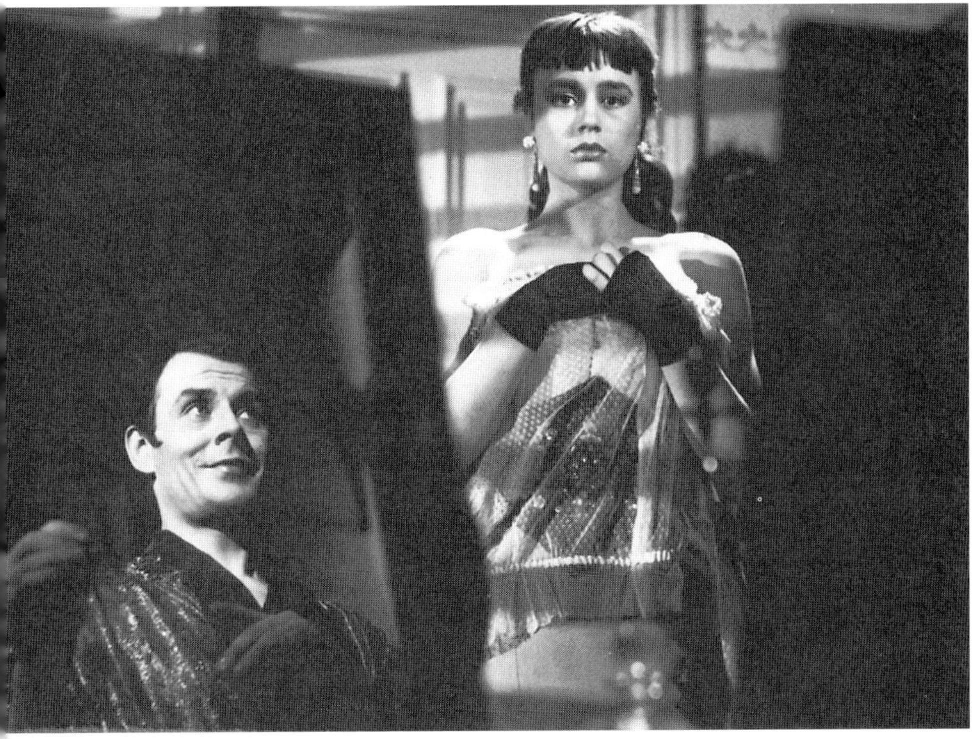

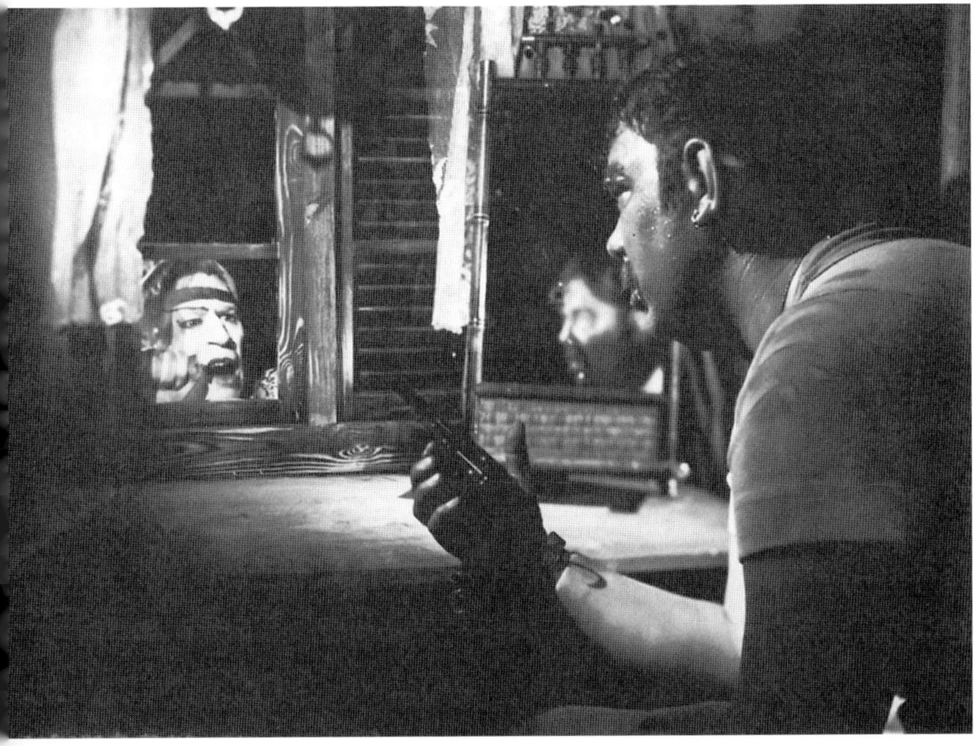

When we had finished filming, Harriet Andersson and I went for a vacation. I had not yet edited the material but was pleased with the work I had done. With pure delight I wrote a comedy in the tower room of the small hotel where we were staying, while Harriet was sunning on the beach below. The story was christened *A Lesson in Love.*

Hard upon the heels of *A Lesson in Love,* I made *Dreams* (*Journey into Autumn*) for Sandrew's Film Company. I had promised the head of the studio, Rune Waldekranz, a comedy, since *Sawdust and Tinsel* was a resounding fiasco. Viewed superficially, *Dreams* consists of two additional variations on themes from *Sawdust and Tinsel.* By this time Harriet and I had terminated our relationship, and we were both feeling quite sad. Our sadness weighs down the film. To be sure, there is an interesting cohesion between the two stories that lead into each other, but *Dreams* is severely wounded by depression and never did take off.

Sawdust and Tinsel received mixed reviews (to put it mildly). A critic, well-respected in Stockholm, said that he "declined an ocular inspection of Mr. Bergman's latest vomiting." This utterance is rather representative of the animosity that was coming at me from many directions. Unfortunately, I cannot claim that it left me unaffected.

With Harriet Andersson in Dreams. *"Our sadness weighs down the film."* ▷

IN *THE MAGIC LANTERN* I wrote that the artistic failure of *The Serpent's Egg* was due mainly to the fact that I set the film in 1920s Berlin. "If I had created the city of my dreams, a city that does not exist and never has, and yet manifests itself acutely with smells and loud sounds, if I had created *that* city, not only would I have been moving in it with total freedom and an absolute sense of belonging but also, more important, I would have brought the audience with me into an alien but secretly familiar world. In *The Serpent's Egg*, however, I ventured into a Berlin that nobody recognized, not even I."

But now I believe the failure lies much deeper. The depiction of time and place might be debatable, but it is hard to deny the care that went into it. Sets, costumes, and casting were done by experts. If you look at *The Serpent's Egg* in pure cinematographic terms, there are excellent aspects of this film and a good dramatic buildup in the unfolding of the plot. The movie does not tire for a moment; rather the opposite. It is overstimulated, as if it had taken anabolic steroids.

But its vitality is powerful on a superficial plane; the failure is hidden underneath.

In an early stage of the planning, I wanted to reactivate my old idea of the two trapeze artists who are stranded because the third member of their act has died. They have been left in a war-threatened city. Their accelerating decline was to be interlaced with the destruction of the city. This theme, found in both *The Silence* and *The Ritual*, is powerful enough for a third application. However, an unfortunate decision made during the planning stage of the screenplay led me astray.

This occurred in the beginning of November 1975. During the previous summer I had read Joachim Fest's biography of Adolf Hitler. I quoted a passage from the book in my workbook:

"The inflation lent a grotesque quality to reality and crushed not only people's incentive to accept the reigning order but also their feeling for permanency in general and made them accustom themselves to living in an impossible atmosphere. This was a complete breakdown of a world's ideas, norms, and morals. The consequences were unfathomable."

Thus this film must take shape in the shadows and in the reality of these shadows. This is damnation, and it's cold in hell because there is no firewood and it is November 1923 and your money is counted by weight. Everything is upside down.

Cast of characters:

ABEL ROSENBERG, 38. Demoted circus artist who, without knowing how it happened, has killed his brother.

HANS VERGÉRUS, same age (or possibly slightly older — perhaps 45). Scientist conducting questionable experiments. Dubious opinions of people and their behavior.

MANUELA BERGMANN, 35. A prostitute going downhill. Badly treated but won't give up. Has five hundred severe wounds leaving long welts on her soul.

" 'The inflation lent a grotesque quality to reality.' " Germany in 1923 is the setting for The Serpent's Egg. ▷

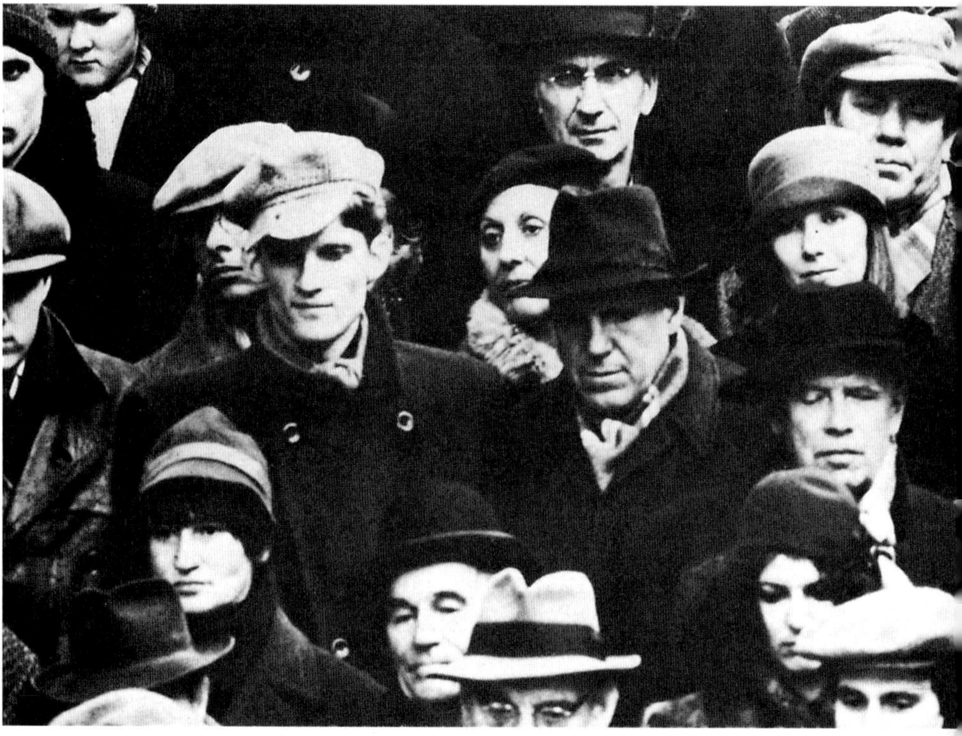

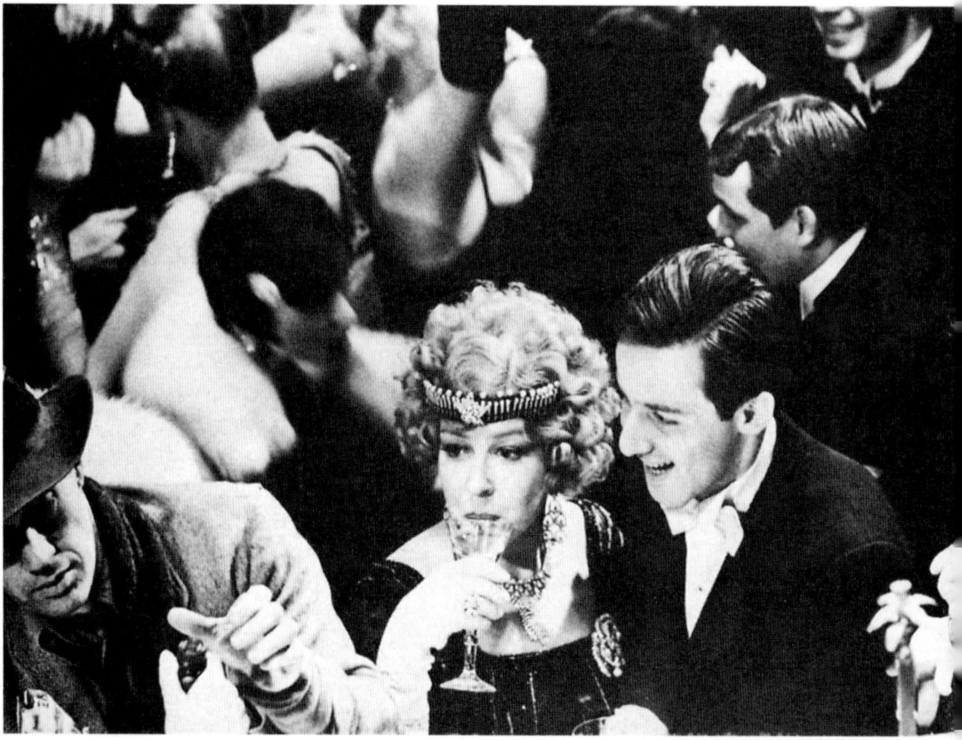

I had not yet been hit with the harsh reality that the whole business concerning my taxes would bring. Those lines about Germany's collapse from Fest's book stimulated my creativity. The hard-to-maneuver balance between order and chaos had always intrigued me. In Shakespeare's later plays lies, among other things, a similar preoccupation with this tension in the break between a world of order, with laws of ethics and social norms, and total collapse, an irresistible chaos that suddenly breaks into a regulated reality and annihilates it.

Without knowing it, however, I already carried failure in my baggage, in my attempt to combine the theme of the two artists in the threatened city with the Vergérus motif, the voyeuristic theme.

I had developed a voyeuristic theme in 1966 when I began writing something, not knowing what it would become:

> He begins to study human faces and reactions while their owners are confronted by experiences he controls. It begins rather innocently: He is showing movies he has shot. One day he takes pictures of a person committing suicide. Then he films a person whom he kills. He shows a woman who is the victim of brutal sexual provocation. Finally he carries out a secret plan: He goes to get a man out of a mental hospital, a man with acute amnesia or some similar disorder. Then he places a woman with him. The two begin to settle into the space that he has put at their disposal. They begin to live together and perhaps to love each other. He notes this with hate and jealousy and begins to intersect and manipulate their activities, creating suspicion and aggression between them. He breaks them down, step by step, so that they destroy each other in the end. Then he has no choice; he must

study himself. He aims the camera at his own person, takes a poison that induces excruciating pain, and notes his gradual failing.

Actually there is a whole movie here. Since then I have repeatedly come back to that very same area: in *Love with No Lovers*, which was never made, and in *Finn Konfusenfej*, for which I did not even complete the screenplay.

But the calamity of *The Serpent's Egg* is that the voyeur motif is totally incompatible with the story of the two artists. They are linked only by my imaginings of a world catastrophe and the collapse of its ideologies. To this, add the collapse of my own private world. On November 19, 1975, came the first memorandum from the tax officials accompanied by quick-as-lightning, coordinated, screaming headlines in the press.

My workbook:

> Afternoon and evening. The fear, the anxiety, the shame. The humiliation. The rage. To have a finger pointed at you and not be able to defend yourself. To be judged in advance by a tribunal that doesn't ask for real reasons. To be perfectly honest, in the beginning I took the whole thing much too lightly. I listened to advice and thought that those giving it surely knew best — this was after all their profession. All was in good order and was being handled in an exemplary manner by qualified people.
>
> But of course this is not the crucial point. The problem is that I react, childishly and self-destructively, in *favor* of those who accuse me. I want to agree; I want to confess; I want to be good; I want to pay for what I've done.

It's a dangerous emotion that suddenly appears out of my dark childhood fears. I feel that I have done something bad. I don't understand what I have done, but I feel guilty. My common sense tries to reason with me, but it's useless; the sense of shame is deeply rooted in me, and the public stigma accentuates my feeling. The weak voice of my common sense is suffocated by shrieks and sobs out of the past — from that time when no appeal was possible, when you were prejudged, as either guilty or not. Then the only thing capable of bringing you peace was punishment, remorse — even if there was nothing to be sorry for — and finally forgiveness, like a sudden grace floating in from nowhere. The voices that had been hard and accusatory suddenly became mild; the icy silence surrounding the criminal broke once the punishment had been executed. Punished, purified, forgiven, no longer struggling on the outside, then reinstated, again a member, again belonging.

That's how I feel, the anxiety rushing around in my entrails, clawing at them; it's as if I had a mad cat in my stomach. My cheeks are blazing from some strange fever that I haven't experienced in forty years but of which I am now reminded with painful conspicuousness.

The hours crawl forward. How will my life turn out after this, will I be able to go on working? Will the desire to work return after this public disgrace? In this reality, will I have the strength to continue playing my games? So this is how things stand now, and this is how it was then, I remember; I am as powerless as I was as a child, as powerless as a person thrown into a strong current that continually pulls him downward. The temptation is to resign oneself, to flee into the darkness, into the paralysis of non-action, into hysteria. The temptation is to give up. Fifty-seven years old and seven years old, at one and the same time, in one and the same moment.

If I at least were able to drum up real disgust for those shrewd bureaucrats who have brought me this torment. But that doesn't work either. The fifty-seven-year-old says lamely, for God's sake, they're doing their job, and the seven-year-old never doubts the authority and infallibility of those meting out justice. The seven-year-old is, of course, always in the wrong. He tells that to the fifty-seven-year-old, and the fifty-seven-year-old believes him and not the voice of his common sense, that calm, factual voice that says the whole thing is a drama with roles and lines of dialogue, a small vexing scene in society's general humiliating comedy-tragedy. Nobody cares; nobody is threatened; nobody feels anything except possibly a touch of malicious joy at someone else's misfortune. Nobody except one from his childhood, the spiritually handicapped clown in his fifty-seventh year who trembles in the face of humiliation, shame, fear, and self-loathing. Hour after hour, day after day.

That's how ridiculous things are.

If I manage to calm down and reflect, I know I can use this as material for the part of Abel Rosenberg. He must feel exactly like this. I can describe it since I know how it feels to be accused, how scary it is, how willing one becomes to receive punishment, willing to the point of longing for the punishment to begin. A tiny joy begins to spread in my whole being for a fraction of a moment. It bubbles up and makes me

"Manuela Bergmann, 35. A prostitute going downhill." Liv Ullmann.
"Abel Rosenberg, 38. Demoted circus artist." David Carradine. ▷

laugh, all by myself. That must be a good sign, after all. A tiny joy in the middle of this sea of anguish. Perhaps the fifty-seven-year-old will be able to regain mastery over the screaming, guilt-addicted child — couldn't that be within the frame of what's possible? Hell, imagine if it were so! Just this brief moment brings sudden appeasement.

Perhaps it's possible to stay here, to remain in place, to fight my impulses, my embarrassment, and my humiliation. To stay, to not run away, to take it all and use it, to be sensible and angry in a healthy, objective way. In spite of everything, can something be done about this?

Two days later I noted: "Oh yes, it was possible to write both yesterday and today, even though it was more an act of will than one of inspiration. It feels a little as if one act were finished."

In actuality, my instrument had already been knocked out of my hands. In spite of this, I played on and put together a screenplay for *The Serpent's Egg* while the lawyers "had meetings," the problems were played down, and conversations with the tax authorities were inititated. I was calm, but the calm was deceptive.

On January 26, 1976, the tax police came and picked me up. We had just finished editing and mixing *Face to Face*. Gunnel Lindblom was ready to begin *Paradise Place* at my company, Cinematograph, and I had set up meetings with her and Ulla Isaksson about the screenplay and casting. I had begun rehearsing Strindberg's *Dance of Death* at the Royal Dramatic Theater, and, finally, the screenplay for *The Serpent's Egg* was complete.

But everything was already wrong. The creative work had

been disturbed. I imagined being able to use a situation that was not yet usable. I let the creativity rush in to help as if it were a doctor, nurse, and ambulance, all at once.

There followed the breakdown and the breaking up of camp. Quite by chance I ended up in Germany with my German film. I had an offer from Dino De Laurentiis, who saw *The Serpent's Egg* as a seductive project. I was able to negotiate a sizable director's fee since I, for the moment, was a "bankable" name with *Cries and Whispers, Scenes from a Marriage,* and *The Magic Flute* under my belt.

I was able to function, yet I was coming undone, a treacherous balance. I felt as if I had been poisoned, and the poison became both fuel and flame. I fought against my experiences and believed that the struggle gave me strength.

When I went to the doctor for a checkup before we started filming, I was told that my blood pressure was abnormally high. I had been walking around Munich feeling feverish and had blamed my suddenly rosy cheeks on not being used to the altitude (six hundred meters — about two thousand feet — above sea level). Until then I had had typically low blood pressure.

I began to eat beta blockers, but that didn't help — I just became schizophrenic.

Today it's easy to see that I reacted irrationally at every turn. My desire then was to make the movie as quickly as possible in order to show the world that I was able to do so. I was intrigued by *The Serpent's Egg.* Everyone encouraged me, telling me that it was a good story. It became a massive, heavy shoot, but I kept convincing myself that I was making my best film ever. I was frenzied and rabid; all my inner safety reserves were rushed into action.

I continued to hold onto the illusion that I was making a masterpiece even during the editing and mixing. At the same

time that I was working on *The Serpent's Egg*, I was also negotiating with the Residenz Theater about a production of
Strindberg's *Dream Play*. That, too, was to be on a grandiose
scale: More than forty of the theater's best actors participated
in a production ultimately studded with insane errors of judgment, not the least of which occurred with the design.

Every morning on my way to the theater, I walked past
the ruins of the old Army Museum. The sight gave birth to
the idea that the ruin with its cupola would be the ideal stage
setting for *A Dream Play*, and so we built the set accordingly.

When I arrived at the theater to inspect the finished scenery, my first impulse was to turn around, go home, and never
come back. The background was gigantic; the actors looked
like tiny ants. The background scenery consumed the whole
play. All we had to do was to open the curtain, show the ruin,
then close it again. The scenery held the spotlight; nothing
else mattered; and the play failed.

I found in an old issue of *Simplicissimus* from 1923 a suggestive charcoal drawing of a heavily trafficked Berlin street in
wintry twilight. Though we had been scouting in Berlin and
other nearby cities for suitable locations, no place could
match the street in that drawing. To top it off, it was magically
named Bergmannstrasse. Through tough negotiating I managed to talk the producer into building the whole street scene
complete with streetcar tracks, backyards, crossing alleys, and
domed portals on the lot of Bavaria Studios. The cost was
astronomical, but I was giddy with feverish enthusiasm.

The Bergmannstrasse came out of the same madness as
A Dream Play did, caused by my high blood pressure and
hypertension.

Warning bells were ringing, but I refused to hear them.

My wife Ingrid and I went to the United States to find an
actor for the male lead, Abel Rosenberg. First, I asked Dustin

Bergmannstrasse on Bavaria Studios' lot, day and night. ▷

Hoffman if he would play Abel. He studied the script and offered a thoroughly intelligent interpretation, but when push came to shove he admitted that he didn't feel he was right for the part and withdrew, assuring me that it would have been fun to work together.

Then I met Robert Redford in Beverly Hills. He was friendly and positive but informed me that he could not see himself playing a Jewish circus performer.

I had great respect for both Redford and Hoffman, but unfortunately, I did not see it as a warning sign that both of them pulled away.

Next I turned to Peter Falk, whom I considered a very fine actor. He was positive about the part; but for very different reasons, not the least of which were contractual, finally he, too, fell by the wayside.

Even in this thorny dilemma, Dino De Laurentiis was utterly loyal and did not give up. In an emergency meeting he came up with another actor, Richard Harris.

Once more all warning signals stopped flashing in my head; I was consumed with bringing *The Serpent's Egg* to fruition.

Richard Harris was soaking in a huge water tank on Malta where he was finishing a film [*Orca*] about a crazy sea captain and his love story involving a giant whale. Dino De Laurentiis had had the water tank specially constructed for the filming, and Harris spent most of his time fully immersed. From there came his message that he would enjoy playing the part and working with me.

Filming was postponed for three weeks. I returned to Munich to keep production going by conducting various screen tests, but everybody was already in position. Bavaria Studios had set the ball rolling long before, and the enormously costly sets were built and in place. From morning until night Sven

"How about Richard Harris?" With Dino De Laurentiis. ▷

Nykvist and I screen-tested costumes, furniture, and masks. Enthusiasm was high, and Bavaria itself offered some diversions while we waited for Richard Harris to emerge from his bath.

In time he did, unfortunately the same evening I was due in Frankfurt to attend a formal ceremony to receive the Goethe Prize.

I made an agreement with my coordinator Harold Nebenzahl (an efficient misanthrope who spoke twelve languages) that he should meet Harris at the Munich airport and have him register at the Hilton, where my wife and I were also staying. Then we could meet for lunch the following day when I returned from Frankfurt.

The next morning we went down to the lobby and waited for Harris (and his lady friend) to appear. We waited in vain. The porter informed us, only when asked point-blank, that Mr. Harris had left early that morning, after booking a room at the Savoy Hotel in London.

In desperation Nebenzahl and I chartered a private plane, flew to London, and went straight to the Savoy, only to be told that Harris had checked in but was not to be disturbed. I rushed out and went for a walk along the Thames to calm my nerves. About ten o'clock that night I called Harris from my room, informing him that we had to stop this game of hide-and-seek. He replied that he was mad as hell that *his* director had not been there to meet him as he arrived in Munich, and he considered the Goethe Prize a poor excuse for my absence. After a while he agreed to meet in his room, where we sat talking until the wee hours. He finally agreed to be in *The Serpent's Egg*, but he needed to make a quick trip to Los Angeles first to settle some business. In a couple of days he'd meet us at Bavaria Studios, and we could then start shooting the film.

Relieved, we returned to Munich, and the entire crew celebrated with cake and coffee.

The following day Dino De Laurentiis called me to say that Richard Harris had contracted pneumonia from some kind of amoeba bacteria in the water tank in Malta, and a long convalescence was expected. We had to find someone else.

At this point the name of David Carradine was mentioned as a possibility. Dino sent me a copy of Carradine's latest film [*Bound for Glory*], which I viewed the next day. It was the story of a country singer and enchanted me. One of the Carradine clan, David Carradine had an exciting look and sang with heartfelt musicality. He reminded me of the Swedish actor, Anders Ek, and the thought that God's finger had finally pointed to the right Abel Rosenberg took hold of me.

Two days later Carradine arrived in Munich. We were finally ready to begin. But when I met him for the first time, Carradine seemed absent-minded and a bit strange. To help him get into the right frame of mind for this film, we launched the shooting with a viewing session of two classic Berlin movies: *Mutter Krausens Fahrt ins Glück* and Ruttmann's *Berlin — die Symphonie der Grosstadt*. The minute the lights in the theater went out, Carradine fell asleep, snoring loudly. When he woke up, I had no chance to discuss his role with him.

Carradine's behavior repeated itself during the filming. He was a night owl and kept falling asleep on the set. He was found slumped just about everywhere, sound asleep. At the same time he was hard-working, punctual, and well prepared. Because of this, among other factors, we finished the film within our planned time schedule. I was pleased, to say the least, and very proud of our accomplishment. I also nourished considerable hope for a positive reaction.

It didn't hit me until much later — *The Serpent's Egg* was

a substantial failure. I made myself immune to the rather tepid reaction from the critics. I remained optimistic, refusing to see the film for what it was. After the film's release, my life began to calm down; then I painfully realized the serious extent of my failure. Still, I do not regret for a moment making *The Serpent's Egg*; it was a healthy learning experience.

IN THE MAGIC LANTERN I wrote about a film I began writing during the summer of 1985 on Fårö Island.

It was to have been about an old maker of silent movies, whose decaying films are found in countless metal cassettes left underneath a summer cottage being restored. A dimly perceived connection runs between his pictures. An expert on deaf-mutes tries to read the actors' lips in the silent films in order to record their lines. Different kinds of montage are tried, which result in various action sequences, all with different outcomes. The project begins to involve more and more people. It grows and thrives, and thus is costing more and more money. It becomes increasingly difficult to handle. Then one day, it all catches fire, the nitrate original as well as the acetate copies, and the whole lot goes up in smoke. The relief is universal.

I put this screenplay aside rather quickly after I had begun to write it. My body reminded me again of the promise of abstinence (from film work) that my soul had forgotten. The idea of attempting to put together a film from fragments, without access to a script, was fascinating, however. It was an idea that I had toyed with once before.

During my second year in Munich (in 1977), I had begun writing a story I called *Love with No Lovers*. It was heavy and

210

formally fragmented, and it mirrored an upheaval that clearly had something to do with my exile. The setting was Munich, and it dealt, as did my silent movie dream, with a large amount of film segments that had been abandoned by the director.

The screenplay for *Love with No Lovers*, finished in March 1978, carries an introduction in the form of a letter to friends and co-workers:

> Whenever I begin working with a play for the stage, I first consider these questions: Why did the playwright write this play, and why did it turn out exactly like this? Now I direct these same questions to myself: Why has B. written this film, and why did it turn out exactly as it did? The answers become uncertain and loaded down with rationalizations after the fact. So if I insist that I was driven by a gratifying disgust to portray certain forms of human behavior, political cynicism, and emotional detachment, then I have only told half the truth. Because I have also a need to show the possibilities of love, the richness of living in the moment, and the human ability to do good.

Nobody in Sweden wanted to invest a penny in *Love with No Lovers*, even though I was willing to put my own money into it. I spoke with Horst Wendlandt, who was the German coproducer of *The Serpent's Egg*, but he had been burned by that experience. Dino De Laurentiis declined as well, and it was soon evident that this large, expensive project would not get off the ground. That was all there was to it. I had been around and knew that the more expensive your projects were, the greater the possibility of refusal.

With Robert Aztorn and Christine Buchegger in From the Life of the Marionettes. ▷

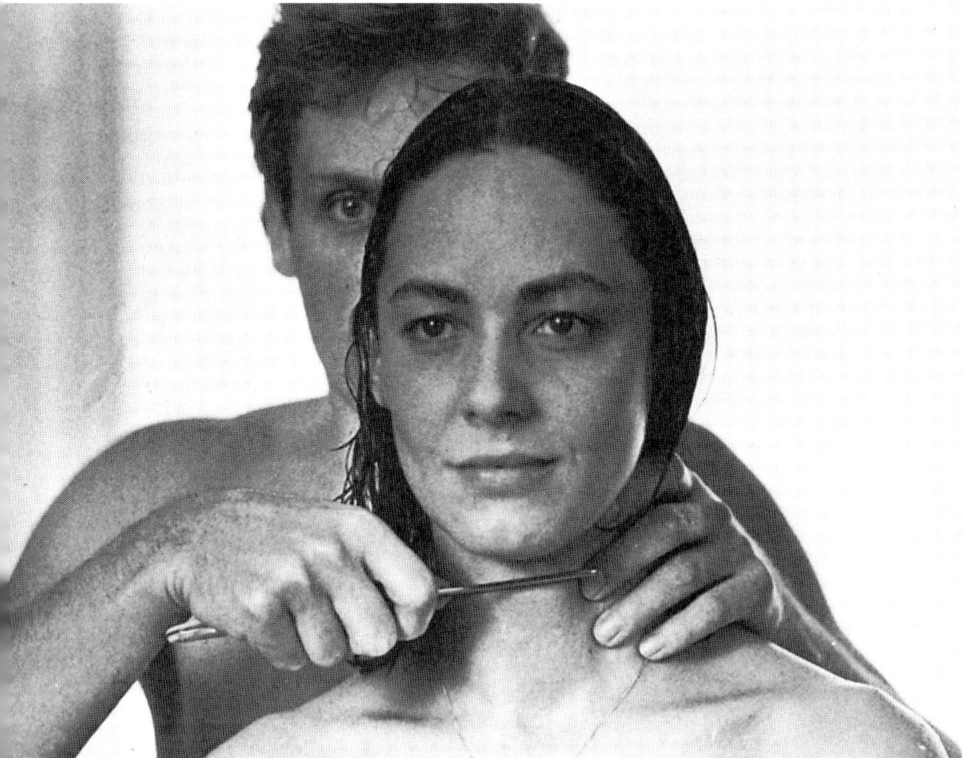

I buried the project without bitterness and didn't think about it further. Later, in order to foster and strengthen the ensemble at the Residenz Theater, I thought it might help if we made a television play together. So I carved the story about Peter and Katarina out of the buried *Love with No Lovers*.

There are a few scenes left from the original script, but, by and large, *From the Life of the Marionettes* is fresh.

The film is based on concrete observations and memories surrounding a theme that had haunted me for a long time: how two human beings who are insolubly and painfully united in love at the same time try to rip themselves free of their shackle.

The main characters of *From the Life of the Marionettes*, Peter and Katarina, appeared previously in *Scenes from a Marriage*, in which they acted as counterpoints to Johan and Marianne in the first episode.

In the earlier film, Peter and Katarina cannot live with each other or apart. They commit cruel acts of sabotage against each other, actions that only two individuals this close could invent. Their time together is a sophisticated and destructive dance of death. When they fight at the dinner table, they hurl the first assault on Johan's and Marianne's marital cardboard world, and Johan and Marianne first witness the purgatory of their every day.

I wrote *Scenes from a Marriage* in six weeks one summer. I wanted to make it for television, a more beautiful everyday product, since we had practically no budget. We planned to create six episodes, each to be rehearsed for five days and then filmed during the subsequent five days. About fifty minutes of film would be made in ten days, which meant that the six episodes would be finished in a little more than two months.

Scenes from a Marriage: *Peter and Katarina Egerman make their first entrance.* ▷

When we actually shot the film, it went much faster than that. Erland Josephson and Liv Ullmann enjoyed their parts as Johan and Marianne and learned them quickly. Suddenly we had a film that had cost practically nothing, which was great since we were broke. (*Cries and Whispers* had not yet been sold.)

All in all, *Scenes from a Marriage* was a pure joy to make because we approached it as a television production and made it without feeling the paralyzing pressure of making a feature film.

From the Life of the Marionettes, however, was not a joy to make. It, too, was made as a television film and was mainly financed by Zweites Deutsches Fernsehen. Outside of Germany, it was unfortunately presented as a feature film.

In *Love with No Lovers*, the main character, Peter, is a desperado who shoots Franz Josef Strauss. While I was writing *From the Life of the Marionettes*, I quickly realized that it was not Strauss Peter ought to shoot.

Peter says that all roads have been closed, that he has no possibility of getting out. Alcohol, drugs, and sexuality offer only the illusion of an exit.

The film poses the question of why Peter, seemingly without reason, ends another human being's life. I offer several different explanations in the film, none of which, purposely, holds water. When I watch the movie today, I feel that the character of Tim, a homosexual, is closest to the truth when he hints that Peter is bisexual. For Peter, the acknowledgment of his split sexuality would possibly have been liberating.

I also offer a glimpse of this explanation in the final analysis made by the doctor, but the whole analysis is a conscious hoax: a cynical codification of a bloody drama in slippery psychiatric terms. The doctor sees what is about to happen, but he lets it go on since he has private designs on Katarina. So, in the end of the film, Peter should have shot the doctor.

From the Life of the Marionettes is my only German film.

The Serpent's Egg may at first glance appear equally German. But I conceived it in Sweden and wrote it at about the same time I was receiving the warning signs of my own personal catastrophe.

The Serpent's Egg is presented from the point of view of an outsider's desperate curiosity, but when I made *From the Life of the Marionettes*, I had to some degree accepted my own life in Germany and no longer had problems with the language. I had been working in the German theater for some time and could tell if what was said sounded right or wrong. I felt that I knew the German people and their culture. I had also already written *Love with No Lovers*, an ambitious attempt to delve more deeply into my German existence.

From the Life of the Marionettes is notable for the rigor with which it was written. After I had written the screenplay, I cut out about 20 percent of the dialogue. Then about 10 percent more was slashed during the actual filming.

Through this editing, the film acquired a compressed form: short episodes with Brechtian texts in between. These texts relate the ongoing events to the final catastrophe.

I have made bad films that are close to my heart, and I have made good films, objectively speaking, to which I am indifferent. Other films, in a comical way, are subject to my own changes of attitude. Sometimes it happens that someone says, "I really liked that film." Then I am instantly happy, and I decide that I also really like that film.

I am rather proud of *From the Life of the Marionettes*. I think it holds its own.

One criticism I can accept is that which deals with the film's

With Walter Schmidinger in Tim's room. ▷

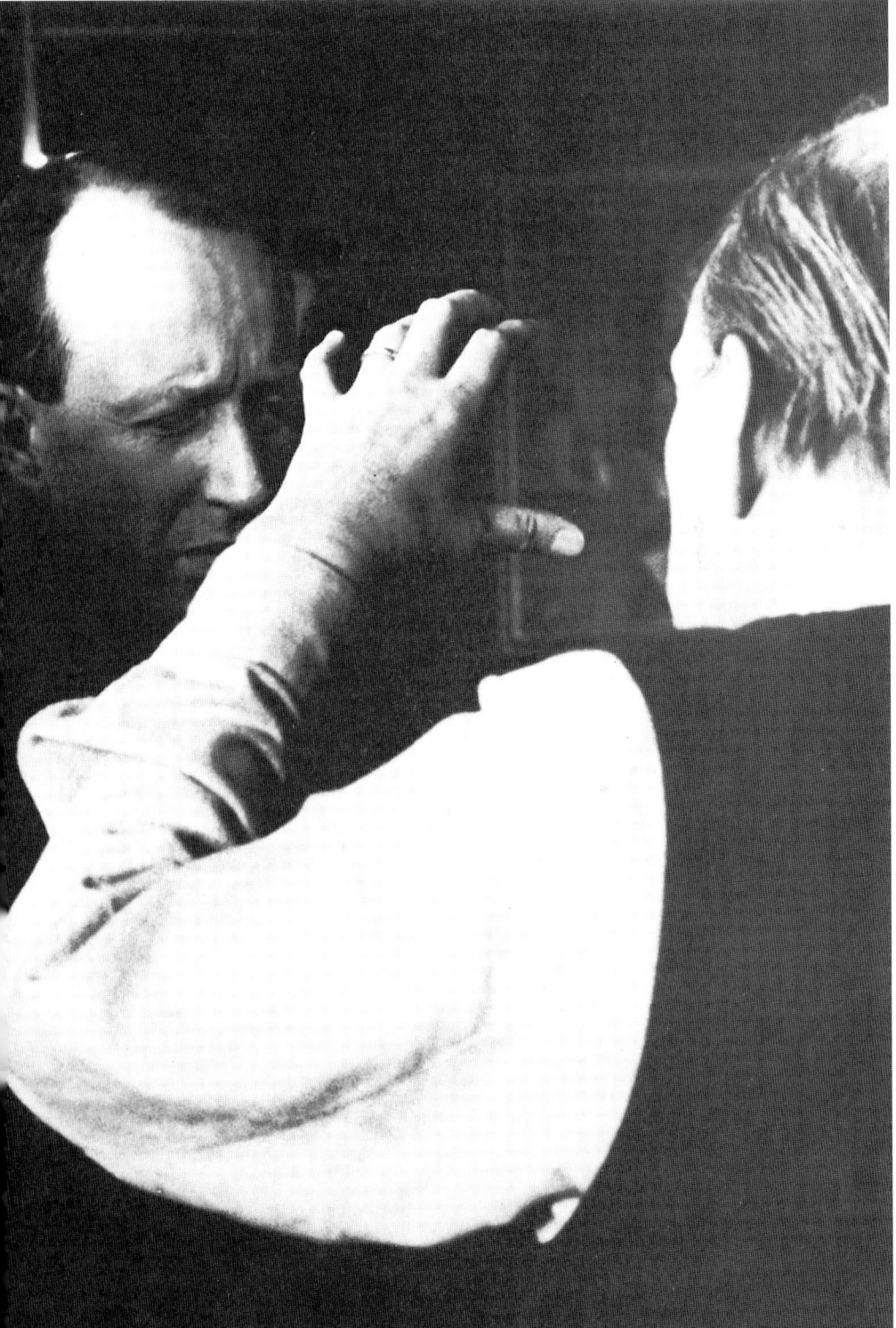

218

constricted form. In my youth, I had staged an adaption of Olle Hedberg's *Rabies*, in Helsingborg, Sweden. The play was taken from one of the later novels in a series Hedberg had written. In a final monologue the main character, Bo Stensson Svenningson, says that we all live in a dark room without windows or doors. But he adds: somewhere there must be a small fissure, invisible to our eyes, which gives us the idea of fresh air.

But in *From the Life of the Marionettes* the characters reside in a hermetically closed room without even this fissure. In retrospect, I can see this modification as a weakness.

Another mistake, as big as a beauty mark, is the letter that Peter writes but never mails. It doesn't make sense psychologically. Only when dictating business letters can Peter formulate what he wants to say. With him, knowledge and the art of self-expression are unthinkable. Unfortunately, on this point I did not follow William Faulkner's sound advice: kill your darlings. In other words, I should have cut it.

Today I would have used my largest pair of scissors. Cutting the sequence would have made the movie ten minutes shorter and much better.

One aspect of the film that came directly from my own life experience is what happens to Peter in the hospital; he cuts off all contact with the external world. I spent some time in a psychiatric clinic after the business about my taxes. I don't remember if it was a painful time. I arose at five-thirty in the morning to be in the bathroom before everybody else — I looked after my physical condition scrupulously. My whole day was carefully divided. I received ten one-tenth-milligram tablets of Valium every day and and an extra dose whenever I needed more.

Peter lives a similar existence. He sleeps with his worn

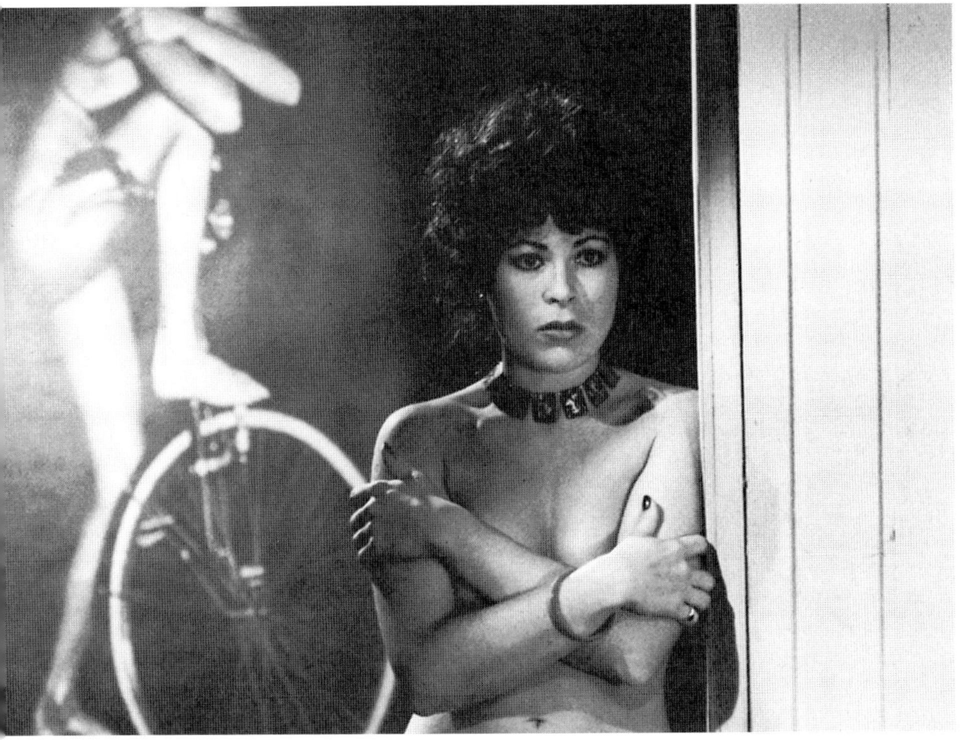
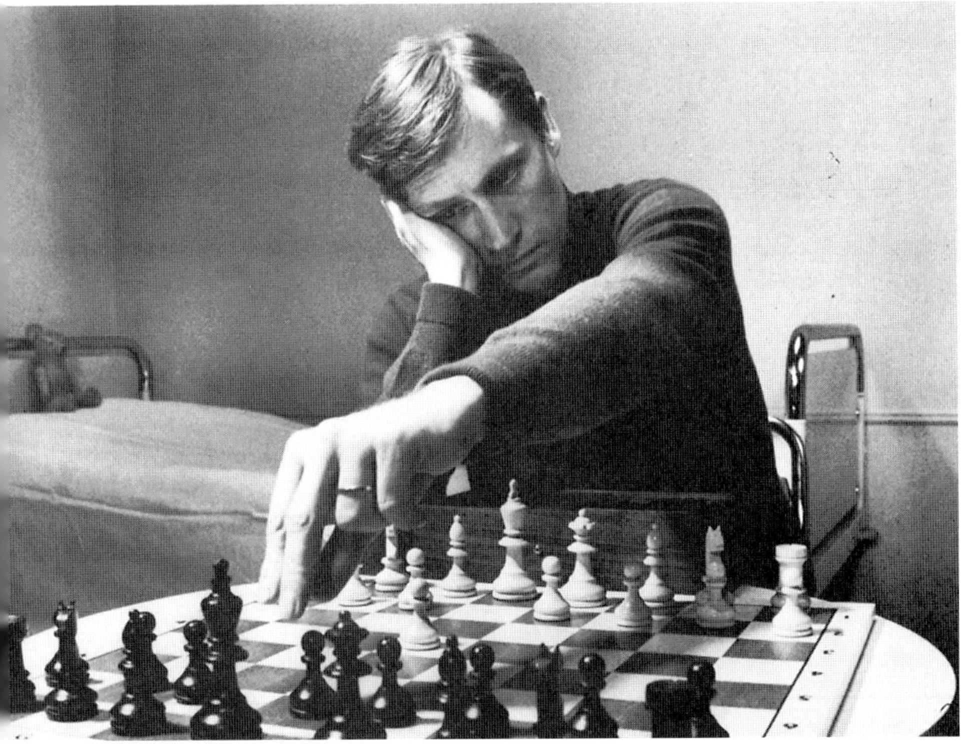

teddy bear from childhood. He plays chess with a computer. For half an hour every morning he stands quietly smoothing his bed.

His wife, Katarina, still lives with him, but now they are distant. She tells her mother-in-law that she leads her life as usual. "But all the time I'm crying inside."

AFTER THE REHEARSAL WAS NOT made as a feature film either. Just like *From the Life of the Marionettes*, it was made for television.

Originally, I imagined the film as a correspondence between an aging director and a young actress. I began writing it but found it boring before long; it would be more fun to see them.

While I wrote, I must have hit a sore nerve or, if you like, an underground vein of water. From my watery unconscious, twisted vines and strange weeds shot up; everything grew into a witch's porridge. Suddenly there appeared the director's former mistress, who is the mother of the young actress. She has been dead for years, and yet she enters the play. On the dark, empty stage of a theater during the quiet hour between four and five in the afternoon, much can return to haunt you.

The result of this brewing was a piece of dramatic television that is about life in the theater.

There are young actors and actresses whom I, a bit absent-mindedly, regard as my children. It happens that they find it useful to have me as a father figure and adopt me. After a while they get angry with me because they don't need a father anymore. I have always liked this role and never felt inhibited by it. Under certain circumstances it can be a safety net for young actors to have a father figure who can stand the rough treatment.

After the Rehearsal was written expressly for the joy of materializing it together with Sven Nykvist, Erland Josephson,

221

and Lena Olin. I have always followed Lena with tenderness and professional interest. Erland has been my friend for fifty years. Sven is Sven. If once in a while I miss working in film, it really is just the collaboration with Sven that I miss.

So *After the Rehearsal* was meant to be a pleasant little episode on my road toward death. We planned to keep the team small. We would rehearse for three weeks, and Sven would film it. We would work in Filmhuset (Film House) and the set was to be simple.

To my surprise, the shooting was completely joyless.

Seeing *After the Rehearsal* now, I find it much better than I had remembered. When you have struggled with a bad shoot, the dispiritedness lingers. It makes you remember the film with greater distaste than necessary.

One frustration I felt concerned a scene with Ingrid Thulin, truly one of the great movie actresses of our time. As a jealous colleague expressed it once: "she is married to the camera." But in this film she couldn't distance herself from her part. When she would say the line "Do you think that my instrument is destroyed forever?" she would begin to cry. I told her, "Please, don't sentimentalize!" To me, it seemed natural for her to say the line with cool observance. Instead she burst out crying every time. Finally I gave up. Perhaps I was upset with Ingrid because I was angry with myself. "Is my instrument destroyed forever?" The question seemed to concern me more than it did her.

Add to this the fact that Erland Josephson was overworked. For the first time during our long collaboration, he was hit by what the Germans call *Textangst* (which literally means *text anxiety* — having trouble learning and remembering lines). The last and most important day brought short-circuiting and blackouts. We muddled through, but that was all.

Lena Olin kept her presence of mind, and in spite of being

relatively inexperienced, she managed gallantly without letting herself be disturbed by our turmoil.

The discomfort of the shoot stuck like glue, and the editing was another wretched experience: there was so much cutting and pasting. *After the Rehearsal*, in the final edited version, ran one hour and twelve minutes. I had been forced to cut at least twenty minutes of the finished material.

Today it is hard to believe that *After the Rehearsal* was actually written as a bit of a black comedy with dialogue in harsh yet comedic language. The film itself is lackluster, with none of the vitality of the original screenplay.

So this was the end.* On March 22, 1983, I wrote in my diary:

> I don't ever want to make films again. I want to quit, *I want peace.* I don't have the strength anymore, neither psychologically nor physically. And I hate the hoopla and the malice. Hell and damnation.

March 25:
> A lousy night; I awoke at three-thirty, nauseous. Then I couldn't get back to sleep. Worry, tension, and fatigue. Finally, I dragged myself out of bed. It's a little better; I am almost functional. Today is overcast, and the thermometer reads zero centigrade. It will probably snow. In spite of the physical discomfort, it was rather fun to work again. But I don't want to make films again. This will be the last time.

March 26 (early morning):
> This film was supposed to be small, fun, and unpre-

*Bergman is referring to the end of his filmmaking career.

Erland Josephson with Lena Olin and Ingrid Thulin in After the Rehearsal. ▷

tentious. What is it now; what will it become? Two
mountainous shadows rise and loom over me. First:
Who the hell is really interested in this kind of intro-
verted mirrored aria? Second: Does there exist a truth,
in the very belly of this drama, that I can't put my
finger on, and so remains inaccessible to my feelings
and intuition? The failure came in our work method:
we rehearsed for three weeks before shooting. I was
sick to death of my lines. We should have thrown
ourselves directly into filming. Then every day would
have held the charm of novelty and excited antici-
pation. But no! Instead we rehearsed, discussed, analyzed, penetrated carefully and respectfully, just as
we do in the theater, almost as if the author were one
of our dear departed. The creativity was thus cas-
trated or had its rump cut off, however you prefer to
look at it.

March 31:

Having now gone carefully through all the takes, I
feel that the work is rather mediocre, a partial failure.
Nothing can be done now; much of what I wrote in
the screenplay on ideas about the profession of filmmaking I no longer believe (there you see how fast it
can happen, how damned fast: what I held as true
yesterday, today I see as banality). Anyway, exhaustion is the main reason I have felt weighed down
during the whole work period. Perhaps being tired
has something to do with my perspective, I don't
know. Katinka* says, summoning all her mild au-

*Katinka Faragò, who has worked closely with Ingmar Bergman since
1954 and has produced some of his films.

thority, that I am wrong in just about everything I say right now about the film. Usually, I am a better self-critic and know rather well how I stand with my results. Oh well, it's not the end of the world. To be honest: Sometimes I think that I ought not to have made it; then I realize that it was better for me that I didn't stay away from it, that I tried.

This evening we had a small farewell party. The atmosphere was tinged with friendly melancholy and tenderness.

I have been thinking, on and off, that I want to quit the theater as well. But with that I'm more uncertain. Sometimes I think of how much fun it is; sometimes I don't want to keep on doing it anymore. My hesitation has to do with my changed attitude toward interpretation.

If I were a musician, I would have no problems. But the whole thing about illusion — all the pretense! The actors act, and as the director I entice them to act. Along the winding roads of creation, we try to elicit emotional impulses that the audience will perceive as emotions, even truth about the characters' lives. It's getting tricky to do this over and over. I feel a growing aversion toward the so-called miracle of creation.

At the same time, certain plays still entice me, but that's because I see specific actors in the roles, actors who possess the rare gift of deep artistic expression. I often find myself turning all this over in my mind, rather quietly. There is no sudden cease-fire. When I am at my desk, on the other hand, I am pleasantly diverted. I write for my own pleasure, not with an eye on eternity.

Closer at hand, I need to reach a decision about how to organize the Epilogue.

Miscreance Credence

NESTLED INSIDE *THE SEVENTH SEAL* lies the one-act play *Wood Painting*, which I wrote for the graduating class of drama students in Malmö. I was teaching at the drama school, and we needed a play for the end-of-the-year student performance in the spring. It was hard to find a play with several equally important parts, so I wrote *Wood Painting* purely as an exercise. It was divided into several monologues, and the number of students determined the number of roles.

Inside *Wood Painting* there are some visual memories from my childhood.

For instance, as I wrote in *The Magic Lantern*, I sometimes accompanied my father when he went to preach in some country church:

> Like all churchgoers have at times, I let my mind wander as I contemplated the altarpieces, triptychs, crucifixes, stained-glass windows, and murals. I would find Jesus and the two robbers in blood and torment, and Mary leaning on St. John: Woman, behold thy son, behold thy mother. Mary Magdalene, the sinner, who had been the last to sleep with her? The Knight playing chess with Death. Death sawing down the Tree of Life, a terrified wretch wringing his hands in the top of it. Death leading the dance to the Land of Shadows, wielding his scythe like a flag, the congregation capering in a long line, and the jester bringing up the rear. The devils keeping the pot boiling, and the sinners hurtling headlong downward into the

depths. Adam and Eve discovering their nakedness. Some churches are like aquariums, not deserts. People are everywhere — saints, prophets, angels, devils, and demons — all alive and flourishing. The here-and-beyond billowing over walls and arches. Reality and imagination merged into robust mythmaking. Sinner, behold thy labors, behold what awaits thee around the corner, behold the shadow behind thy back!

I had acquired a huge record player, and I bought Carl Ferenc Fricsay's recording of Carl Orff's *Carmina Burana*. I used to let Orff thunder forth in the morning before I set off for rehearsal.

Carmina Burana is inspired by medieval songs written by minstrels who, during the years of the plague and the bloody wars, joined the big, wandering crowds of homeless men and women traipsing across the lands of Europe. Among the crowd were scholars, monks, priests, and jesters. A few could write, and they created songs that were sung at church festivals and fairs.

What attracted me was the whole idea of people traveling through the downfall of civilization and culture, giving birth to new songs. One day when I was listening to the final choral in *Carmina Burana*, it suddenly struck me that I had the theme for my next film!

Then I thought that I would make *Wood Painting* my point of departure.

In the end, *Wood Painting* wasn't of much use. *The Seventh Seal* took off in another direction; it became a kind of "road movie," traveling without constraint in time and space. It makes great big sweeps and takes full responsibility for these sweeps.

When I turned in the screenplay to Svensk Filmindustri,

Nils Poppe as Jof. The vassal and the knight with Albertus Pictor, the church painter (Gunnar Björnstrand, Max von Sydow, and Gunnar Olsson). ▷

234

I was met with a thumbs-down from every imaginable hand. Then *Smiles of a Summer Night* happened. It opened the day after Christmas 1955 and became, in spite of all overt and covert misgivings, a genuine success.

In May 1956 it was shown at the Cannes Film Festival. When it received the prize, I went straight to Malmö and borrowed money from Bibi Andersson, who at the moment was the richest one of us. Then I flew down to see the head of Svensk Filmindustri, Carl Anders Dymling. I found him sitting in a hotel room in Cannes, overexcited and out of control, selling *Smiles of a Summer Night* dirt cheap to any horse trader who happened to show up. He had never experienced anything like it. His innocence nearly matched his cockiness.

I placed the refused screenplay for *The Seventh Seal* in his lap and said, "Now or never, Carl Anders!" He said, "Sure, sure, but I have to read it first." "You must have already read it since you turned it down." "That's true, but maybe I didn't read it carefully enough."

For him to agree to let me do the film, I had to promise to make the film quickly, in thirty-six days, not including days spent traveling to and from the exteriors. It had to be an extremely inexpensive production. When the high from Cannes had turned into a hangover, *The Seventh Seal* was considered narrow, exclusive, and a hard sell. Two months after the deal was made, however, our camera was rolling.

We were given studio space in place of some other film that was supposed to have been made. It is remarkable with what merry lightheartedness I was able to start a shoot as complicated as this one back then.

Everything was filmed at Film City with the exception of three scenes we shot at Hovs hallar: the prologue, the ending, and Jof's and Mia's supper in a wild strawberry patch located there. For the outdoor scenes we moved within a very confined space, but we had good luck with the weather and were able to shoot from sunrise to late at night.

All the other sets were constructed within the studio area. The stream in the dark forest where the wanderers meet the witch was created with the help of the fire department and actually caused some violent overflows. If you look carefully, you will see a mysterious light reflecting from behind some trees. That is a window in one of the nearby high-rise apartment buildings.

The final scene when Death dances off with the travelers was, as I said, shot at Hovs hallar. We had packed up for the day because of an approaching storm. Suddenly, I caught sight of a strange cloud. Gunnar Fischer hastily set the camera back into place. Several of the actors had already returned to where we were staying, so a few grips and a couple of tourists danced in their place, having no idea what it was all about. The image that later became famous of the Dance of Death beneath the dark cloud was improvised in only a few minutes.

That's how things can happen on the set. We made the film in thirty-five days.

The Seventh Seal is one of the few films really close to my heart. Actually, I don't know why. It's certainly far from perfect. I had to contend with all sorts of madness, and one can detect here and there the speed with which it was made. But I find it even, strong, and vital. Furthermore, in this film I passionately cultivated my theme to the fullest.

Since at the time I was still very much in a quandary over religious faith, I placed my two opposing beliefs side by side, allowing each to state its case in its own way. In this manner, a virtual cease-fire could exist between my childhood piety and my newfound harsh rationalism. Thus, there are no neurotic complications between the knight and his vassals.

Also, I infused the characters of Jof and Mia with something that was very important to me: the concept of the holiness of the human being. If you peel off the layers of various theologies, the holy always remains.

I also added a playful friendliness to the family picture. The child brings about the miracle, and the juggler's eighth ball stands still in the air for one breathtaking moment, a microsecond.

The Seventh Seal doesn't chafe anywhere.

But I had recklessly dared to do what I wouldn't dare to do today. The knight performs his morning prayer. When he is ready to pack up his chess set, he turns around, and there stands Death. "Who are you?" asks the knight. "I am Death."

Bengt Ekerot and I agreed that Death should have the features of a white clown. An amalgamation of a clown mask and a skull.

It was a delicate and dangerous artistic move, which could have failed. Suddenly, an actor appears in whiteface, dressed all in black, and announces that he is Death. Everyone accepted the dramatic feat that he was Death, instead of saying, "Come on now, don't try to put something over on us! You can't fool us! We can see that you are just a talented actor who is painted white and clad in black! You're not Death at all!" But nobody protested. That made me feel triumphant and joyous.

I still held on to some of the withered remains of my childish piety. I had until then held a totally naïve idea of what one would call a preternatural salvation.

With Death (Bengt Ekerot) in The Seventh Seal. ▷

My present conviction manifested itself during this time.

I believe a human being carries his or her own holiness, which lies within the realm of the earth; there are no other-worldly explanations. So in the film lives a remnant of my honest, childish piety lying peacefully alongside a harsh and rational perception of reality.

The Seventh Seal is definitely one of my last films to manifest my conceptions of faith, conceptions that I had inherited from my father and carried along with me from childhood.

When I made *The Seventh Seal*, both prayers and invocations to something or someone were central realities in my life; to offer up a prayer was a completely natural act.

In *Through a Glass Darkly*, my childhood inheritance is put to rest. I maintained that every conception of a divine god created by human beings must be a monster, a monster with two faces or, as Karin puts it, the spider-god.

In a joyful scene with the painter of churches, Albertus Pictor, I present without any embarrassment my own artistic conviction. Albertus insists that he is in show business. To survive in this business, it's important to avoid making people too mad.

The character of Jof is a forerunner of the boy in *Fanny and Alexander* — the one who is so irritated because he is constantly being assaulted by ghosts and demons and must forever associate with them although they frighten him. At the same time he can't keep from telling wild stories, mostly to make himself seem important. Jof is both a braggart and a seer. Jof and Alexander are in turn related to the child Bergman. I did see a vision or two, but more often I embellished my stories. When my visions ran dry, I made some up.

As far back as I can remember, I carried a grim fear of death, which during puberty and my early twenties accelerated into something unbearable.

With Inga Landgré and Max von Sydow. ▷

The fact that I, through dying, would no longer exist, that I would walk through the dark portal, that there was something that I could not control, arrange, or foresee, was for me a source of constant horror. That I plucked up my courage and depicted Death as a white clown, a figure who conversed, played chess, and had no secrets, was the first step in my struggle against my monumental fear of death.

There is a scene in *The Seventh Seal* that used to fill me with fear and, at the same time, fascination. It is when Raval dies behind the tree in the dark forest. He burrows his head into the ground and howls with fright.

Originally, I had planned to make this a close-up, but I soon discovered that the sense of the horrible was reinforced by distance. When Raval died, I let the camera keep rolling for some reason, and over the mysterious glen in the forest, there was a sudden pale sunlight. It looked like a stage set. The whole day had been overcast, but at the precise moment when Raval died, the light appeared as if previously arranged.

My fear of death was to a great degree linked to my religious concepts. Later on, I underwent minor surgery. By mistake, I was given too much anesthesia. I felt as if I had

disappeared out of reality. Where did the hours go? They flashed by in a microsecond.

Suddenly I realized, *that is how it is.* That one could be transformed from *being* to *not-being* — it was hard to grasp. But for a person with a constant anxiety about death, now liberating. Yet at the same time it seems a bit sad. You say to yourself that it would have been fun to encounter new experiences once your soul had had a little rest and grown accustomed to being separated from your body. But I don't think that is what happens to you. First you *are*, then you are *not.* This I find deeply satisfying.

That which had formerly been so enigmatic and frightening, namely, what might exist beyond this world, does not exist. Everything is of this world. Everything exists and happens inside us, and we flow into and out of one another. It's perfectly fine like that.

At Svensk Filmindustri, *The Seventh Seal* suddenly became part of the pomp and splendor of an anniversary celebration focusing on the golden age of Swedish film. This was a catastrophe for the film; it was not made for such activities. The gala premiere held a murderous atmosphere for a serious art film, complete with a society audience, a flourish of

△
"The image that later became famous of the Dance of Death beneath the dark cloud was improvised in only a few minutes."

trumpets, and a speech by Carl Anders Dymling. It was devastating. I did what I could to stop the onslaught but ultimately was powerless. Their boredom and their malice poured relentlessly over everything.

Later, once it was released, *The Seventh Seal* swept like a forest fire across the world. I was met with strong responses from people who felt that the movie struck right at their own inner doubts and agony.

But I will never forget that solemn gala premiere.

IF YOU DON'T COUNT the epilogue that I tacked loosely onto *Through a Glass Darkly*, you could say that the film is above reproach both technically and dramatically. It is my first real small ensemble drama and leads the way for *Persona*. I had made a decision to compress the drama. This is immediately apparent in the first scene: four human beings come out of a roaring sea, appearing from nowhere.

Even on the surface, *Through a Glass Darkly* is obviously the beginning of something new, perhaps not yet worked out here. The technical staging can hardly be faulted; it is rhythmically irreproachable. Every shot sits just right. The fact that Sven Nykvist and I have laughed many a time at our not always successful lighting is another story. At that point in our collaboration, we began to have intense discussions about lights and lighting. These discussions led to a totally different concept of cinematography; the results can be seen in the later *Winter Light* and *The Silence*. So, from a cinematographic point of view, *Through a Glass Darkly* marks the end of a stage, of earlier attitudes. For me, it stands as a conclusion.

The epilogue has, with some justification, been criticized for being loosely tacked onto the end. In this scene between David and Minus, the boy's final line is "Daddy spoke to me!" I suppose that was written out of my need to be didactic. Perhaps I put it there in order to say something that had not yet been said; I don't know. I feel ill at ease when confronted with the epilogue today. Throughout the film runs a false

243

tone, hardly detectable to others, which may account for the scene.

It must be kept in mind that the preceding year (1959) I had made *The Virgin Spring*, a movie which improved my status, at that time, especially when it received an Oscar.

Today I take full responsibility for the religious problem I set up in *The Seventh Seal*. A genuine romantic piety rendered the special luster there.

But with *The Virgin Spring* my motivation was extremely mixed. The God concept had long ago begun to crack, and it remained more as a decoration than as anything else. What really interested me was the actual, horrible story of the girl and her rapists, and the subsequent revenge. My own conflict with religion was well on its way out.

In Vilgot Sjöman's book about *Winter Light*, entitled *Diary with Ingmar Bergman*, there is a discussion that hints at a connection between *The Virgin Spring* and *Through a Glass Darkly*. He wrote that I had planned *Winter Light* as the last part of a trilogy that began with *The Virgin Spring* and *Through a Glass Darkly*.

Today I see this view as a rationalization created after the fact. I tend to look skeptically at the whole trilogy concept. It was born during my conversations with Sjöman and was

△
Through a Glass Darkly: *"Four human beings come out of a roaring sea."*

fortified when the screenplays for *Through a Glass Darkly*, *Winter Light*, and *The Silence* were published together in a book. With Vilgot's help I wrote an introductory note that explained:

> These three films deal with reduction. THROUGH A GLASS DARKLY — conquered certainty. WINTER LIGHT — penetrated certainty. THE SILENCE — God's silence — the negative imprint. Therefore, they constitute a trilogy.

This note was written in May 1963. Today I feel that the "trilogy" has neither rhyme nor reason. It was a *Schnaps-Idee*, as the Bavarians say, meaning that it's an idea found at the bottom of a glass of alcohol, not always holding up when examined in the sober light of day.

Through a Glass Darkly is mainly connected to my marriage to Käbi Laretei and our life together.

Between the two of us, we had, as I wrote in *The Magic Lantern*, developed a complicated, staged relationship. We were confused and at the same time exceptionally successful. We were also enormously fond of each other. Moreover, we spoke about everything and anything that occurred to us. But in reality we had no common language. We couldn't communicate.

Our acquaintance began by correspondence. We exchanged letters for almost a year before we even met. For me, it was an exalting experience to have an emotionally and intellectually charged, richly endowed correspondence partner. I have not reread our letters, but I believe that before long I was using a vocabulary that I would not have dared to employ earlier in my life.

The reason was that Käbi was very expressive in a literary sense. She possessed an extraordinary keenness for the Swedish language, which may stem from the fact that she had been forced to learn and conquer it.

I see in my diary from that time that I used words I would not dream of using today. I note a dangerous tendency toward a flowery literary language.

The more Käbi and I watched the erosion of the collaboration into which we put so much effort, the more we tried to improve it superficially with verbal cosmetics.

I used this personal experience later, in *Autumn Sonata*. Viktor, the minister, tells his wife, Eva: "Furthermore, I have nourished unrealistic hopes and dreams. And some kind of longing, too, for that matter." Then Eva says:

> Those are very beautiful words, aren't they? I mean they are words that don't mean anything. I was raised on beautiful words. The word "pain," for instance. Mother is never mad or disappointed or unhappy, she "feels pain." You, too, have a lot of words like that. Since you are a preacher, it's probably a kind of occupational disease. If you say that you long for me when I'm standing right here in front of you, I am suspicious.
>
> Viktor: You know very well what I mean.
>
> Eva: No. If I knew, you would never think of saying that you long for me.

Making *Through a Glass Darkly* was like taking inventory before a sale. I was anxious about the enormous changes both my wife and I had made when we broke away from our earlier lives and came together in a totally new life-style. I feared it would turn out to be what it was: a perilous gamble.

◁ The Virgin Spring: *"The actual, horrible story of the girl and her rapists, and the subsequent revenge" (Max von Sydow, Birgitta Pettersson, and Birgitta Valberg).*

Out of my fear grew the slightly too beautiful words, the slightly too grandiose formulations, and the slightly too pretty shape of *Through a Glass Darkly*.

All this is clearly seen in a diary notation Vilgot Sjöman made in the beginning of his book about *Winter Light*:

> Dinner at the home of Ulla Isaksson. Ingmar and Käbi come over for coffee. Differences over artistic interpretation. Käbi speaks about Hindemith; Ingmar about direction and interpretation — then he tells wild and outrageous stories about animals he has filmed: the snakes in *Thirst*, the squirrel in *The Seventh Seal*, the cat in *The Devil's Eye*. Suddenly the conversation takes a turn and is now about suffering.

When I first read these words in Vilgot's book, I thought that Vilgot, goddamn him, had seen right through us. He had identified the game between Käbi and me.

Today I know that Vilgot didn't have the faintest suspicion. But the scene speaks its own uncomfortable language.

Through a Glass Darkly was a desperate attempt to present a simple philosophy: God is love and love is God. A person surrounded by Love is also surrounded by God. That is what I, with the assistance of Vilgot Sjöman, named "conquered certainty." The terrible thing about the film is that it offers a horrendously revealing portrait of the creator and the condition he was in at the start of the film, both as a man and as an artist. A book would have been much less revealing in this case, since words can be more nebulous than pictures.

So here we started with a falsehood, largely unconscious, but a falsehood nevertheless. In a weird way, the film floats a couple of inches above the ground. But falsehood is one thing, the weaving of illusions another. The illusion maker is conscious of what he is doing, as is Albert Emanuel Vogler in *The Face*. Therefore *The Face* is an honest film, whereas *Through a Glass Darkly* is a conjurer's trick.

The best thing about *Through a Glass Darkly* also emanated from Käbi's and my relationship. Through Käbi I learned much about music. She helped me find the form of the "chamber play." The borderline between the chamber play and chamber music is nonexistent, as it is between cinematic expression and musical expression.

When the film was in its planning stages, it was called *The Wallpaper*. I wrote in my workbook: "It's going to have a story that moves vertically, not horizontally. How the hell do you do that?" The note is from New Year's Day 1960, and even if it was strangely expressed, I understood exactly what I meant: a film that went into an untested dimension of depth.

My workbook (middle of March):

A god speaks to her. She is humble and submissive toward this god whom she worships. God is both dark and light. Sometimes he gives her incomprehensible instructions, to drink saltwater, kill animals, and so on. But sometimes he is full of love and gives her vital experiences, even on the sexual plane. He descends and disguises himself as Minus, her younger brother. At the same time the god forces her to swear off marriage. She is the bride awaiting her groom; she must not let herself be defiled. She pulls Minus into her world. He follows her willingly and eagerly since he exists on the border of puberty. The god throws suspicion on Martin and David and creates the wrong impression of them in order to warn her. On the other hand he endows Minus with the strangest qualities.

Harriet Andersson as Karin: "The borderline that she crosses is the bizarre pattern on the wallpaper." ▷

What I wanted, most deeply, was to depict a case of religious hysteria or, if you will, a schizophrenic individual with heavily religious tendencies.

> Martin, the husband, struggles with this god in order to win Karin back to his world. But since he is the type of person who needs that which is tangible, his efforts are in vain.

Then I find this in my workbook:

> A god descends into a human being and settles in her. First he is just an inner voice, a certain knowledge, or a commandment. Threatening or pleading. Repulsive yet stimulating. Then he lets himself be more and more known to her, and the human being gets to test the strength of the god, learns to love him, sacrifices for him, and finds herself forced into the utmost devotion and then into complete emptiness. When this emptiness has been accomplished, the god takes possession of this human being and accomplishes his work through her hands. Then he leaves her empty and burned out, without any possibility of continuing to live in this world. That is what happens to Karin. And the borderline that she crosses is the bizarre pattern on the wallpaper.

Parallel with the carefully chosen words exists a contrasting harsh concept of how the god I have created actually looks.

In my workbook at the time there is even a small reckoning with Bergman himself:

> The strange experience of Frank Martin's *Petite symphonie concertante*. It began extremely pleasantly, and

I found it both beautiful and moving. Then it hit me all of a sudden that *this music was like my films.* At some point I said that I wanted to make films the way [Béla] Bartók writes music. But the truth is that I make films the way Frank Martin has composed his *Symphonie concertante,* and that is not fun at all. I can't say that it's bad music, rather the opposite. It is irreproachable, both fine and moving, and also utterly refined, so far as the musical effects go. But I have a strong suspicion that this music is superficial, that he employs ideas that are not completely thought through, that the music deploys more effect than it can defend. Käbi says that this is not so. But I wonder about it anyhow and am rather sad.

This was written around the end of March 1960 before *Through a Glass Darkly* had taken on a definite shape. I was still on my way toward a different film:

> Karin wants Martin, her husband, to worship the god; otherwise the god might turn dangerous. She tries to force Martin to do so. He finally gets David to help him give her an injection. Then she disappears directly into her world behind the wallpaper.

April 12, I write in my workbook:

> Don't sentimentalize Karin's illness. Show it in all its ghastly glory. Don't try to effect a lot of subtle ties from her experience with the god.

Good Friday, 1960:
> Feel desire for work and concentration. Possibly also for various deviltry and mischief though it remains to

be seen what will come out of it. I have been pondering over the film and think: If we force ourselves to imagine a god, if we try to materialize him, he immediately becomes a rather repulsive figure with many faces.

I was touching on a divine concept that is real, but then I smeared a diffuse veneer of love all over it. I was really defending myself against what was threatening me in my own life.

The character of David, Karin's father and a successful author, became a problem. In him, two forms of unconscious lying came together: my own and actor Gunnar Björnstrand's. Our combined efforts created a dreadful stew.

Gunnar had converted to Catholicism, certainly with deep honesty and a passion for truth. Under this circumstance, I handed him a text that is totally impossible because of its superficiality. Today I realize that I didn't let him say one true word.

He portrays a best-selling author: here I wrote of my own situation — that of being successful yet not being recognized or respected. I let David explore my aborted suicide in Switzerland during the time before *Smiles of a Summer Night*. The text is hopelessly cynical. I let David draw an extraordinarily dubious conclusion from his suicidal attempt: in seeking his own death he finds renewed love for his children.

Out of my own obviously horrible situation in Switzerland came absolutely nothing. It was a dead end. But Gunnar experienced the monologue's gospel of conversion as if it were his own. He thought it was splendid.

It was poorly done and poorly played.

For the part of Minus, I chose an actor who had just finished drama school and was not mature enough for the com-

The old shipwreck by the seashore. Minus and Karen (Lars Passgård and Harriet Andersson). ▷

plications of the role: the crossing over of borders, the debauchery, the contempt for his father yet the longing for contact with him, the bond with his sister, the need for productivity. Lars Passgård was a moving, fine human being, and he slaved like a dog. But it should have been a young version of the actor Bengt Ekerot.

Over the years I have developed more skill in choosing the right actors for the right parts. Passgård and I did the best we could. He is totally without blame for our failure.

So I had my string quartet. But one instrument, Björnstrand, played false notes all the time, and the other instrument, Passgård, certainly followed the written music but had no interpretation.

The third instrument, Max von Sydow, played with purity and authority, but I had not given him the elbowroom he needed.

The miraculous thing is that Harriet Andersson played Karin's part with sonorous musicality. She needed no coercion and went without visible steps in and out of her prescribed reality. She portrayed Karin with a clear tone and a touch of genius. Through her presence the product becomes bearable.

She also portrayed fragments of another film that I was going to write but never did.

IT IS SATISFYING to see *Winter Light* after a quarter of a century. I believe that nothing in it has eroded or broken down.

My first notes on the film are from March 26, 1961. Under the heading "Conversations with God," it says in my workbook: "Sunday morning. Symphony of psalms. Work with *The Rake's Progress*." I was struggling with Stravinsky's *The Rake's Progress* at the Stockholm Opera, and it was like rock blasting. I had to learn the music by heart, and I don't have a knack for remembering music easily. "One has to do what is necessary. When nothing is necessary, one can do nothing."

I go into an abandoned church in order to converse with God; I want to get some answers. To finally give up either my resistance to God or my unceasing conflict. Either to bond to the stronger, to the father, to the need for security or to reveal his being as a jeering voice from centuries gone by.

The drama takes place at the demolished high altar in this deserted church. Individuals appear and disappear. But always there is this Self in the center who threatens, rages, prays, and tries to find some clarity in his perplexity. To make a day scene and a night scene at the high altar, the latter being the climactic ending: "I won't let go of your hand until you bless me." The Self enters the church, locks the door, and remains there in a fever. The despairing silence of the night, the graves, the dead, the organ pipes soughing, the rats, the smell of decay, the hourglass, and the pervading panic that particular night. This is Gethsemane, the judgment, the crucifixion. "God, my God, why have you deserted me?"

Hesitatingly, the Self leaves its old skin, that gray nothing, behind.

Christ, he is the good shepherd and he whom the Self cannot love. The Self must hate him. The Self digs up the grave, walks down into it, and awakens the Dead One.

As I began to imagine this drama, it took shape in my mind as a medieval play. All scenes occurred in front of the altar. The only aspect to change was the lighting, showing the dawn, twilight, and so on.

I'd rather carry my heavy inheritance of universal terror than submit to God's demands for surrender and worship. This marks the end of the first movement. The conversation with the churchwarden's wife, on the other hand, is totally real. She has come to close up because nobody is expected to come during the week. She busies herself inside. Then the church doors close with a bang, and the Self is left alone.

Christ, most beloved. Suffering is not difficult if you know your mission. True suffering comes from knowing the commandment of love and seeing how human beings betray themselves and each other when it comes to love. How they defile love. Christ's clear-sightedness must have caused his greatest suffering.

I was at this point alternating between my own self and a fictitious self in an uninhibited yet confusing way:

I must get inside *Through a Glass Darkly*. I must grab hold of a door that is absolutely not a door to secrets. It's imperative that I defend myself against all false doors, all tricks. I have had power and am prepared to relinquish it. Now nothing is simple, and neither is anything certain. Nothing happens through the dramatic action. It is always a question of erosion, of moving away. The moment the movement stops, I am dead. An acceleration to greater speed, on the other hand, blurs the vision, and I become uncertain about where I am going.

When the wife enters the church, the scene develops into an obvious story. The drama begin to take shape:

> The morning of the second day, the minister is awakened by someone knocking loudly on the church door. It is his wife, trying to get in. She is creating such an uproar that he simply does not dare let her remain standing outside. She enters with her hands and feet wrapped in bandages and wounds on her forehead. Her eczema is acting up. She is restless, afraid, and at the same time resigned. These two people love each other and give each other definite proof of their love and solidarity. But her denial is complete — there is no God. Therefore, to her, his waiting in the church is absurd, something that makes no sense. Her suffering is physically evident, and her decision to stay there with him unshakable.
>
> He then turns his hatred toward her. In the evening she leaves him, in bitterness. The sun turns blood-red. All around, everything lies in a disturbing twilight. Completely still and without a tremor in his voice, he

delivers his hatred for God and his hatred for Christ. The day draws to a close; the silence roars. He lies down to sleep at the foot of the altar. This is the darkest night, the night of annihilation. This is the empty and chilling harbinger of death, a spiritual death, a putrefying death.

Time moved on. Toward midsummer I wrote:

An endless row of mindless jobs lie as obstacles to making this film in my way. It weighs heavily on me, leaving me with a bad conscience and feeling rather dejected. My film is collecting dust, turning to sludge. It's no good.

Now I see this in the film: After the church services, the fisherman and his wife go to see Pastor Ericsson. Mrs. Fisherman speaks to the pastor about her husband's anxiety. Pastor Ericsson, deeply absorbed in an attack of the flu, answers by speaking about the omnipotency of love. The fisherman says nothing. The wife announces that he must drive her home to assume her duties as wife and mother. She will come back in half an hour or so.

I've decided that the woman with the bandaged hands is not his wife but his mistress. His wife has been dead for four years. His mistress, Märta, is a skinny, tormented, and lonely woman who has no faith. She represses great anger inside. She goes to communion out of love, in order to get close to her lover.

I believe that I should not begin to write this drama before I truly love my characters, before I can seriously wish them well in their sorrow. I don't want to force the drama into lightheartedness.

We went to Torö in the beginning of July, and there I started writing *Winter Light*. By July 28 I had finished. That was fast for a story so tricky, not because of a complicated plot but because of its simplicity.

My original thought was for the drama to take place in an abandoned church, which had been closed up and was waiting to be restored, with a ruined organ and rats running between the pews. It was a good idea! A man locks himself in an abandoned church and is finally alone with his hallucinations. This required only one set: a closed space depicting the small church with its high altar and its triptych. Only the lighting effects any changes in the room to signify dawn, the bright sun, sunset, the darkness of night. Then there are the strange sounds of the wind and the silence.

But the film became a bigger and wilder idea, perhaps more theatrical than most films. The shifting from religious themes to utterly worldly events demanded another setting. And another kind of lighting. This is where the break from *Through a Glass Darkly* becomes so radical.

Through a Glass Darkly affected an emotional tone both romantic and coquettish, something that one can hardly accuse *Winter Light* of doing. The two films belong together only when one sees *Through a Glass Darkly* as the starting point for *Winter Light*. Already I had divorced myself rather violently from my approach in *Through a Glass Darkly*. But I had not yet acknowledged this out loud.

Outside resistance to *Winter Light* was strong; criticism had already begun at the production level. But Svensk Filmindustri's head of production, Carl Anders Dymling, was seriously ill, and I found myself in the position of being able

"The role of Tomas Ericsson made harsh demands on him." With Gunnar Björnstrand in Winter Light. ▷

to do what I wanted. It was time to risk a death-defying leap. Or, to use the actor Spegel's words in *The Face*: "A sharp knife-edge to scrape out all impurity."

I have always tried to make my films appealing in some way to my audience. But I was not so stupid as to believe that *Winter Light* would be a public favorite. Unfortunate, perhaps, but inevitable. Even Gunnar Björnstrand had great difficulties with his part. We had worked together on a long line of comedies, but the role of Tomas Ericsson made harsh demands on him. Gunnar found it painful to portray a person who was unsympathetic to such a degree. His inner turmoil became so acute that he had trouble remembering his lines, a problem that had never happened before. Furthermore, he had health problems, and for his sake we worked relatively short day shifts. We shot exteriors in Dalecarlia [Sweden] — in an area abutting Orsa Finnmark. The November days were short there, yet the light was extremely gratifying even with its peculiar slant.

Not one shot was taken in direct sunlight. We filmed only when it was overcast or foggy.

A Swedish man in the midst of a Swedish reality experiencing a dismal aspect of the Swedish climate. In general, the film lacks highly dramatic moments.

But there is one such moment, and it comes when Tomas and Märta Lundberg are stopped at a railway crossing. He tells her that it was his father who wanted him to become a clergyman. Then a train arrives with freight cars that look like enormous coffins. It is the only moment with strong visual and acoustic effects. Otherwise the film is simple. Beneath the simplicity, however, there lies a complexity, which is hard to define.

It seems like a religious conflict, but it goes farther than that. The pastor is dying emotionally. He exists beyond love, actually beyond all human relations.

His hell, because he truly lives in hell, is that he recognizes his situation.

Together with his wife he has maintained a kind of fiction. The fiction is "God is love and love is God."

The wife contracts cancer, and her suffering deepens their relationship. Through her pain he experiences feelings of tenderness and human reality, a reality he has hardly ever been in touch with. He becomes real through his sorrow over his powerlessness over his wife's suffering.

His wife and he have been two of a kind, two damaged children who have found each other. They give each other a bearable existence.

Their idealism is fragile but real. Supported by her, he extols a romanticized ideal and begins a modest revival in the area. People listen to their pastor with renewed interest. He speaks eloquently, and his wife is very beautiful. A mild wind sweeps over the congregation. The couple visit different cottages, speaking with old people and singing psalms. One can imagine that their roles give them a deep satisfaction.

Then his wife dies, and his life dies with her. He becomes a relentless taskmaster. His mildly deceitful wife is dead, and God the Father is fading.

He bleeds to death emotionally, since there never was any real substance to his childish feelings. He lives alone for two years after his wife's death. Then Märta takes hold of him. She has loved him all the time, even when he was married and unattainable. As a minister and a teacher in a small community, they have been in contact frequently. The winter, the silence, their loneliness, and a mutual hunger drive them into each other's arms.

In the church: Tomas (Gunnar Björnstrand). Märta (Ingrid Thulin). ▷

Märta has her psychosomatic illness — eczema. He begins to pull away since he finds her illness horrifying. She realizes with striking perception the lovelessness of their relationship. But she is stubborn. This man is her mission. There is a mixture of honesty and banter to her credo: I prayed for a mission and I got you! When she kneels to say her prayers, she is not turning to God for guidance. The kneeling is a gesture dictated by the church. She prays for faith and security.

When Tomas stands by the rapids and guards Jonas's corpse, he sees with a clarity that is etched in his mind the fiasco of his life. An hour later he takes revenge on the one who loves him. Then the cowardly being can no longer keep quiet; to his own surprise, he hears himself say: "The reason, the decisive reason, is that I don't want you."

> Märta (to herself): I understand that I have made mistakes. All the time.
>
> Tomas (pained): I have to go now. I'll talk to Mrs. Persson.
>
> Märta: No, I have made mistakes. Every time I felt hatred toward you, I made an effort to transform that hatred into compassion. (Looks at him.) I have felt sorry for you. I am so used to feeling sorry for you that I am unable to hate you even now. (She smiles apologetically — her crooked, ironic smile. He looks quickly at her: her hunched shoulders, her head straining forward, her large immobile hands, the look in her eyes that is suddenly unprotected and burning, her earlobes poking out through unkempt hair.)
>
> Märta: What will you do *without me?*
>
> Tomas: Ah! (Disdainful. He bites his lip. A heavy distaste works upward from his innards to his mouth.)

"Not one shot was taken in direct sunlight." With Sven Nykvist. ▷

Märta (lost): Oh no, you won't be able to get along. You won't make it, dearest little Tomas. Nothing can save you now. You'll hate yourself to death.

He stands up and walks toward the door. During these moments he has time to imagine an even more horrible life — life without her. For him it is irrevocably over; death reigns in the schoolroom. He turns around as he reaches the door and hears himself say, "Do you want to come along to Frostnäs? I'll try to be nice."

(She looks up. Her severe face has an expression of being turned off, being closed up.)
Märta (stiffly): You really want me to? Or is it only some new fear that's passing through you?
Tomas: Do what you want, but I am asking you.
Märta: Yes. Of course, I'll come. I have no choice.

What has happened is a draining. Not only for him but also for her. He throws out words, and she sits there defenseless. She realizes suddenly that she is guilty of wrongdoing, that there has been a brutal egoism in her emotional gale.

At three o'clock the same afternoon, Tomas and Märta arrive in Frostnäs. Church bells are ringing, and peace reigns between them as they walk quietly side by side in the twilight. Algot Frövik's reflections on forlornness offer welcome relief. Tomas believes for a brief moment that Christ and he have suffered the same pain: "God, my God, why have you abandoned me?"

Darkness falls over both Frostnäs and Golgotha.

Frövik has already seen this change in Tomas, and for a

few seconds even Tomas grasps the bizarre camaraderie felt through suffering.

Everything is burned clear, and personal growth now becomes a possibility. For the first time in his life, Pastor Ericsson makes his own decision. He goes through with his service for no other reason than that Märta Lundberg is present.

If one has religious faith, one would say that God has spoken to him. If one does not believe in God, one might prefer to say that Märta Lundberg and Algot Frövik are two people who help raise a fellow human being who has fallen and is digging his own grave.

At that point it doesn't matter if God is silent or if he is speaking.

I wrote in *The Magic Lantern:*

> While I was preparing *Winter Light,* I went around looking at churches in Uppland in the early spring. In most cases, I borrowed the key from the organist and sat for a few hours in the church, watching the light travel across the space inside and thinking of how I would end my film. Everything had been written down and planned, except the ending.
>
> One Sunday, I phoned Father early in the morning and asked him if he would like to come with me on an outing. Mother was in the hospital after her first heart attack, and Father had isolated himself. His hands and feet had grown worse, and now he wore orthopedic boots and walked with a stick. Out of self-discipline and sheer willpower, he continued his duties in the parish of the royal palace. He was seventy-five.
>
> It was an early spring day with mist and bright light

reflecting off the surrounding snow. We arrived in plenty of time at the little church north of Uppsala to find four churchgoers ahead of us waiting in the narrow pews. The churchwarden and the sexton were whispering on the porch while a female organist was rummaging in the organ loft. Even after the summoning bell had faded away over the plain, the pastor still had not appeared. A long silence ensued in heaven and on earth. Father shifted uneasily in his seat and muttered to himself and me. A few minutes later we heard the sound of a car speeding across the slippery ground outside; a door slammed, and after a minute the pastor came puffing down the aisle.

When he got to the altar rail, he turned around and looked at his congregation with red-rimmed eyes. He was a thin, long-haired man, his trimmed beard scarcely covering his receding chin. He swung his arms like a skier and coughed, the hair on the crown of his head curly, and his forehead turning red. "I am sick," said the pastor. "I have a high fever and a chill." He sought sympathy in our eyes. "I have permission to give you a short service; there will be no communion. I'll preach as best I can, then we'll sing a hymn and that will have to do. I'll just go into the sacristy and put on my cassock." He bowed and for a few moments stood irresolutely as if waiting for applause or at least some sign of approval, but when no one reacted, he disappeared through a heavy door.

Father rose from his seat in the pew. He was upset. "I must speak to that man. Let me pass." He got out of the pew and limped into the sacristy, leaning heavily on his stick. A short and agitated conversation followed.

◁ *"I prayed for a mission and I got you!" Gunnar Björnstrand and Ingrid Thulin.*

A few minutes later, the churchwarden appeared. He smiled with embarrassment and explained that there would be a communion service after all, and an older colleague would assist the pastor.

The introductory hymn was sung by the organist and us few churchgoers. At the end of the second verse, Father came in, in white vestments, with his stick. When the hymn was over, he turned to us and spoke in his calm free voice, "Holy, holy, holy Lord of Hosts, heaven and earth are full of thy glory. Glory be to thee, O Lord most High."

Thus it was that I discovered the ending to *Winter Light* and a rule I was to follow from then on: *irrespective of anything that happens to you in life, you hold your communion.*

Other Films

BIRGER MALMSTEN PLANNED to visit a childhood friend of his, a painter living in Cagnes-sur-Mer. We traveled together and found a small hotel in the mountains high above the carnation fields with a commanding view of the Mediterranean.

My second marriage had hit rock bottom. So my wife and I tried to revitalize our love by writing letters to each other. At the same time I began to think back to our time in Helsingborg. I sketched a few scenes from a marriage. Much inside me insisted on being expressed, both my personal concept of my place in the world of art and my marital problems of infidelity (and fidelity). More specifically, I wanted to make a film with music streaming through it and out of it.

The symphony orchestra in Helsingborg, though severely lacking in sophistication, exuberantly played the canon of major symphonies. As often as time and circumstances allowed, I sat in on orchestra rehearsals. For their season finale they planned to perform Beethoven's Ninth. I was allowed to borrow the score from the conductor, Sten Frykberg, and could actively follow, note by note, the musicians and the members of the unpaid but passionate amateur choir. It was a powerful and touching event. I thought it was a magnificent idea for a film.

It seemed so natural that I tripped over the idea. I changed the theatrical people in my autobiographical film to musicians and gave it the title *To Joy* after Beethoven's symphony.

I thought my idea utterly brilliant. In relation to my profession, I obviously was not suffering from any neuroses at all. I worked because it was fun and because I needed money.

How many carats the work contained was something I rarely considered. When in this intoxicated state, I could become totally enveloped in my own sense of brilliance.

There is in *To Joy* a discussion of the importance of being in place punctually when the rehearsal begins and being diligent. As I wrote in *The Magic Lantern* about the years in Helsingborg: "Our rehearsal periods were short, our preparations were almost nonexistent. What we presented was hastily assembled consumer goods. I think that was a good learning experience, for us very useful. Young people should constantly be faced with new tasks. Their instruments must be tried and hardened because technique can be developed only through steady contact with an audience."

That the film's young violinist plays Mendelssohn's Violin Concerto with about the same lackluster skill as I exhibited in *Crisis* is just part of the whole story.*

To Joy is a hopelessly uneven film, but it has a few shining moments. A good scene is the confrontation at night between Stig Olin and Maj-Britt Nilsson. It is good because Maj-Britt Nilsson's adept acting enriches the scene. The clear and honest depiction of a complicated relationship echoes the conflicts in my own marriage.

But *To Joy* is also an impossible melodrama. A kerosene stove explodes portentously in the beginning of the film, and Beethoven's Ninth Symphony is shamelessly exploited. I do understand the techniques used in both melodrama and soap opera quite well. One who uses melodrama as it should be used can implement the unrestrained emotional possibilities available in the genre. Melodrama enables one, as it did me in *Fanny and Alexander*, to revel in total emotional freedom,

---

*Crisis was the first film Bergman directed, in 1945.

To Joy: *Maj-Britt Nilsson, Stig Olin, and Victor Sjöström.* ▷
Summer Interlude: *"We filmed it in Stockholm's outer archipelago. . . . A touch of genuine tenderness is achieved through Maj-Britt Nilsson's performance."* ▷▷

but it is crucial to know where to draw the line between what is acceptable and what is downright ridiculous.

I did not know that when I made *To Joy*. The connection I made by juxtaposing the wife's death with Beethoven's "An die Freude" was careless and unbelievably frivolous. My original story worked better. It simply ended with the couple splitting up. They remain with the orchestra, but she receives an offer in Stockholm, which hastens their breakup.

Sadly, I couldn't handle such a simple, harsh finale to the story.

A general weakness reigns in my films from this period. I had trouble trying to depict the happiness of youth. I believe the problem is that I myself never felt young, only immature. As a child, I never associated with other young people. I isolated myself from my peers and became a loner. At the same time I became dangerously enchanted with the Swedish novelist and playwright Hjalmar Bergman and his elaborately constructed tales of youth. His influence can be seen in *Illicit Interlude (Summer Interlude)* and created, I believe, the most serious flaw in *Wild Strawberries*.

The world of youth was alien to me. I stood on the outside, looking in. When I had to formulate dialogue for my young characters, I reached for literary clichés and adopted a coquettish silliness.

In *To Joy* I presented a series of events that should have been detached and realistic — the scenes demanded distance and perspective — but verged instead on the highly personal. I couldn't provide a solid foundation for this material, and therefore the house of cards collapsed.

I learned quickly, and already in *Summer Interlude* [1950] the shape of the personal message was much clearer as I managed to hold it at arm's length.

Summer Interlude has a long history. Its origin, I see now, lies in a rather touching love affair that I had one summer when my family resided on Ornö Island. I was sixteen years old and, as usual, was stuck with extra studies during my summer vacation and could only occasionally participate in activities with people my own age. Besides, I did not dress as they did; I was skinny, had acne, and stammered whenever I broke my silence and looked up from reading Nietzsche.

It was a fantastic life of laziness and self-indulgence in a pristine, sensuous landscape. But as I said, I was rather lonely. On the far end of this so-called Paradise Island, toward the bay, there lived a girl who was also alone. A timid love grew between us, as often happens when two young lonely people seek each other out. She lived with her parents in a large, strangely unfinished house. Her mother was a somewhat faded yet rare beauty. Her father had suffered a stroke and sat immobile in the large music room or on the terrace facing the sea. Important ladies and gentlemen came for visits to see and admire the exotic rose garden. Actually, it was a little like stepping straight into one of Chekhov's short stories.

Our love died when autumn came, but it served as the basis for a short story that I wrote the summer after my exams. When I went to Svensk Filmindustri to work as a script slave, I retrieved it and fleshed it out into a movie script. It was entangled in itself and filled with flashbacks, which I couldn't find my way out of. I wrote several versions, but nothing fell into place. Then Herbert Grevenius came to my aid. He chiseled away all the superfluous episodes and pulled out the original story. Thanks to his efforts, I finally got the screenplay approved for production.

We filmed it in Stockholm's outer archipelago. The landscape had a special mixture of tempered countryside and wilderness, which played an important part in the different

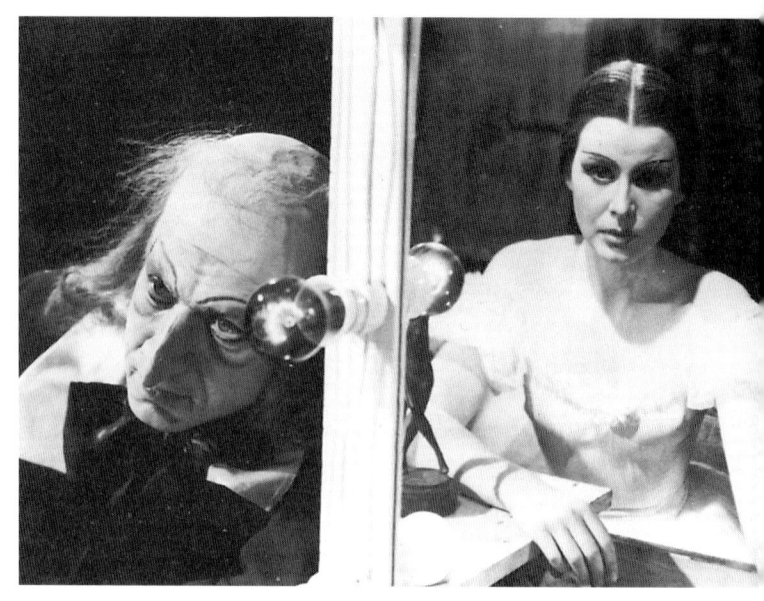

time schemes, in the luminescence of summer and in the autumnal twilight. A touch of genuine tenderness is achieved through Maj-Britt Nilsson's performance. The camera catches her with an affection that is easy to comprehend. She embraced the girl's story and lifted it higher with her brilliant mixture of playfulness and seriousness. The filming became one of my happy experiences.

But harsher times were ahead. The film crisis, promising a total standstill in motion picture production, was fast approaching, and Svensk Filmindustri was in a hurry to produce the spy thriller *This Can't Happen Here* (also known as *High Tension* in the United States) with Signe Hasso, imported from Hollywood. I agreed to direct it for financial reasons and practically went straight from one shoot into another. *Summer Interlude* was put aside. It was *This Can't Happen Here* that counted.

For me the whole thing was torturous, a good example of how bad you can feel when you must do something you do not want to do. It was not the assignment per se that was making me sick. Later, during the time when movie production was shut down, I put together a series of commercials for the soap *Bris* (Breeze), and I had a lot of fun challenging stereotypes of the commercial genre by playing around with the genre itself and making miniature films in the spirit of Georges Méliès. Originally, I accepted the *Bris* commercials in order to save the lives of myself and my families. But that was really secondary. The primary reason I wanted to make the commercials was that I was given free rein with money and could do exactly what I wanted with the product's message. Anyhow, I have always found it difficult to feel resentment when industry comes rushing toward culture, check in hand. My whole cinematic career has been sponsored by private capital. I have never been able to live on my beautiful

◁ Summer Interlude: *Maj-Britt Nilsson with Stig Olin and Annalisa Ericson in the dressing room mirrors.*

eyes alone! As an employer, capitalism is brutally honest and rather generous — when it deems it beneficial. Never do you doubt your day-to-day value — a useful experience which will toughen you.

This Can't Happen Here, as I said before, was complete torture from beginning to end.

I was not at all averse to making a detective story or a thriller; that was not the reason for my discomfort. Neither was Signe Hasso the reason. She had been hailed as an international star who Svensk Filmindustri, with incredible naïveté, hoped would make the film a raging success all over the world. Therefore we filmed *This Can't Happen Here* in two languages: Swedish and English. Signe Hasso, a talented and warm person, unfortunately felt poorly during the entire filming. We were never sure from one day to the next whether she would be euphoric or depressed on the set. It was one difficulty, of course, but not the deciding factor.

A creative paralysis hit me after only four days of shooting.

That was exactly when I met the exiled Baltic actors who were going to participate. The encounter was a shock. Suddenly I realized which film we ought to be making. Among these exiled actors I discovered such a richness of lives and experiences that the unevenly developed intrigue in *This Can't Happen Here* seemed almost obscene. Before the end of the first week, I demanded to see Svensk Filmindustri's chief executive, Carl Anders Dymling, and pleaded with him to cancel the project. But our train was running its course and could not be stopped.

At about this point I had a violent attack of influenza, and from that arose sinus trouble that raged almost comically and tormented me throughout the rest of the filming. My very soul resisted this film, hiding in the deepest darkness of my sinus and nasal passages.

The Bris (Breeze) *soap commercials: "Miniature films in the spirit of Georges Méliès," here with a three-dimensional film-within-a-film.* ▷
This Can't Happen Here: *the obscene intrigue (Signe Hasso and Ulf Palme). Exiled Baltic actors. A seemingly idyllic interlude with Signe Hasso and Alf Kjellin.* ▷▷

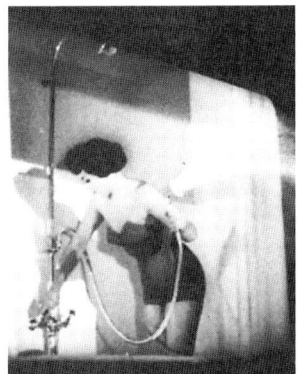

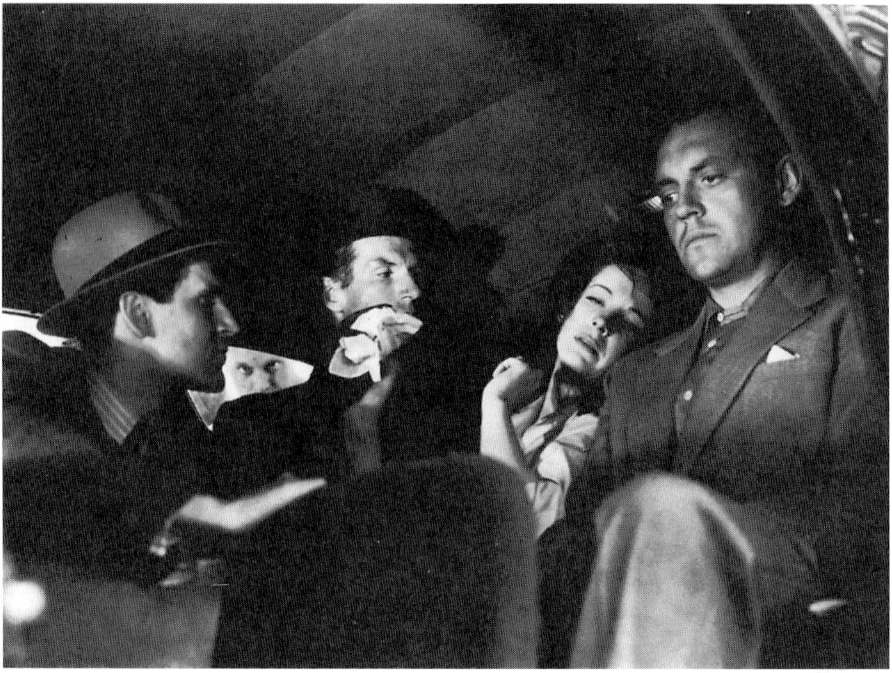

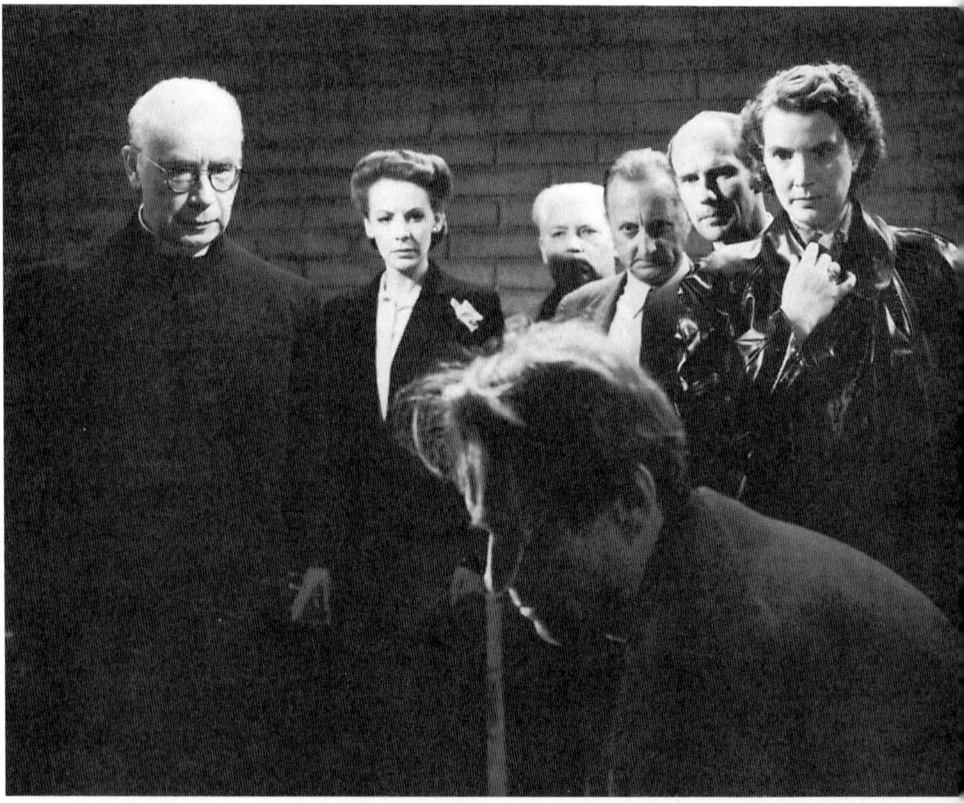

Few of my films do I feel ashamed of or detest for various reasons. *This Can't Happen Here* was the first one; I completed it accompanied by violent inner opposition. The other is *The Touch*. Both mark the very bottom for me.

My punishment did not fail to come from the outside as well. *This Can't Happen Here* opened in the fall of 1950 and was regarded as a fiasco, a well-deserved failure, in the eyes of both the critics and the public. During that time *Summer Interlude* lay there, waiting. It would not be released until a year later.

My reputation as a movie director had the chance to be saved if I made another film. With this in mind, I decided to make *She Danced One Summer* for Sweden's Folkbiografer. For some reason this picture's production was exempted from the general motion picture moratorium. But at the last minute, the head of production, Karl Kilbom, got cold feet. He wanted to see a "beautiful" film, not some "neurotic vulgarity such as, for example, *Thirst*." I was fired from the project. However, the determining screen test with Ulla Jacobsson (who rose to international stardom after the film) had already been made.

Instead my next film was *Secrets of Women (Waiting Women)*, and we were given a head start the day after the production ban was lifted. The idea for the film came from my wife at the time, Gun Hagberg. Before we met, she had married into a large family with a big summer place on the Danish island of Jylland. Gun told me how one evening the women of the clan remained sitting at the table after the evening meal and how they began to really talk to each other. With great openness they spoke of their marriages and their loves. I thought this an excellent framework for a film consisting of three stories.

My financial situation after the production standstill forced me to sign a second-rate (to put it mildly) contract with Svensk Filmindustri. I was painfully aware that I had to come up with a successful film. In other words, a comedy seemed an absolute necessity.

Such a comedy was manifested in the third episode of the film: Eva Dahlbeck and Gunnar Björnstrand in the elevator. For the first time, I heard an audience laugh at something I had created. Eva and Gunnar had experience in comedy and knew exactly the many ways to skin a cat. That this little comedy routine in the narrow space of the elevator was funny is completely thanks to them.

The second episode is more interesting to me. For a long time I had considered making a movie without dialogue. In the 1930s, a Czech movie director, Gustav Machaty, made two films — *Ecstasy* and *Nocturno* — which were both visual narratives, practically without dialogue. I saw *Ecstasy* when I was eighteen years old, and it deeply affected me. This was partly a natural reaction because, for once, one was allowed to see a nude woman on screen, but more important, because the movie told nearly everything through images alone.

I recognized in Machaty's technique something from my childhood. I had once built a miniature movie theater out of cardboard. It had a few rows of seats in front, an orchestra pit, curtains, and a proscenium. I made tiny balconies for the sides. On a sign outside I wrote Röda Kvarn (Red Mill), the name of a popular movie theater in Stockholm.

For film, I drew comic strips on long pieces of paper, which I then pulled through a container fastened behind the cut-out square that was my "silver screen." I made up stories and placed text cards between the pictures but limited myself rather consciously to as few text interruptions as possible. I soon discovered that it was possible to tell stories without text, exactly as in *Ecstasy*.

Waiting Women: *the five women. The three episodes: Jarl Kulle and Anita Björk. Maj-Britt Nilsson. Eva Dahlbeck and Gunnar Björnstrand.* ▷

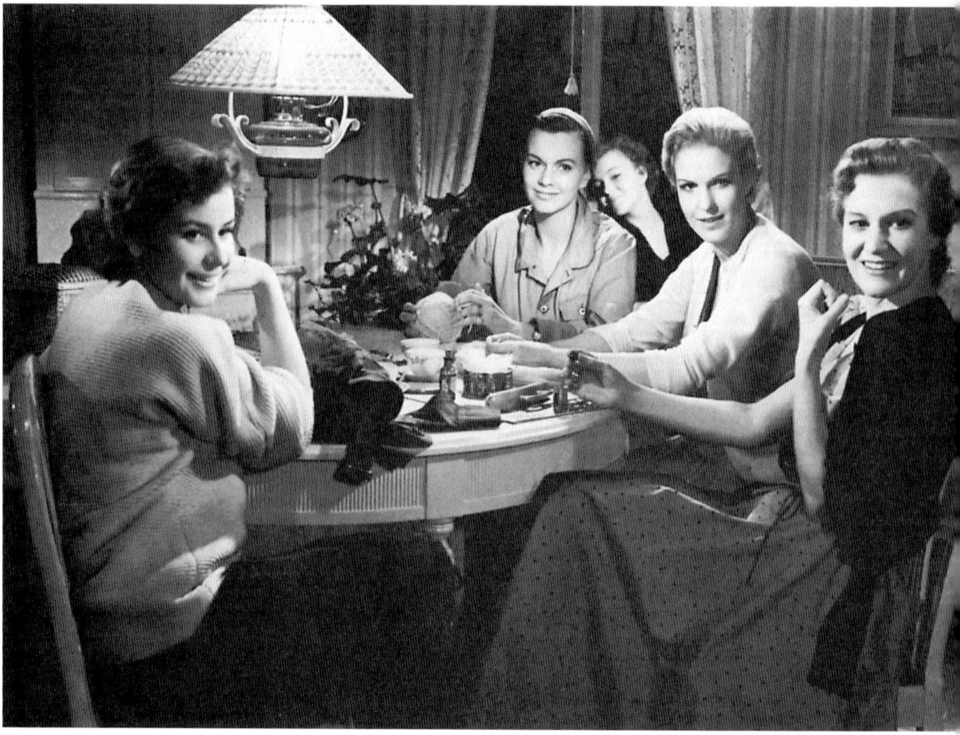

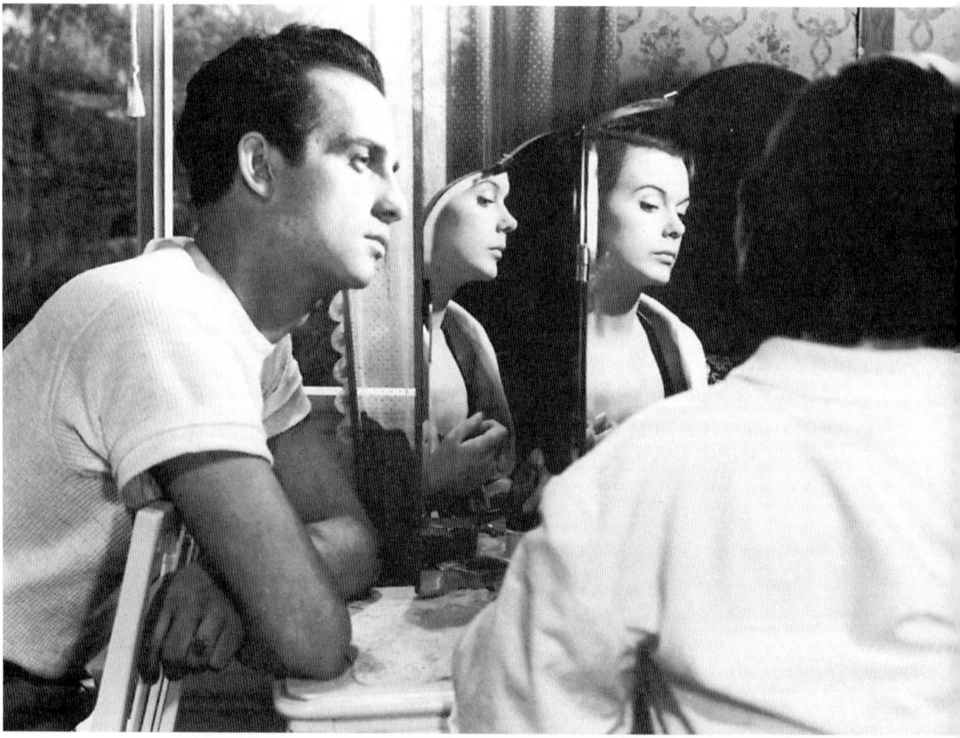

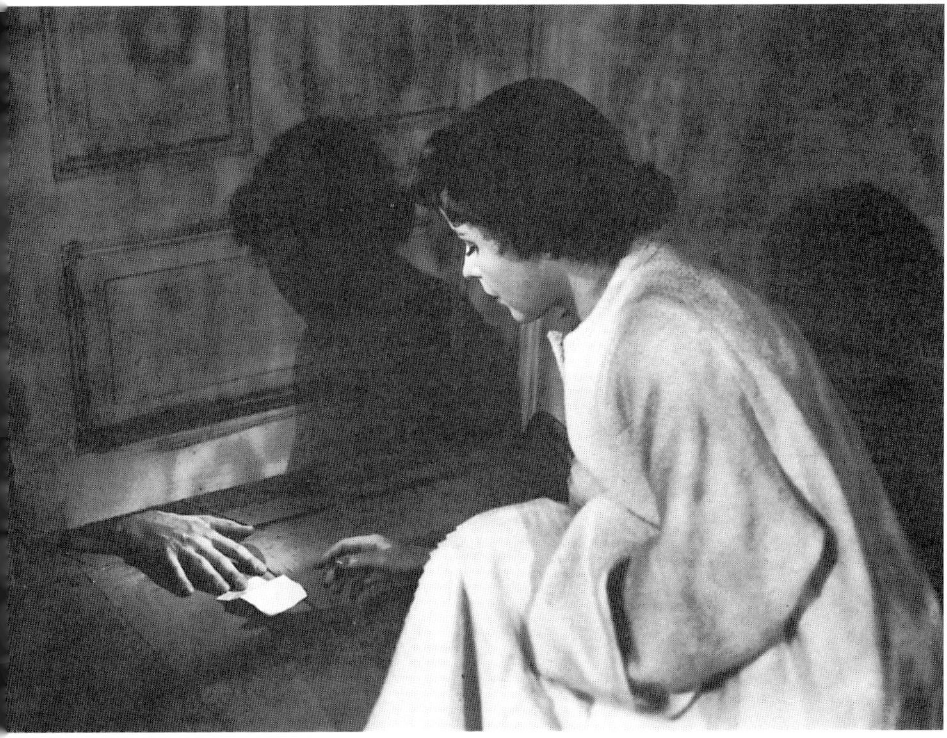

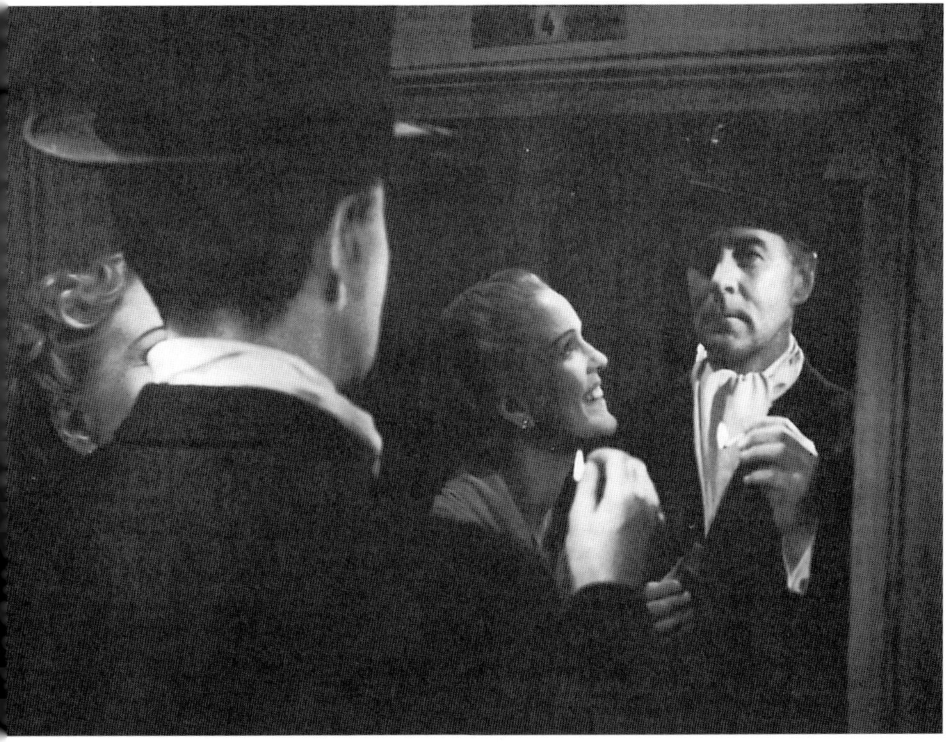
4

While preparing *Waiting Women*, I regularly met with the writer Per Anders Fogelström. He was working on a story about a girl and a boy who run away from home together and live in the wilderness of the archipelago before returning to civilization. Together we wrote a screenplay. We delivered it to Svensk Filmindustri along with detailed "directions for use." My intention was to make a low-budget film under a relaxed schedule, far from the soundstages and with the smallest crew possible. *Monika* (*Summer with Monika*) was given the green light to be the second film on my slave contract. Harriet Andersson and Lars Ekborg took a screen test on one of the sets for *Waiting Women*. Again, I went directly from finishing one film to starting another.

I have never made a less complicated film than *Summer with Monika*. We simply went off and shot it, taking great delight in our freedom. And the public success was considerable.

It was immensely gratifying to bring out a natural talent such as Harriet Andersson and watch how she behaved in front of the camera. She had acted in the theater and in variety shows and had played small parts in light comedy films such as *Mrs. Andersson's Kalle* and *The Beef and the Banana*. She had also been given, after some hesitation, the ingénue role in Gustaf Molander's *Defiance*. When I went to make *Summer with Monika*, the skepticism was thick in the executive production offices. I asked Gustaf Molander about using Harriet. He looked at me and winked. "If *you* believe you can get something out of her, I suppose it would be nice." Only later did I grasp the amiable but improper insinuation in my older colleague's remark.

Harriet Andersson is one of cinema's geniuses. You meet only a few of these rare, shimmering individuals on your travels along the twisting road of the movie industry jungle.

◁ Summer with Monika: *before and after. Lars Ekborg, Harriet Andersson.*

Here is an example of her talent: The summer has ended. Harry is not at home; Monika goes on a date with a guy named Lelle. At the coffee shop he drops a coin into the jukebox. With the swing music resounding, the camera turns to Harriet. She shifts her glance from her partner straight into the lens. Here is suddenly established, for the first time in the history of film, shameless, direct contact with the viewer.

"She shifts her glance from her partner straight into the lens." Harriet Andersson. ▷

SHAME (*THE SHAME*) PREMIERED ON September 29, 1968. The following day I made this entry in my workbook:

> I'm sitting on Fårö Island, waiting. Just as I wished, I am totally isolated, and it feels rather good. Liv is in Sorrento at the festival. Yesterday, the film opened both in Stockholm and in Sorrento. I'm sitting here waiting for the reviews. I'm going to take the ferry at noon to Visby and buy the morning and evening papers at the same time.
>
> It feels good to do this alone. It is good not to have to show my face. Because I am tormented. It's an incessant ache tinged with fear. I don't know anything yet. Nobody has said anything. But intuitively I feel very depressed. Because I do believe that the reviews will be lukewarm when they aren't clearly disparaging. And this time, especially, it will be difficult not to be affected by the criticism. Of course everyone would like to enjoy critical and public success all the time. But it has been a long time now for me. I have a feeling that I am being pushed aside. Things are quiet and very polite around me. It's hard to breathe. How am I to go on?

Finally, I couldn't wait any longer. I called the main office of Svensk Filmindustri and asked to speak to the head of Public Relations. He was out on a coffee break. Instead, I spoke to his secretary:

Oh, yes, she had not read the reviews yet, no. They were good, though, five stars in the evening paper *Expressen*, but nothing to quote, no. Yes, Liv was good, of course, though we know how they write.

By this time I had a fever of 104 degrees and put down the receiver. My heart was beating as if it wanted to jump out of my mouth from shame, exhaustion, and a sense of ennui. All due to my desperation and hysteria. No, I am not particularly happy.

Both passages show two things: 1) the agony of a movie director awaiting his reviews, and 2) his belief that he had made a good film.

When I see *Shame* today, I find that it can be divided into two parts. The first half, which is about the events of the war, is bad. The second half, which is about the effects of war, is good. The first half is much worse than I had imagined; the second much better than I had remembered.

There are bits and pieces of the first half that are all right. The movie begins well. The couple's situation and background are effectively established. The good part of the film starts with the moment the war is over and the pain of the aftermath sets in. It begins in a potato field, where Liv Ullmann and Max von Sydow move in oppressing silence.

One might say that the authenticity of the second half is disturbed by an overblown scheme involving a wad of paper money that changes hands several times. This scheme reflects an influence from American dramaturgy of the 1950s.

For a long time before making this film I had carried around the notion of trying to focus on the "little war," the war that exists on the periphery where there is total confusion, and nobody knows what is actually going on. If I had been more patient when writing the script, I would have

depicted this "little war" in a better way. I did not have that patience.

To tell the truth, I was exorbitantly proud of this film. I also felt I had made a contribution to the current social debate (the Vietnam war). I convinced myself that *Shame* was well made. I had suffered under the same delusion after finishing *A Ship Bound for India*. And the same thing would happen to me again later when making *The Serpent's Egg*.

To make a war film is to depict violence committed toward both groups and individuals. In American film, the depiction of violence has a long tradition. In Japan, it has developed into a masterful ritual, matchlessly choreographed.

When I made *Shame*, I felt an intense desire to expose the violence of war without restraint. But my intentions and wishes were greater than my abilities. I did not understand that a modern portrayer of war needs a totally different fortitude and professional precision than what I could provide.

Once the outer violence stops and the inner violence begins, *Shame* becomes a good film. When society can no longer function, the main characters lose their frame of reference. Their social relations cease. The people crumble. The weak man becomes ruthless. The woman, who had been the

△
Shame: *"The first half is much worse than I had imagined."*

stronger, falls apart. Everything slips away into a dream play that ends on board the refugee boat. Everything is shown in pictures, as in a nightmare. In a nightmare, I felt at home. In the reality of war, I was lost.

(During the whole screenwriting period, the story was called *Dreams of Shame*.)

In other words, we are talking about a poorly constructed manuscript. The first half of the film is really nothing more than an endlessly drawn-out prologue that ought to have been over and done with in ten minutes. What happens later could have been built upon, fleshed out, and developed as much as was needed.

I didn't ever see that. I didn't see it when I wrote the screenplay; I didn't see it when I shot the film; I didn't see it when I edited it. During that time I lived with the idea that *Shame* was self-evident and emotionally logical all the way through.

That during the course of working one does not see anything wrong with the mechanics of the script is probably due to a self-protective reflex that functions throughout a long and complicated procedure. This defensive mechanism quiets the critical superego. With your self-critical inner voice hollering in your ear, shooting a film would probably become much too heavy and painful to bear.

"The good part of the film starts the moment the war is over and the pain of the aftermath sets in." With Max von Sydow, Gunnar Björnstrand, and Liv Ullmann. ▷

THE PASSION OF ANNA (*A PASSION*) WAS MADE on Fårö Island during the fall of 1968 and carries traces of the winds that were blowing in those days both in the real world and in the world of film. In some respects, therefore, it looks very dated. In other ways it is powerful and shows a break with accepted film practices. I look at it with mixed feelings.

On a superficial level it's obvious to see, the hair and fashion styles of the actresses link the film to that time period. The difference between a dated film and a timeless one apparently is measured by the length of the skirts, and it cuts me to the quick when I see Bibi Andersson and Liv Ullmann, two grown women, appearing in the childish, extreme miniskirts of the time. I seem to remember putting up a weak resistance, but, when confronted with the power of two women, I unfortunately gave in. That misfortune was not noticeable then but revealed itself later, like writing in invisible ink.

The Passion of Anna is in some ways a variation of *Shame*. It depicts what I really wanted to show in *Shame* — the violence manifested in an underhanded way.

Actually, it is the same story but told more credibly.

I had kept a detailed workbook in which I had taken notes, which are interesting to read now. As early as February 1967, there are notes that show me laboring with the idea of Fårö as the setting for the Kingdom of Death. Someone walks across the island out of a longing for something that exists far away. Several stops along the journey. Simple, frightening, and strangely exciting.

There you have the basic concept, and it remained as the basis for the finished movie. But suddenly the concept grew in every possible direction. For a while I worked on a complicated project that revolved around two sisters, a dead Anna and a living Anna. Two stories alternating in counterpoint to each other.

On June 30, 1967, my workbook contains the following statement: "One morning I awakened and decided to abandon the story about the two sisters. It feels too large, too unwieldy, and too uninteresting from a cinematic point of view."

Nothing of the screenplay existed at the time but a detailed outline, in which both story lines were composed of long sequences of dialogue. So when the European Radio Union ordered a television play, it did not take me more than one week to extract *The Reservation* from my notes and put a piece of theater on its feet. It is therefore understandable that *The Reservation* and *The Passion of Anna* are so closely associated.

The rest of my enterprise consisted of extensively reshaping what would turn out to be *The Passion of Anna*. This process went on all summer long, and in the fall we began filming.

The Kingdom of Death continues to show up again and again in my notes. Today I regret that I didn't hang onto my original vision more strongly.

Instead, a different movie emerged out of the original vision of the Kingdom of Death. Among other things, the connection to *Shame* became increasingly important.

In both films the landscape is the same, but the undeniable threats seen in *Shame* are much more subtle in *The Passion of Anna*. Or as it says in the text: the warning signs lie beneath the surface.

The dream in *The Passion of Anna* begins where the reality

of *Shame* ends. Sadly, it is not especially convincing. The fatally stabbed lambs, the burning horse, and the hanged puppy suffice to create the nightmare. The ominous false suns in the introduction have already established the mood and tone of the film.

The Passion of Anna could have been a good film, had the traces of the 1960s not been so evident. They leave an imprint, not only because of the skirts and hairdos, but, even more essentially, because of the important formal elements: the interviews with the actors and the improvised dinner invitation. The interviews should have been cut out. The dinner party should have been vastly different, much tighter.

It is regrettable that I frequently became so worriedly didactic. But I was scared. You are scared when you have, for a long time, been sawing off the branch upon which you sit. *Shame* was truly not a success. I worked under the pressure of a firm demand that my film be comprehensible. I could possibly defend myself by saying that, in spite of this, it took all my courage to give *The Passion of Anna* its final shape.

The four leading characters in the film use Johan (Erik Hell) as an accomplice in their game. There exists a parallel between Johan and the fisherman Jonas in *Winter Light*. Both become victims of the characters' paralysis and inability to engage in human emotional experience.

My philosophy (even today) is that there exists an evil that cannot be explained — a virulent, terrifying evil — and humans are the only animals to possess it. An evil that is irrational and not bound by law. Cosmic. Causeless. Nothing frightens people more than incomprehensible, unexplainable evil.

The filming of *The Passion of Anna* took forty-five days and was quite an ordeal. The screenplay had been written in a white heat. It was more a description of a series of moods than a traditional, dramatic film sequence. Ordinarily, I solved any anticipated technical problems immediately in the writing stage. But here I chose to deal with the problems during filming. To some extent this decision was made because of a lack of time, but mostly I felt a need to challenge myself.

The Passion of Anna was also the first true color film Sven Nykvist and I did together. In *All These Women* we had filmed in color according to the established rules. This time we wanted to make a film in color as it had never been done before.

Contrary to our usual collaborative experiences, we found ourselves in endless conflicts. My intestinal ulcer acted up, and Sven had vertigo. Our ambition was to make a black-and-white film in color, with certain hues emphasized in a strictly defined color scale. It turned out to be difficult. The color negative exposed slowly and demanded a totally different lighting than it would today. The poor results of our efforts confused us, and, regretfully, we argued often.

It was also 1968. The seeds of rebellion from that year began to reach even the crew at Fårö.

Sven had an assistant photographer with whom we had worked on several earlier films. He was a short man with round glasses, like a military serviceman. Nobody had been more diligent and industrious than he. Now he was transformed into an active agitator. He called big meetings. He declared that Sven and I behaved like dictators and that all artistic decisions should be made by the whole crew.

I declared that those who did not like our way of working could return home the next day with their salaries intact. I was not going to change my method and schedule of shooting

The Passion of Anna: *the four leading actors. Erland Josephson. Bibi Andersson. Max von Sydow. Liv Ullmann.* ▷

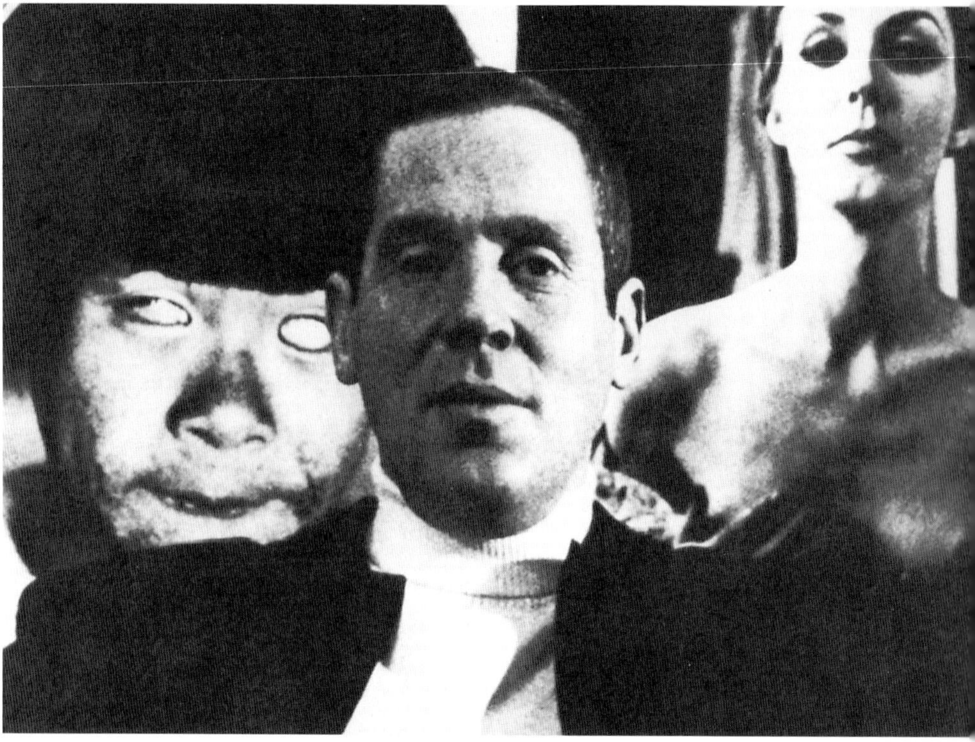

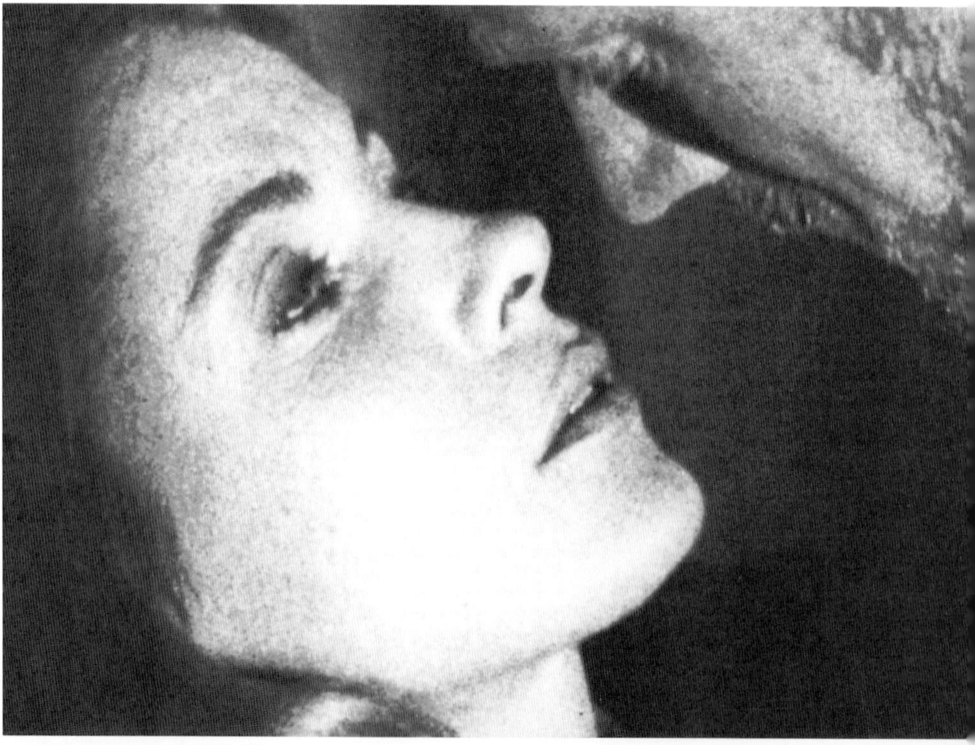

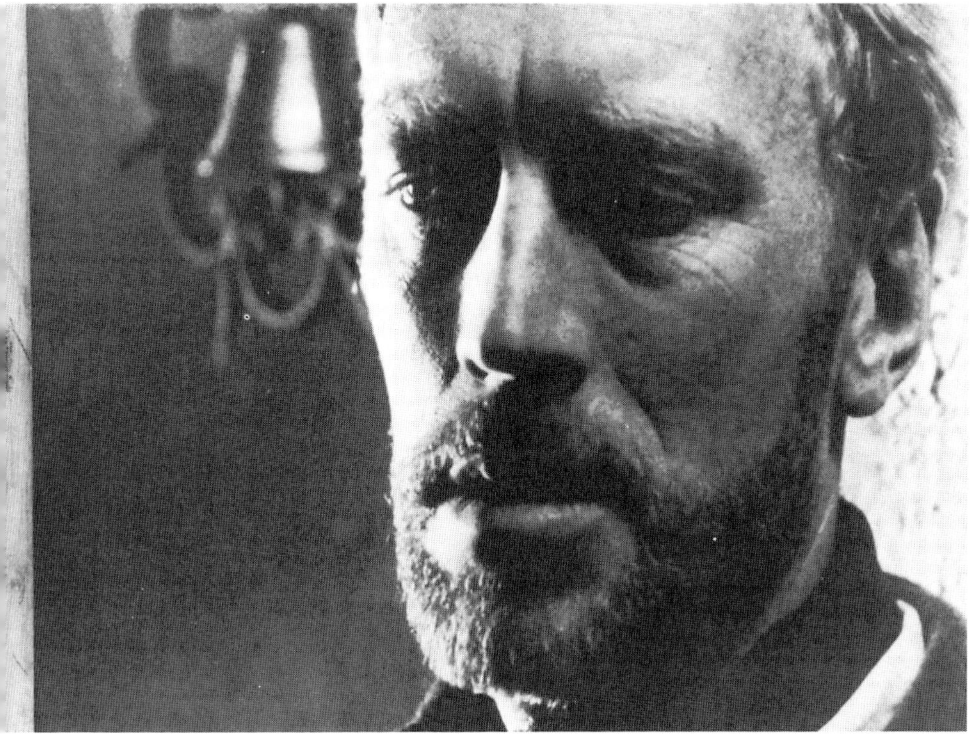

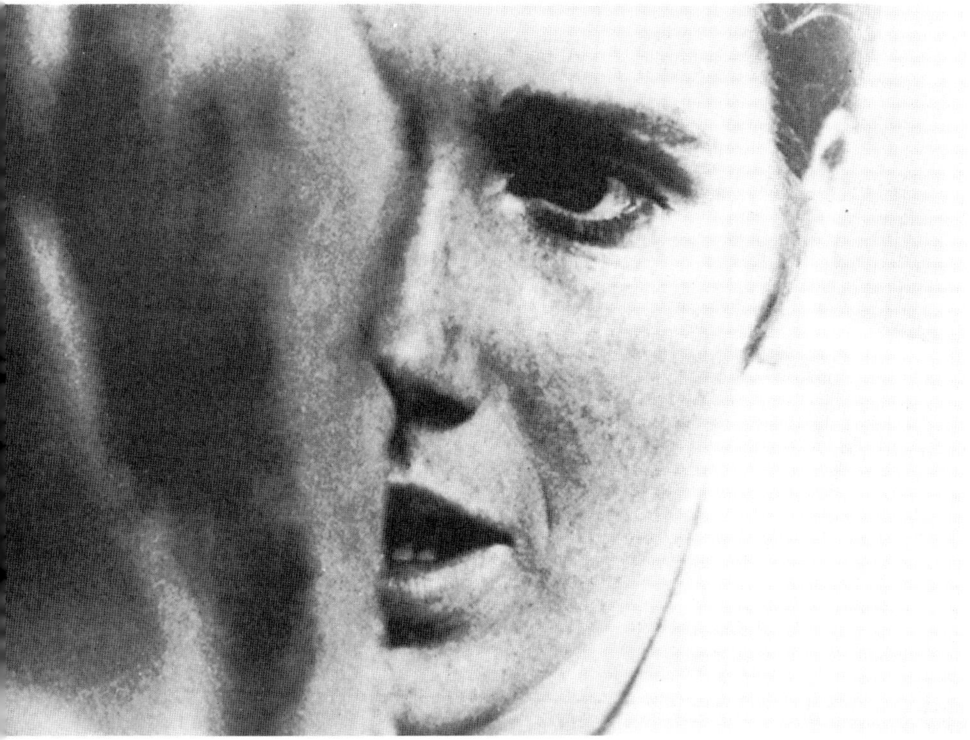

and did not intend to accept artistic decisions from the crew.

Nobody wanted to go home. I saw to it that our agitator was assigned to other duties, and the filming of *The Passion of Anna* continued without any further protest meetings.

The filming, however, became one of the worst I have ever experienced, equal to *This Can't Happen Here*, *Winter Light*, and *The Touch*.

I HAD NOT SEEN *Brink of Life* (*So Close to Life*) since I made it in the fall of 1957. But this fact did not stop me from speaking of it in derogatory terms. When Lasse Bergström and I finished our taped conversations about my films and turned off the machine for good, we discovered to our amazement that *Brink of Life* had not been mentioned, not one word, not even a footnote. We agreed that this omission was strange indeed. So I finally decided to see the film, but at that point I uncovered a stubborn resistance inside me, one hell of a resistance, and I don't know why.

I watched the film alone in my screening room on Fårö and was surprised by the resentment I felt. The film had been an assignment: I had promised (I no longer remember why) to make a film for Sweden's Folkbiografer. I read Ulla Isaksson's fine short story collection, *Aunt of Death*, and was captivated by two of the stories, which, if put together, could be made into a screenplay. The screenwriting proceeded quickly and was fun (as it always is with my friend Ulla). I was given the crew I wanted; Bibi Lindström built a manageable maternity ward; everybody was in a good mood; and the work proceeded swiftly. Why so apprehensive? Oh yes! I can see weaknesses and shortcomings, more clearly now than thirty years ago, but how many films from the 1950s still hold up today? Our criteria have changed (and in film and theater this happens at a dizzying speed). A definite advantage to directing a stage performance is that it dives into the ocean of oblivion and disappears. Films live on. I wonder how this book would have turned out if my opus had

311

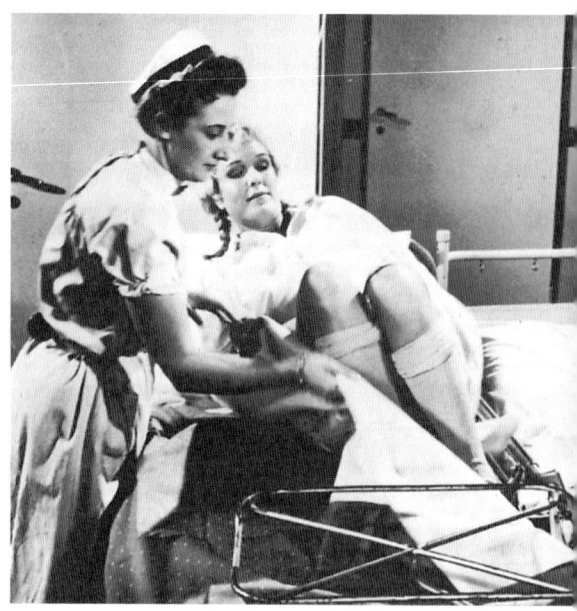

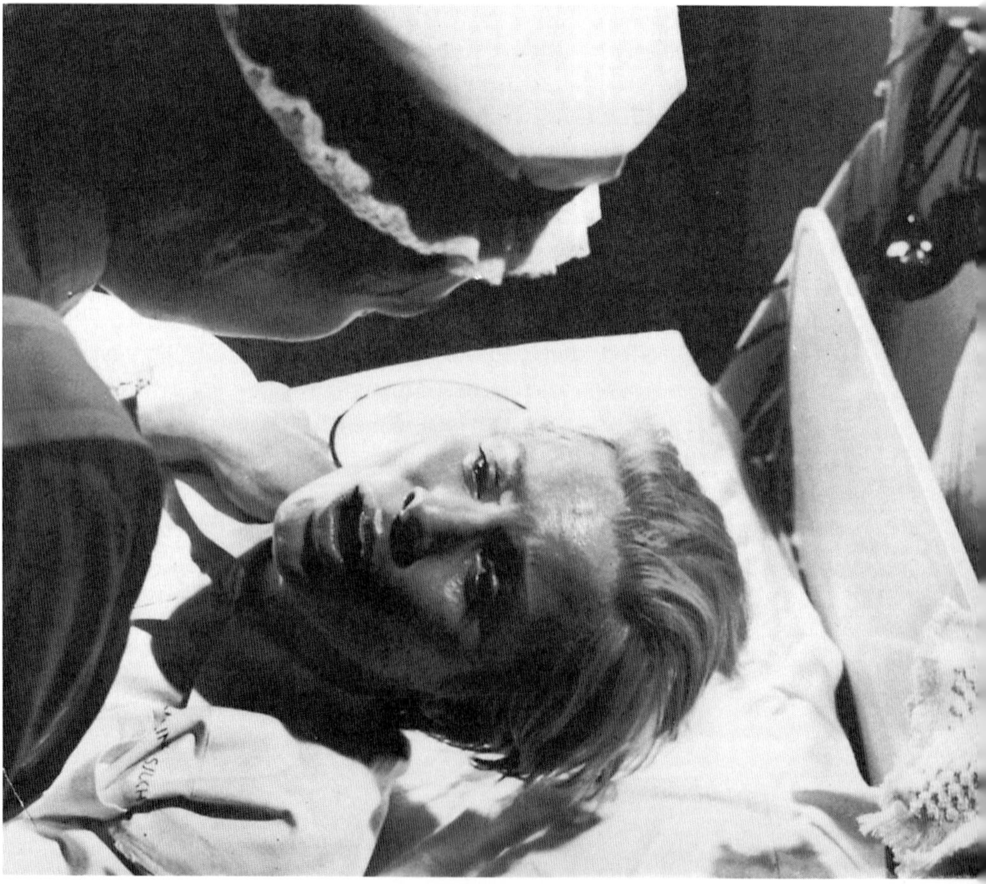

disappeared, and I had based my comments solely on note-books, photographs, newspaper reviews, and faded memories?

But *Brink of Life* exists exactly as it was seen and heard at the premiere on March 11, 1958, and I sat watching the same film years later in the darkness, alone and influenced by no one. What I saw was a well-told but a bit too long-winded story about three women in a maternity ward. Everything was honest, warmhearted, and intelligently done, with first-class performances, but too much makeup, a deplorable wig on Eva Dahlbeck, poor cinematography in parts, and a few too many literary references. When the movie ended, I sat there, surprised at myself and a little annoyed — I suddenly *liked* the old film. It was nicely behaved and accurately done and in all probability very useful when it was running in the movie theaters.

I recall that there had been medical attendants stationed in the theaters. People had a tendency to faint from pure fright. I also recall that the medical adviser for the film, Dr. Lars Engström, allowed me to be present during a birth at the Karolinska Hospital. It was a traumatic and edifying experience. Even though I was the father of five children by that time, I had never been present at any of the births (that's how things were back then). Instead, I got drunk or played with my miniature electric trains or went to the movies or rehearsed or worked on a movie or, inappropriately, paid attention to other women. I don't quite remember the details. Anyhow, the delivery at Karolinska Hospital was splendid and not the least complicated. The mother was young and plump and gave birth with both screams and laughter. The atmosphere was exhilarating. I came close to fainting twice, and finally I had to leave the room and hit my head against

◁ Brink of Life: *"The actresses remain its biggest asset." Bibi Andersson. Eva Dahlbeck. Ingrid Thulin.*

a wall in order to come around. Then I went back to my work, a bit shaken but immensely grateful.

I don't want to pretend that filming proceeded without complications. Folkbiografer owned a long, narrow studio, which was once a school gymnasium, deep down in the basement of an old ramshackle building in the Östermalm area of Stockholm. The adjacent spaces were rudimentary or nonexistent. The ventilation was questionable — the air came in at sidewalk level, pulling in the exhaust from passing cars. It was cramped, dirty, and dilapidated. The Asian flu was raging at the time, and we all fell like dominoes, but we could not cancel or postpone since the actors had contracts for other work immediately following this shooting. To carry on filming with a fever of 104 degrees would seem impossible. It turned out to be perfectly possible. Everyone walked around with masks. From time to time (rather frequently) we went behind the sets, where laughing gas was kept. Laughing gas is as addictive as dope, though it has a shorter effect.

Max Wilén, the cameraman, turned out to be an adequate craftsman without any sensitivity or joy. We carried out a gloomy collaboration with sullen but polite decorum. The laboratory was also a disaster (scratches and dirt on the developed film).

All together, the film isn't much. The actresses remain its biggest asset. Just as in other pressured situations, these women proved their professionalism, inventiveness, and unshakable loyalty. They had the ability to laugh in the face of trouble. They had sisterhood. Consideration and caring for each other.

Actors, yes, they deserve a special chapter, but I don't know if I'd be able to explain and illuminate how each one influenced the origin and composition of my films.

How would *Persona* have looked if Bibi Andersson had not

played Alma, and what would have become of my life if Liv Ullmann had not committed herself both to me and to Elisabet Vogler? And no Harriet in *Summer with Monika?* Or *The Seventh Seal* without Max von Sydow? Victor Sjöström in *Wild Strawberries?* Ingrid Thulin in *Winter Light?* I would never have dared to make *Smiles of a Summer Night* without Eva Dahlbeck and Gunnar Björnstrand.

I often saw the actors outside the studios in other contexts besides work, but my motives still revolved around my films. Ah, the grandmother, Gunn Wållgren, is a natural. Of course, she must play the grandmother in *Fanny and Alexander.* Without Lena Olin and Erland Josephson, I would never have written *After the Rehearsal* because these two actors inspired me and gave me the desire to make it. Ingrid Bergman and Liv Ullmann were necessary for *Autumn Sonata.* So many mornings, lunch hours, and deliberations. So much joy, confusion, and tenderness. All this devotion — once the shooting ended — changed in intensity and manner and stabilized or paled or disappeared. Love, touching, and kissing and perplexity and tears. The four women in *Cries and Whispers*: Kari Sylwan, Harriet Andersson, Liv Ullmann, Ingrid Thulin. I have a behind-the-scenes photograph taken during the filming; they are sitting in a row on a low couch, all clad in black, and solemn; Harriet is made up and dressed as a corpse. Suddenly they begin to bob up and down on the couch. It has strong springs, and all four of them bob up and down, bump into each other, and laugh. What an assembly of female experience and what great professional accomplishment.

Gunnar Björnstrand regarded me with a darkly narrowed look, his mouth smiling sarcastically; we were two samurai in wild combat, a fight-to-the-end warrior's story. Then he fell ill and had difficulty memorizing his lines; he suffered a catastrophic opening night at a private theater, and, to top it off, he was panned by a couple of fastidious drama critics in Stockholm. I wanted very much for him to be part of my last film since we had worked together throughout my career. (Our collaboration began in 1946 when he played Mr. Purman in *It Rains on Our Love*.) So I wrote a part especially for Gunnar, moderately adjusted to his handicap. He played the head of the theater in *Fanny and Alexander*, business manager, director, and Père Noble in one person. The theatrical group in the film performs *Twelfth Night*. Gunnar plays the clown. At the end he sits on a small ladder with a lighted candle on his balding head and a red umbrella opened in his hand. He sings: "For the rain it raineth every day." It rains, and everything is beautiful and touching, and done in the good taste of Gunnar Björnstrand. All day long, the cameraman making our documentary kept his camera unremittingly aimed at Gunnar. Nobody, not even I, knew that he was immortalizing this remarkable day at the South Theater.

Gunnar had a difficult time. He had trouble with his memory and his coordination. There were endless retakes, but neither he nor I had the faintest intention of giving up. He fought heroically with his handicap and his failing memory; he fought and did not give in for a moment. Finally all of the clown was on reel. The triumph was complete.

In the documentary about the filming of *Fanny and Alexander* — a documentary that runs a little over two hours — the central position is Gunnar Björnstrand's struggle and triumph. I had edited the footage down from a considerable amount of material, thousands and thousands of feet, into a film within the film, about twenty minutes long.

To be on the safe side, I asked Gunnar and his wife to approve the sequence on him. They said they were satisfied. I was happy; I felt that I had built a monument to a great actor's last victory, not just any kind of victory but a victory at the highest artistic level. Later on, Gunnar's widow retracted her approval and demanded that the part with the song of the clown be taken out. Regretfully, I saw myself forced to comply with her request. But we kept the negative. Gunnar Björnstrand's greatest triumph as an actor shall not perish.

When it comes to the director's choices and the genesis of a new theatrical production, the actors' influence can be even more important. Jarl Kulle's King Lear, Peter Stormare as Hamlet, Bibi Andersson portraying the Legend. I am sitting opposite Gertrud Fridh in the green-painted canteen at the Malmö theater. We linger over old memories. We have worked together for so many years, first in Gothenburg, then in Stockholm and Malmö. We gossip and talk nonsense. The winter of southern Sweden can be seen through the large, dirty windows facing the Theater Park, a stingy, bluish shimmer; the ceiling lights have already been turned on. Gertrud's face is illuminated twice — by the cold light from outside and by the warm lights above; her voice is tired but purrs on intensely; her gray-green eyes shine with a special luster. Suddenly I think: There she sits, my Célimène! Gertrud is perfect for Célimène in *The Misanthrope*. Next year I plan to direct *The Misanthrope*, and you have to play Célimène, you do want to, don't you, Gertrud? Oh yes, she would like to, but right at this moment she is not completely sure of who Célimène is, and what kind of a figure is the Misanthrope? Yet Ingmar looks happy and eager, so I don't have the heart to express any doubt. Yes, Gertrud Fridh, the fire, the welding flame that burns her so terribly and so frighteningly. Hedda Gabler, the big tragic tone, the humor, the cruel playfulness. Yes!

When I directed *A Dream Play* a few years ago, the small

Gunnar Björnstrand in A Lesson in Love, Sawdust and Tinsel, The Seventh Seal, Smiles of a Summer Night, The Magician, *and* The Ritual. *His last triumph:* Fanny and Alexander. ▷

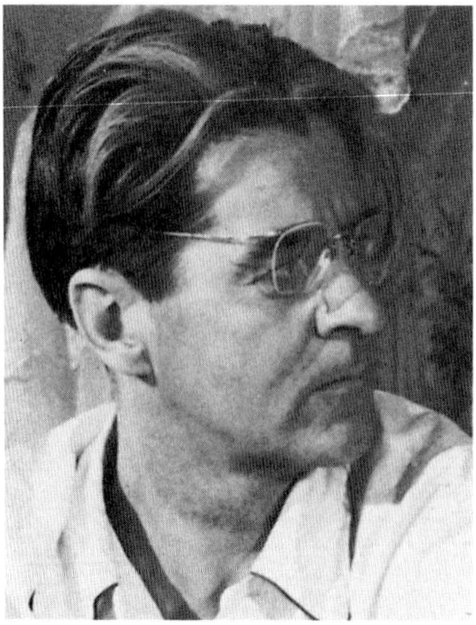

but crucial role of the dancer was played by a young actress, Pernilla Östergren. She had just played a cheery nursemaid who walks with a limp in *Fanny and Alexander*. Now we were rehearsing *A Dream Play*. I watched Pernilla, her strength, her eagerness, and her straightforwardness (even when she did something wrong, it was good). It struck me suddenly that *finally*, after many years of waiting, the Royal Dramatic Theater had a new Nora! I grabbed hold of her after rehearsal and told her that in three years or at the most four, she would play Nora.

The theater is carried by the strength of its actors. Directors and art directors can do whatever they want; they can sabotage themselves, the actors, and even the playwrights. When the actors are strong, that's when the theater thrives. I remember a production of *Three Sisters* that had been analyzed and rehearsed to death, ground down to snuff by an old, disillusioned European director. The diligent actors submissively walked around like sleepwalkers, bored stiff. A queen dressed in black rose above this grayness, uncompromising and furiously alive: Agneta Ekmanner.

I am fully aware that what I have just written does not bear any connection to my contemplation of *Brink of Life*. Yet perhaps it does. Most of the time, I write my own screenplays. I write, and then I *rewrite*. My workbooks bear witness to the lengthy process (often to my surprise later). The dialogue is put through a strict regimen, is put on a diet, made denser, fleshed out, and erased; words are tried and replaced. In the final round, big chunks disappear ("kill your darlings"). By the time the actors finally take over, transforming my words through their own expression, I have, in general, lost contact with the original meaning of the lines. These artists give new life to the scenes that I have nagged to death. I feel happy but reserved and yet satisfied; oh, did I write that? Oh yes,

◁ *With Gertrud Fridh: "The fire, the welding flame that burns her." Pernilla Östergren: "A cheery nursemaid who walks with a limp in* Fanny and Alexander.*"*

of course, that's exactly what I meant to say, though I had forgotten it during the long and extremely solitary process of revision.

In the case of *Brink of Life,* the situation was totally different. I felt a responsibility toward the words that Ulla Isaksson had written. I had to master a reality that was both familiar and alien: women and childbirth. I found myself literally "on the brink of life." Many of the side effects of childbirth were unexpected: one hospital room contained six new mothers and newborn children only hours old. Swelling breasts, sour milk stains everywhere, innumerous physical conditions, the content and attentive animal side of the vocation. I felt nauseous and could only relate all this to my own inadequate experiences as a daddy, eternally awkward, eternally fleeing.

Ingrid Thulin plays Cecilia, who is only in her third month and close to losing her baby. She throws off the covers and sees, in terror and with cold sweat pouring, that the bed and sheets are covered with blood, all the way up to her breasts. Our technical consultant, a midwife who was present on the set every day, created the blood (from an ox, slightly diluted with some chemical dye to give the right tint). I remember my sudden nausea at the sight and the personal memory that resurfaced from my past of a terrified girl crouching over the toilet with blood gushing out between her legs.

Although I handled the words and actions of Ulla Isaksson's characters with relentless professionalism and with teeth clenched, I sometimes thought in desperate moments that had I known, really known, what I was getting into, I would not have done it. I swam like a person drowning, searching for a bottom to stand on but finding none there. To top it all off, I had an attack of that devilish Asiatic flu. And, of course, I was totally knocked out.

The four actresses were kind and remained untroubled by

my impediments. They could see that I was not feeling well. In spite of the demands of acting, they treated me with indulgent kindness. I was grateful; I am nearly always grateful for the tolerance of my actors. When we part after a period of collaboration, I find myself in the grips of severe separation anxiety and an ensuing depression. People sometimes seem surprised that I abstain from attending opening nights and wrap parties. There is nothing strange about it. I have already cut the emotional ties of our relationship. It hurts me, and I cry inside. In such a state, who wants to go to a party?

After the Rehearsal is actually a dialogue between a young actress and an old director:

> Anna: How can you know for sure that you say the right thing to an actor?
> Vogler: I don't know it. I feel it.
> Anna: Aren't you ever afraid of feeling the wrong thing?
> Vogler: When I was younger and had reason to be afraid, I didn't understand that I had reason to be afraid.
> Anna: The road for many good directors is lined with humiliated and crippled actors. Have you ever taken the trouble to count your victims?
> Vogler: No.
> Anna: Perhaps you haven't left any victims behind you?
> Vogler: I don't think I have.
> Anna: How can you be so sure?
> Vogler: In life, or let us say in the real world, I believe there are human beings who do carry in

themselves injuries from my rampaging, just as I carry injuries from their treatment of me.

Anna: Not in the theater?

Vogler: No. Not in the theater. Perhaps you wonder how I can be so sure, and now I am going to tell you something that sounds both sentimental and exaggerated but which, nevertheless, is absolutely true. I love actors!

Anna: Love?

Vogler: Exactly. I love them. I love them as much as anything in the world; I love their profession; I love their courage or their contempt of the world or whatever they want to call it. I love their deception but also their coldhearted sincerity, which stops at nothing. I love it when they try to manipulate me, and I envy them their gullibility and their keen insight. Yes, I love these actors without reservation; I love them magnificently. Therefore I cannot do them harm.

◁ After the Rehearsal: *"Actually a dialogue between a young actress and an old director." Lena Olin and Erland Josephson.*

THE OUTLINE FOR *AUTUMN SONATA* was written March 26, 1976. Part of the story is the whole tax evasion scandal that fell upon me in the beginning of January: I ended up at the Karolinska Hospital's psychiatric clinic, then at the Sophia-hemmet, and finally on Fårö. After three months the indictment was repealed. The charge was reduced from that of a serious crime to one of simple tax understatement. My initial reaction was euphoria.

This is what it says in my workbook:

> The night after the acquittal, when I cannot go to sleep in spite of sleeping pills, it occurs to me that I want to make a film about the mother-daughter, daughter-mother relationship, and I must have Ingrid Bergman and Liv Ullmann in the two roles, and no one else. Eventually, there may be room for a third character.
>
> It should look something like this: Helena,* who is not a devastating beauty like her ancient namesake, is thirty-five years old and married to a gentle pastor named Viktor. They live in the parsonage near the church and lead a quiet life among their congregation and with the changing seasons ever since their small son died of an unexplained illness. He was six years old when he died and named Erik. Helena's mother

*In the actual film, this character is called Eva, and Helena is the name of Eva's handicapped sister.

326

is a concert pianist, now touring around the world. She is expected to arrive soon for her annual visit with her daughter. Actually, she has not come to see them for a few years, so there is a great to-do in the parsonage, elaborate preparations, and happy but anxious expectations. Helena has waited a long time for this meeting with her mother. She also plays the piano, and her mother usually gives her lessons. Therefore, sincere joy pervades this visit that both mother and daughter have looked forward to with both anxiety and fervor. The mother is in a splendid mood. At least she manages to act as if she were in a splendid mood. She finds everything arranged perfectly; even the hard wooden board (for her back) has been placed in her bed in the guest room. She has brought goodies from Switzerland.

The church bells ring. Helena wants to take her mother to the grave, Erik's grave. Helena goes there every Saturday. She admits that Erik visits her there sometimes, that she can feel his small, cautious caresses. Her mother finds this fixation on the dead child alarming, and she tries, carefully choosing her words, to make Helena see that she and Viktor should adopt or try to have another child. Then later, Helena plays something for her mother, and her mother pays her a number of compliments. But, to insure the purity of the piece, she plays it again herself, thereby crushing her daughter's meek interpretation, quietly but effectively.

The second act begins with the mother fighting insomnia. She takes sleeping pills, she reads her books, she murmurs her prayers, but she still can't sleep. Finally she gets up and goes into the living room. Helena hears her, and here follows the grand unmasking. The two women talk about their relationship. For the first time Helena dares to tell the truth of how she really feels. Her mother is completely shaken up by all the hatred and contempt that Helena reveals.

Then it is the mother's turn to speak about herself, her bitterness, her loathing, her despair, her loneliness. She speaks of the men in her life, about their ultimate indifference, and how they humiliate her by always chasing after other women. But the scene becomes even more profound: *The daughter finally gives birth to the mother.* Through this reversal they unite for a few brief moments in perfect symbiosis.

Nevertheless, the mother leaves the next morning. She can't stand the hush or her raw feelings. She arranges it so that someone sends her a telegram saying she must return to work immediately. Helena overhears the telephone conversation. Her mother has left, it is Sunday, and Helena prepares to go to church to listen to her husband's sermon.

Instead of just two characters in the film, they became four. That idea that Helena gives birth to her mother is a difficult one to convey and one which, I'm sad to say, I abandoned. Characters have a way of following their own paths. In the old days I tried to control and force them, but over the years I became wiser and learned to let them behave as they wished. The result: their hate becomes cemented. The daughter can never forgive the mother. The mother can never forgive the daughter. Forgiveness can be found only through connection with the fourth character, a sick girl.

Autumn Sonata was conceived in one night, in a matter of

hours, after a period of total writer's block. The lingering question is, why this: Why *Autumn Sonata?* It contained nothing that I had been thinking about before.

The idea of working with Ingrid Bergman was an old desire, but that did not initiate this story. The last time I had seen her was at the Cannes Film Festival at the screening of *Cries and Whispers.* She had snuck a letter into my pocket, in which she reminded me of my promise that we would make a film together. Once long ago we had planned to adapt Hjalmar Bergman's novel *The Boss, Mrs. Ingeborg* to film.

A puzzling element remains: Why did I choose this story, and why was it so complete? It was more finished in the outline than in its final execution.

I wrote the screenplay for *Autumn Sonata* in a few weeks in order to have something up my sleeve in case *The Serpent's Egg* flopped with a somersault. My decision was final: I would never work again in Sweden.

That is the reason I made the strange arrangement to shoot *Autumn Sonata* in Norway. As it turned out, I felt perfectly content to work in the primitive studios on the outskirts of Oslo. Built in 1913 or 1914, the buildings have been left just as they were. Of course, when the wind blew in certain directions, the air traffic passed right overhead, but otherwise it was old-fashioned and cozy. Everything we needed was available there, even though the place was dilapidated and had not been kept up. The crew members were friendly but a little amateurish.

The actual filming was draining. I did not have what one would call difficulties in my working relationship with Ingrid Bergman. Rather, it was a kind of language barrier, but in a profound sense. Starting on the first day when we all read the script together in the rehearsal studio, I discovered that she had rehearsed her entire part in front of the mirror,

Autumn Sonata: *"I must have Ingrid Bergman and Liv Ullmann in the two roles, and no one else."* ▷

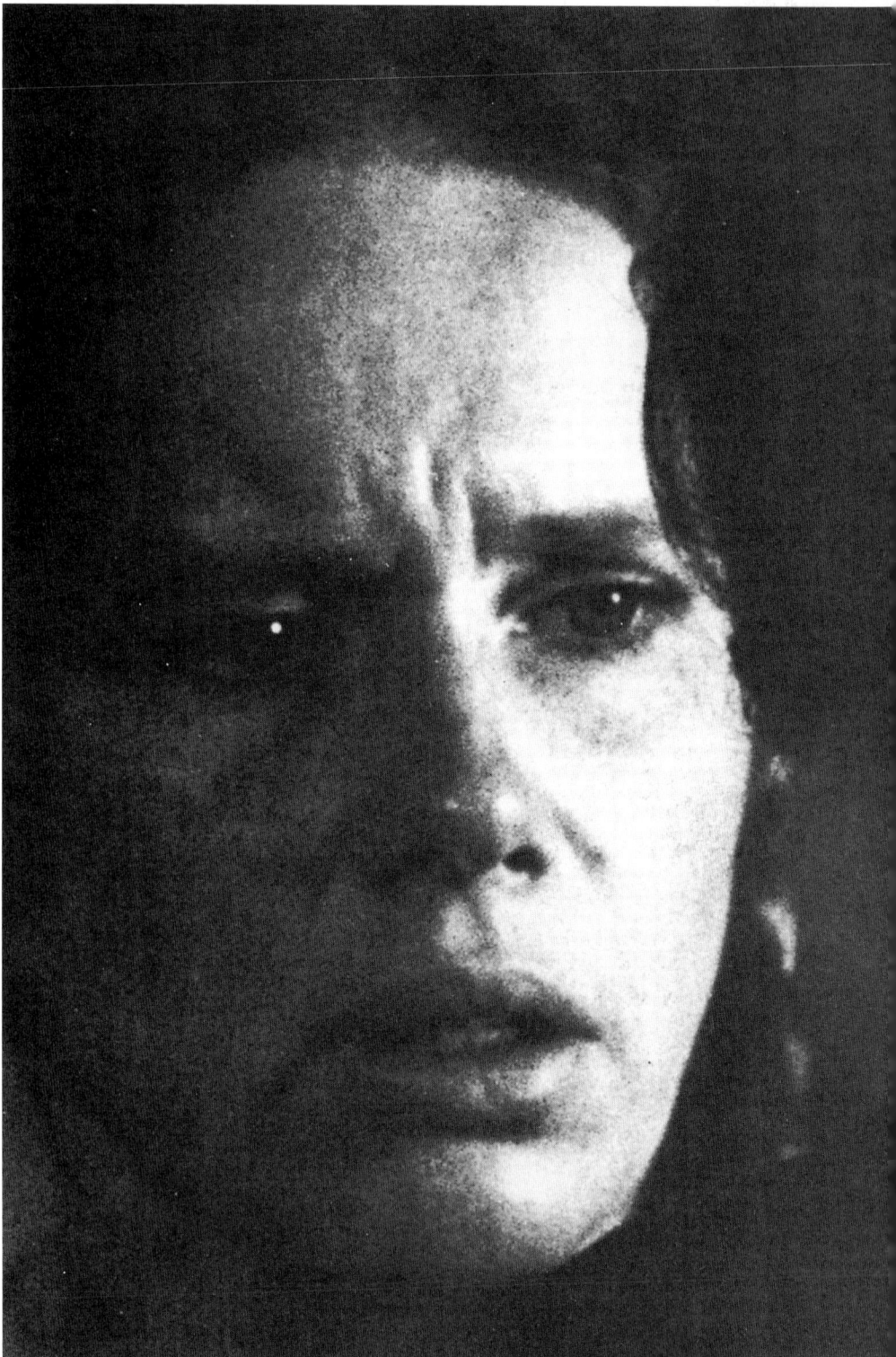

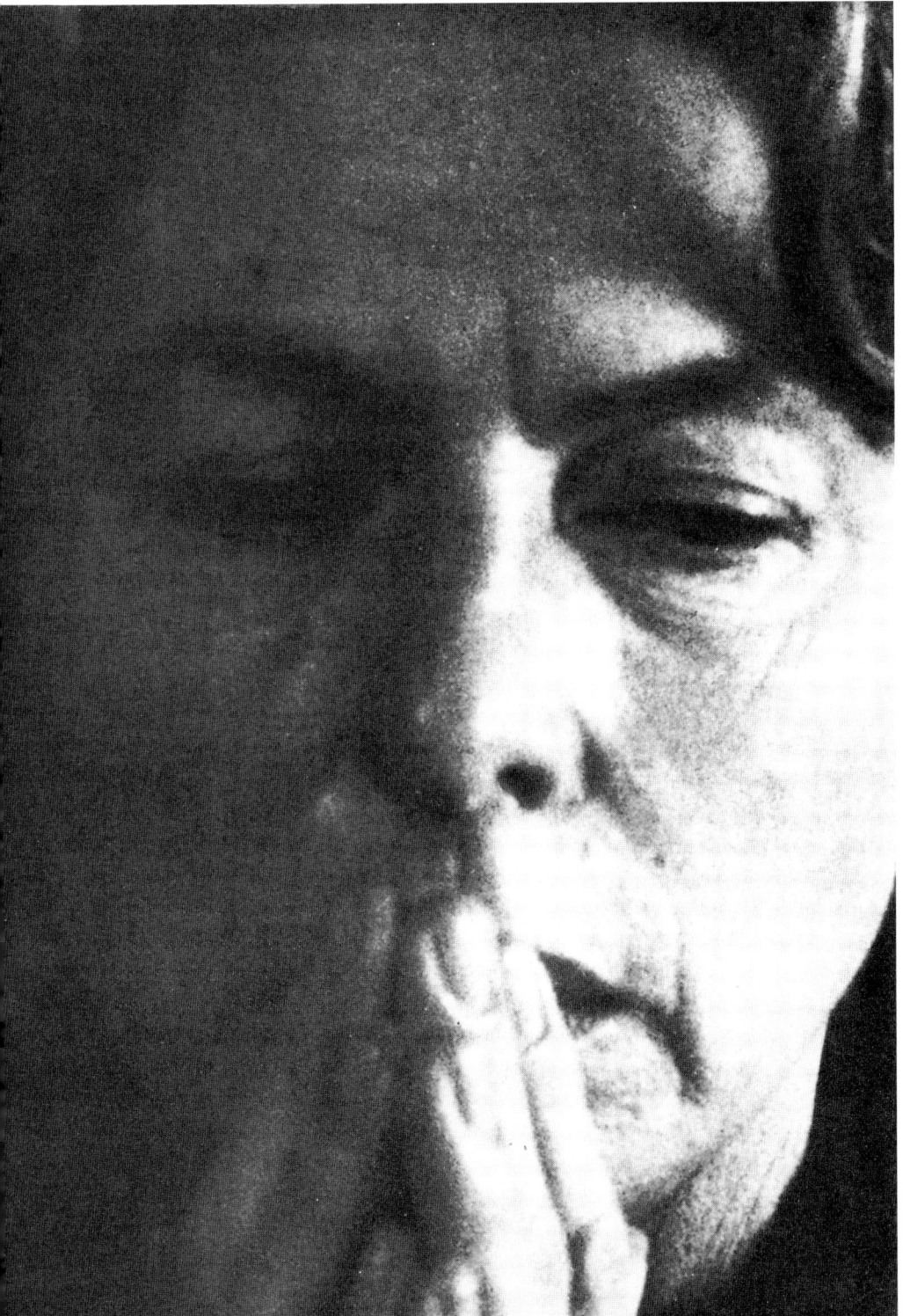

332

complete with intonations and self-conscious gestures. It was
clear that she had a different approach to her profession
than the rest of us. She was still living in the 1940s.

I believe that she possessed some sort of inspired system
of working, albeit a strange one. In spite of her mechanisms
for receiving director's cues not being placed where one expected to find them — and where they ought to be — she
still must have been somehow receptive to suggestions from
two or three of her former directors. After all, she had done
excellent work in several American films.

In Hitchcock's films, for instance, she is always magnificent.
She detested the man. I believe that with her he never hesitated to be disrespectful and arrogant, which evidently was
precisely the best method to make her listen.

I discovered early into our rehearsals that to be understanding and offer a sympathetic ear did not work. In her
case I was forced to use tactics that I normally rejected, the
first and foremost being aggression.

Once she told me: "If you don't tell me how I should do
this scene, I'll slap you!" I rather liked that. But from a strictly
professional point of view, it was difficult to work with these
two actresses together. When I look at the film today, I see
that I left Liv to shift for herself when I ought to have been
more supportive. Liv is one of those generous artists who
give everything they have. In a few scenes, she sometimes
goes astray. That is because I paid too much attention to
Ingrid Bergman. Ingrid also had some trouble remembering
her lines. In the mornings she was often crabby and angry,
which was understandable. She lived with constant anxiety
over her own illness* and at the same time found our way

*At the time she made *Autumn Sonata*, Ingrid Bergman was fighting
cancer. She died in 1982.

Halvar Björk and Liv Ullmann. With Ingrid Bergman. ▷

of working unfamiliar and frightening. But she never made any attempt to back out. Her conduct was always extraordinarily professional. Even with her obvious frailties, Ingrid Bergman was a remarkable person: generous, grand, and highly talented.

A French critic cleverly wrote that "with *Autumn Sonata* Bergman does Bergman." It is witty but unfortunate. For me, that is.

I think it is only too true that Bergman (Ingmar, that is) did a Bergman.

If I had had the strength to do what I intended to do at the beginning, it would not have turned out that way.

I love and admire the filmmaker Tarkovsky and believe him to be one of the greatest of all time. My admiration for Fellini is limitless. But I also feel that Tarkovsky began to make Tarkovsky films and that Fellini began to make Fellini films. Yet Kurosawa has never made a Kurosawa film.

I have never been able to appreciate Buñuel. He discovered at an early stage that it is possible to fabricate ingenious tricks, which he elevated to a special kind of genius, particular to Buñuel, and then he repeated and varied his tricks. He always received applause. Buñuel nearly always made Buñuel films.

So the time has come for me to look in the mirror and ask: Where are we going? Has Bergman begun to make Bergman films?

I find that *Autumn Sonata* is an annoying example.

What I will never know is this: How did it happen that this film was *Autumn Sonata?* If you carry around a story inside long enough or keep dwelling on a certain subject as happened with *Persona* or *Cries and Whispers*, it is possible to discern how a film evolved and why it ended up as it did. But how did *Autumn Sonata* suddenly burst forth, looking the way it does, like a dream? . . . And perhaps that is its weakness: it should have remained a dream. Not a film of a dream but a dream of a film: two characters. Background and everything else ought to have been pushed to the side. Three acts in three kinds of lighting: one evening light, one night light, and one morning light. No cumbersome sets, two faces, and three kinds of lighting. Without a doubt that is how I first imagined *Autumn Sonata*.

There is something close to an enigma in the concept of the daughter giving birth to the mother. Therein lies an emotion that I was not able to realize and carry through to its conclusion. On the surface, the finished film resembles the outline, but actually that is not the case.

I am drilling, and either the drill breaks or else I don't dare drill deeply enough. Or else it is because I don't have the strength, or I don't realize that I should drill deeper. Then I pull up the drill and don't take that extra dizzying step. I pull up the drill and declare myself satisfied. That is an unerring symptom of creative exhaustion, exceedingly dangerous because it doesn't hurt.

Farces Frolics

DURING THE STRIKE in the Swedish film industry in 1951,* I made a series of commercials for the soap *Bris* (Breeze). They rescued me from a severe financial setback. Even today when I look at them, I still feel a touch of my earlier enthusiasm. They do not reflect any lack of ambition or any laziness. They are unusual and were made in good spirits. One can even overlook the fact that they promoted a soap that practically tore the skin off your body.

The comedies that I produced were made for the same reasons as the soap commercials. Their purpose was to make money. This doesn't embarrass me in the least. Most projects in the world of film come into being for that very reason.

My own relationship to comedy has been complicated, however, and the difficulties go way back in time. As a child I was considered sullen and too sensitive. From an early age onward it was said that "Ingmar has no sense of humor."

My brother, on the other hand, was an excellent "entertainer." Even at a very young age, he was a brilliant conversationalist at dinner, terribly funny, sarcastic, and witty, although over time his jokes became rather bitter.

Yet I wanted very much for people to laugh at my jokes. I made several attempts to create something funny. In

---

*The Swedish film industry experienced a ten-month-long work stoppage beginning January 1951, in protest of a steep amusement tax levied solely on motion pictures. Like many Swedish film directors, Bergman faced the prospect of unemployment. The offer to direct several commercials made him "absurdly grateful," as he once expressed it.

Helsingborg I directed two New Year's revues for which I wrote a few skits that I thought were hilarious. But nobody cracked even a smile, and I brooded a good deal over how others could so easily make people laugh. Even if my life had depended on it, I couldn't figure out how they did it.

At the Gothenburg City Theater I watched all of Torsten Hammarén's rehearsals for a production of the classic French farce *Bichon*. He was an exceptional comedy director with a matchless talent for knowing exactly when to push our laugh button. He could effectively choreograph a comedy situation in which the actors began all the way on stage left and then let the gag explode in the middle, twelve seconds later.

The classic French farces are not for a moment meaningful. They are built entirely around a comical situation. Everything is mathematically constructed to culminate in a precise situation designed to release the laughter.

In *Waiting Women* I took my first real stab at comedy. The elevator scene with Eva Dahlbeck and Gunnar Björnstrand is based on a real-life experience. My second wife and I decided to be reunited in Copenhagen after a marital row, and we planned to stay at the home of good friends who had gone off to the country. We ate an excellent dinner at a restaurant and went back to the apartment in high spirits and rather excited. I brought out the key, put it in the lock, and then it broke off and got stuck in the lock. We were forced to sit in the stairwell all night until the superintendent deigned to get up the following morning. But the night was not wasted because we suddenly received an unexpected opportunity to really talk to each other.

I made note of the fact that, without a doubt, herein lay the basis for a solid comedy situation.

During this time Eva Dahlbeck and Gunnar Björnstrand

A Lesson in Love: *"In a scene meant for farce, Eva tries to hang herself. In that same moment Gunnar declares his love for her."* ▷

both had contracts with Svensk Filmindustri. So it seemed natural that I write a script for them.

There was something fateful about the meeting between the three of us: me, Eva, and Gunnar. Both of them were talented and creative actors. They felt immediately that although I had perhaps not yet written a spectacular text, the collaboration offered them great opportunities. On my part I was panic-stricken as I attempted for the first time to make a comedy. With overt confidence in me and great tact, they taught me how I should go about it.

They played off each other so perfectly in the elevator sequence that I came to write it as a fully developed comedy, *A Lesson in Love*. In a scene meant for farce, Eva tries to hang herself. In that same moment Gunnar declares his love for her. The ceiling collapses, and the whole incident becomes funny. When we went to shoot the scene, I got cold feet. I told Eva and Gunnar that I had reread the scene in the script and found it totally impossible, boring, poorly written; we would have to do it some other way. Eva and Gunnar protested in unison. They asked me to leave the set, go into town, and find something else to do. "Give us an hour or so to work on it. When we are ready, we'll play the scene for you."

That is how it happened. And all at once I had a revelation: ah yes, it is possible to do it like this! I could not have received a better lesson. The trust, the security, the lack of tension, and the professionalism were forever established between us and became a stable foundation for the comedies we did together, not the least of which is *Smiles of a Summer Night*.

I went to the premiere of *A Lesson in Love*. On edge, I paced back and forth in the foyer of the movie theater Röda Kvarn, like a lost soul. Suddenly I could hear from inside the theater one roaring wave of laughter after another. And

I said to myself: It's not possible! *They are laughing.* They are laughing at something I have created.

Smiles of a Summer Night began to form inside me at the beginning of 1955. I had directed Molière's *Don Juan* and *The Teahouse of the August Moon* by John Patrick at Malmö City Theater and had also done *Wood Painting* in March.

I went to Switzerland to stay at a gigantic luxury hotel with the weighty name of Monte Verità. It was preseason. I soon discovered that there were only about ten guests and that they had kept the large hotel open despite the fact that renovations were being done before the tourist season began.

The mountains depressed me, especially since the sun dropped quickly behind the Alps at three o'clock in the afternoon. I did not talk to anyone, but I did take long walks and tried to establish a daily routine. Nearby was a very chic nursing home for aristocrats with syphilis. The patients took their daily walks at the same time as I did. It was an incredible sight: these people arrived, half dead, in varying stages of deterioration. Each one with his valet or nurse staggered along the road in a landscape quivering with the coming of spring.

Out of desperation I rented a car and drove to Milan. I went to La Scala and sat in the last row to see a terrible performance of Verdi's *Sicilian Evening Song*. When after this excursion I returned to Monte Verità and the mountains and the lunatics, I was sinking fast.

I have often toyed with the idea of suicide, especially when I was younger and my demons threatened to overtake me.

I surrendered myself completely to the idea that the moment had arrived. I was going to get in my car, take my foot off the brake, and drive over the edge of the serpentine roadway leading up to the hotel. This way it would look like an accident. Nobody would have to feel sad or guilty.

Right then a telegram arrived from Stockholm with the

message that I must call Carl Anders Dymling at Svensk Filmindustri immediately.

I had written Dymling an optimistic letter from Ascona in which I told him that I was working on *Smiles of a Summer Night*. There would be important roles for both Eva Dahlbeck and Gunnar Björnstrand. It was to be a very commercial piece. A finished screenplay would be ready in April. We could definitely begin shooting by midsummer.

When I got hold of Dymling on the telephone, he asked me to return home — not to continue working on *Smiles of a Summer Night* but in order to work with Alf Sjöberg. The screenplay was called *Last Couple Out* (after a children's game). It had been floating around Svensk Filmindustri for a long time in synopsis form. For my efforts, they would pay me more than required by my current slave contract. They were also in a hurry. Relieved, I postponed my suicide and returned home.

Working rapidly, Sjöberg and I started churning out the script for *Last Couple Out*, from which Sjöberg later wrote his own version. I did not care one whit about *Last Couple Out*. But if Svensk Filmindustri and Sjöberg wanted to film it, I was happy to take the money.

And I graciously spent my extra income at a tourist hotel in Dalecarlia, called the Siljansborg. I had often gone there and stayed in a small double room on the top floor with a view of Lake Siljan and the elongated mountains. I packed up my yellow manuscript paper, two sweaters, a dark suit, and a tie. At this hotel they liked the guests to dress for dinner.

It was like coming home to a sudden and unexpected security. My work on *Smiles of a Summer Night* had gotten blocked among the syphilis victims. All I had done was sketch out the different characters and their relationships to one another. I had established the equation, and I even knew the solution. But then I had gotten stuck.

Staying at the same hotel were not only the author Sven Stolpe and his lovely wife, Karin, but also a young girl who had suffered shock from a severe poisoning from the penicillin prescribed for her allergy complications. We were two solitary figures who found each other. In the afternoons we went driving through the early spring days past places from my childhood around Lake Siljan and along the riverbanks. All at once it became a merry game to write.

When I returned to Stockholm in the middle of March, I had the finished manuscript in my suitcase, exactly as I had promised. It was immediately accepted by the studio.

At that time there were no long preparations before a film took flight, but, starting at the planning stage, this film became expensive. It was to be a period piece, which involved more days of shooting in the schedule than usual. Including the time spent traveling to film on location, it would require close to fifty days.

Smiles of a Summer Night further develops themes from *A Lesson in Love*. It explores the frightening insight that it is possible for two people to love each other even when they find it impossible to live together. It also contains a bit of nostalgia, looking back at my own life and my relationship with my daughter, full of great confusion and sorrow.

We started shooting around midsummer. Immediately, my old stomach demon acted up. I was sick during the entire shooting and was apparently in a rotten mood. Evidently I did not bother the actors whom I have always tried to protect from my unpleasantness. But those who remember insist that I carried on like the devil himself with the production people, the lab, the sound department, and especially the administration.

My assistant, Lennart Olsson, took copious notes in a voluminous but unpublishable notebook during the filming, in

Smiles of a Summer Night: *Ulla Jacobsson and Eva Dahlbeck. Ulla Jacobsson. Björn Bjelfvenstam, Harriet Andersson, and Ulla Jacobsson. Jarl Kulle, Gunnar Björnstrand, and Margit Carlqvist.* ▷

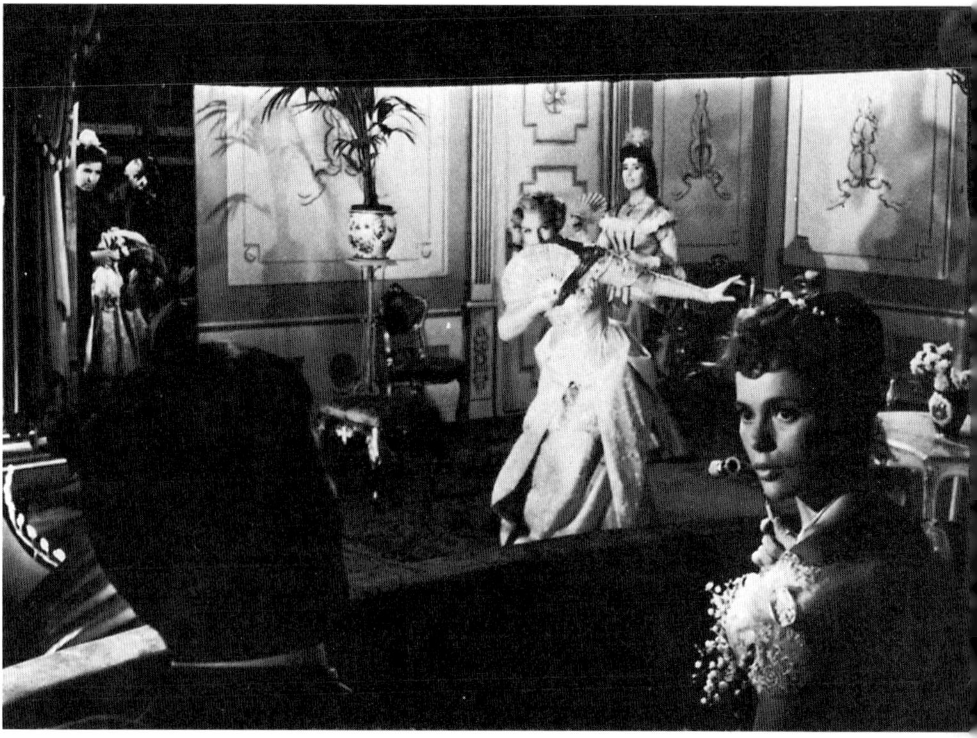

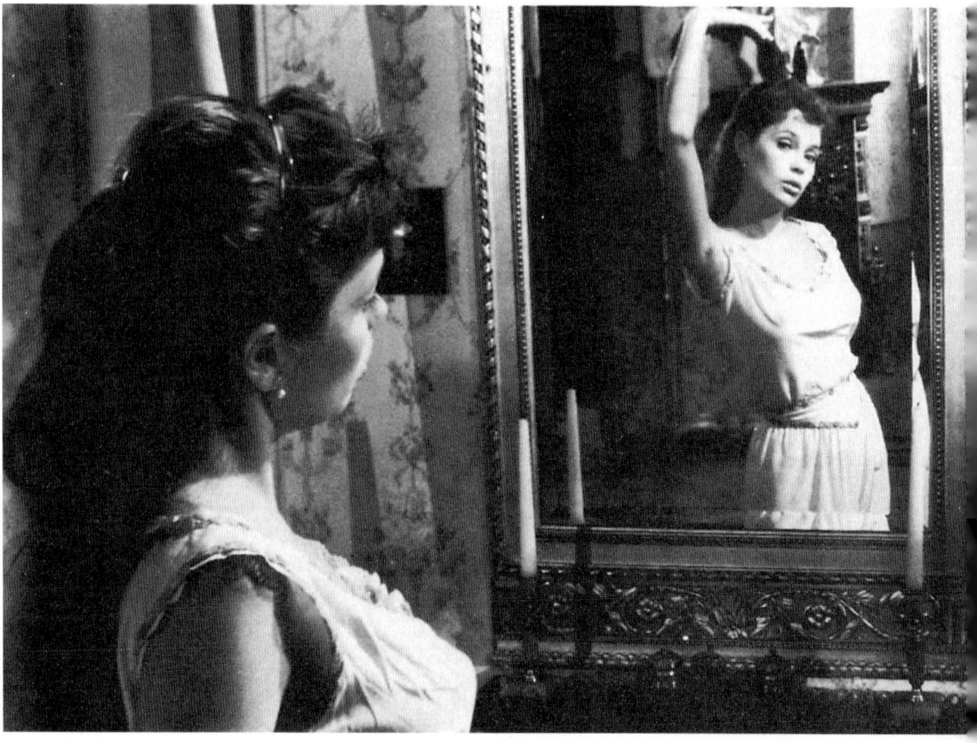

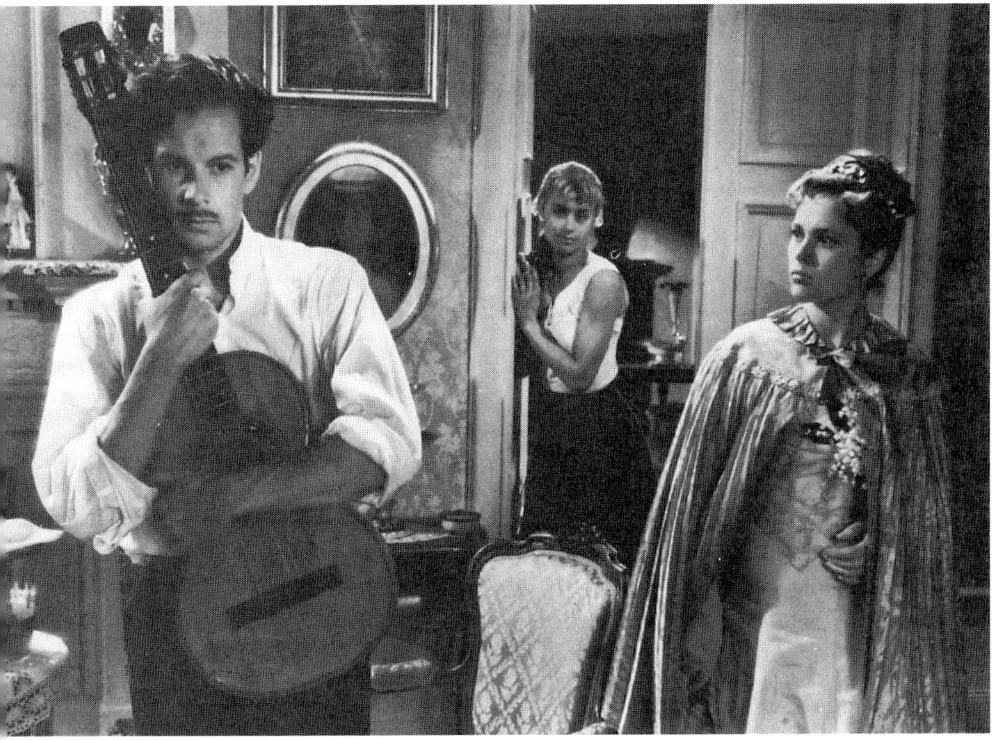

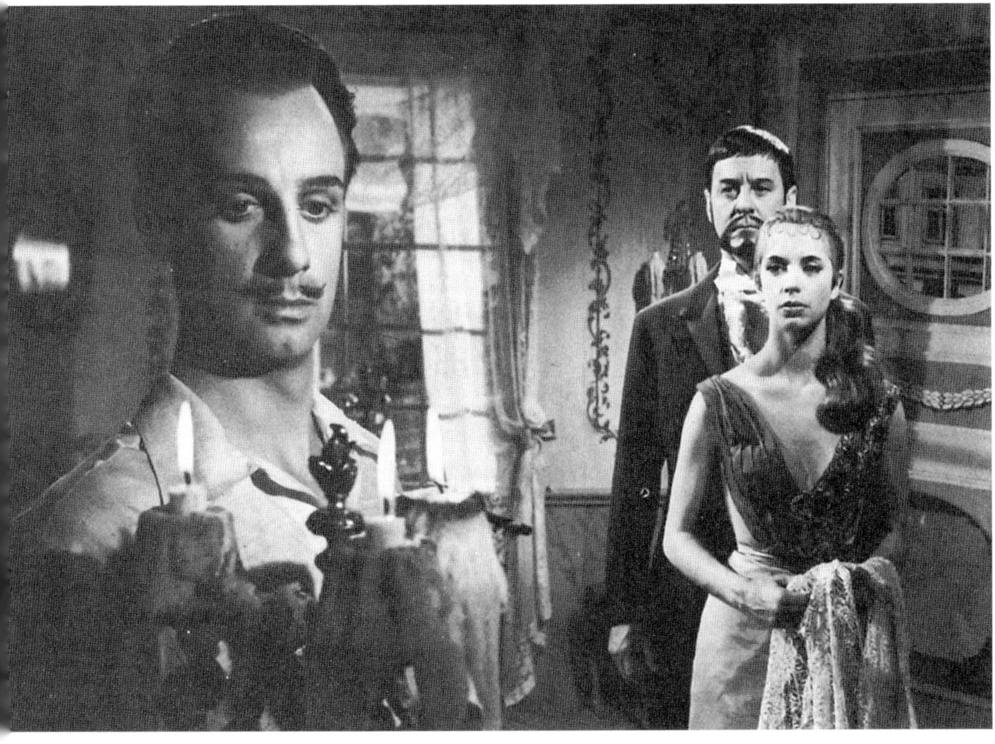

which he accounted for every scene with sketches of the sets and stage directions.

It is as ambitious and boring as Xenophon's *Anabasis*. But in the middle of the technical accounts that fill page after page after page, it says: "Everyone is now exhausted. Katinka bursts into tears if you just tell her to shut up."*

The filming went on uninterrupted, and we were lucky enough to have good weather. The actors enjoyed what they were doing, and the film became a success in spite of my bad temper, my sickness and depression. The last day of filming I weighed only 57 kilos (a little more than 125 pounds). Everyone, including me, thought that I had stomach cancer. I was checked into a hospital and was thoroughly examined. The diagnosis: I was unbelievably healthy.

The Devil's Eye continues my line of comedies. The studio had bought the rights to a dusty Danish comedy called *The Return of Don Juan*. Dymling and I entered into a shameful agreement. I wanted to direct *The Virgin Spring*, which he detested. He wanted me to direct *The Devil's Eye*, which I detested. We were both very satisfied with our agreement through which both could be made, and each one of us felt that we had fooled the other. In reality I had only fooled myself.

Waiting Women had been made solely in order to earn money for Svensk Filmindustri. That it became a great, calculated gimmick from beginning to end is another story. In *The Magic Lantern*, I wrote: "Sometimes considerably more courage is required to put on the brakes than to fire the rocket. I lacked this courage and realized, only too late, what kind of film I should have made."

---

*Olsson is referring to Katinka Faragò, Bergman's longtime assistant and sometime producer.

All These Women: *without brakes on the bed canopy.* ▷

I WAS TWELVE YEARS OLD when I saw *The Magic Flute* for the first time at the Royal Opera House in Stockholm. It was a lengthy and unwieldy production. The curtain came up for a brief scene and then went down again immediately. The orchestra huddled in its pit. There was a commotion behind the curtain with stage technicians bustling about, hammering parts constructed earlier. After an interminable wait, the curtain went up for the next brief scene.

Mozart wrote *The Magic Flute* for a theater using an interchangeable backdrop and movable wings, which facilitated rapid scene changes. That machinery still existed at the Opera House, but it was not being used. The revolution in set design that occurred in the 1920s had left disastrous consequences. The scenery became multidimensional, and well it should! It was solidly constructed — one could even hide out there — but consequently it was heavy, cumbersome, and hard to move.

I had begun to attend the Royal Opera House regularly in the fall of 1928. If you sat in the third balcony on the side, it was relatively cheap. It was even cheaper than going to the movies. Sixty-five öre [approximately thirteen cents] at the opera. Seventy-five öre [approximately fifteen cents] for a movie. I became a frequent operagoer.

I already had my puppet theater. I mainly performed whatever stories I could find in the collections of children's fairy tales. There were four of us about the same age who were involved with the theater. My sister and I spent most of our time on it. My best friend and her best friend were zealous co-workers.

It was a large puppet theater with a wide repertoire. We made everything ourselves: the puppets, the costumes for each puppet, the scenery, and the lights. We had a revolving stage, a set that could be lowered, and a curved panoramic backdrop. We became increasingly sophisticated in our choice of plays. More and more, I began to look for plays that required complicated lighting and frequent changes of scenery. Therefore, it seemed rather natural that *The Magic Flute* began to occupy a large place in the imagination of the head of this theater.

One evening the director saw *The Magic Flute* performed and decided to do a production of the play. Unfortunately, the project fell through because it was too expensive for us to purchase a complete recording of the opera.

The Magic Flute became my companion through life.

In 1939 I was employed as a production assistant at the Opera House. In 1940 a revival of the old, heavy production was set into action. In my role of assistant to the director I stood in the lighting booth to the left of the stage in the first entrance of the wings. Working there were an old gentleman called "The Fire Chief" and his son. Both of them looked as if they had grown up in the cramped corridor between all the levers. My job was to stand there with the piano score in my hand and signal them in the booth when it was time to change the lighting.

Sometime later I went to the Malmö City Theater. On the main stage, at least two operas were produced each season, and I voted ardently for us to stage *The Magic Flute*. I was eager to direct it myself.

That would probably have happened, had the theater not

contracted with a German opera director of the old school for a whole year. He was around sixty years old and had directed during his lengthy career most operas in existence. It was natural that he direct *The Magic Flute*, a monumental mastodon of a performance with heavy sets. For me, the disappointment was twofold.

There is another line that merges with my love for *The Magic Flute*. As a boy I loved to roam around. One October day I set out for Drottningholm [in Stockholm] to see its unique court theater from the eighteenth century.

For some reason the stage door was unlocked. I walked inside and saw for the first time the carefully restored baroque theater. I remember distinctly what a bewitching experience it was: the effect of chiaroscuro, the silence, the stage.

In my imagination I have always seen *The Magic Flute* living inside that old theater, in that keenly acoustical wooden box, with its slanted stage floor, its backdrops and wings. Here lies the noble, magical illusion of theater. Nothing *is*; everything *represents*. The moment the curtain is raised, an agreement between stage and audience manifests itself. And now, together, we'll create!

In other words, it is obvious that the drama of *The Magic Flute* should unfold in a baroque theater with the efficiency and incomparable machinery of a baroque theater.

The seed was sown by the end of the 1960s. For years the Swedish Radio orchestra had performed public concerts at the Circus in Djurgården. For the musicians it might have been an uncomfortable locale, but for the music it was wonderful; the acoustics were great, with the music resounding from under the cupola. One evening I ran into the then head of the Swedish Radio music department, Magnus Enhörning. We sat chatting during the intermission, and I pointed out

◁ The Magic Flute *with chimes.*

that this would be the perfect place to stage Stravinsky's *Oedipus Rex.* "Let's do it," he said.

Before then I had directed a production of *The Rake's Progress.* I had also done the folk musical *The Värmlanders,* as well as *The Merry Widow* at the Malmö City Theater — that was the total extent of my experience in musical theater.

Enhörning asked if I had any other suggestions to propose, and I heard myself say, "I want to do *The Magic Flute.* I want to do *The Magic Flute* for television."

"Good. Let's do that, too," said Enhörning, and that's the long and short of how we reached our decision. The Swedish television station estimated that a production of *The Magic Flute* would cost the dizzying sum of half a million Swedish crowns [about $100,000]. Furthermore, culture in general and the opera in particular were being hotly debated in the mass media, which since 1968 had become militant and anti-elitist. In this situation an expensive opera production was not a sure thing.

Without the undying enthusiasm of Magnus Enhörning, *The Magic Flute* would never have been made. He was untiring, and not having been born yesterday, he knew every trick in the book, and he also knew how to go about making the best decisions.

First of all we needed a conductor. I asked Hans Schmidt-Isserstedt, an old friend. In his inimitable accent he replied: "Nein, Ingmar, nicht das alles noch mal!" ["No, Ingmar, for the last time, no!"]

That was exactly how to respond to the paradox of *The Magic Flute:* musically it is insanely difficult. Despite this fact, the conductor is seldom rewarded for his efforts.

Next I turned to Eric Ericson whom I admired and respected as choirmaster and conductor of the oratorios. He responded with a definite no. But I did not give up. He

◁ *Eric Ericson conducts: "He possessed all the talents I wanted in a conductor."*

possessed all the talents I wanted in a conductor: a tingling warmth in his approach to music, a passion for interpretation, and — most of all — a feeling for the natural voice, which he had developed during his fabulous career as choirmaster. Finally, he accepted.

Since we were not performing *The Magic Flute* on a stage but in front of a microphone and camera, we did not need large voices. What we needed were warm, sensuous voices that had personality. To me it was also absolutely essential that the play be performed by young actors, naturally close to the dizzy, emotional shifts between joy and sorrow, between thinking and feeling. Tamino must be a handsome young man. Pamina must be a beautiful young woman. Not to speak of Papageno and Papagena. I was totally convinced that the three women must be young, happy, and virtuous. Little darlings, dangerous flirts, with a true sense of comedy, but also fiercely sensual. The three young men had to be little rascals, and so on.

After a considerable amount of time, we managed to assemble the entire group, a very Nordic ensemble. The singers and musicians then met for our very first rehearsal. I outlined what I wanted to bring out and emphasize in this production: an intimate atmosphere, a human quality, a sensualness, a warmth, and a close contact with the audience. The artists all responded with enthusiasm.

My main goal was to portray as intimately as possible the characters in the fairy tale. The magic and the scenic details happening as if only in passing: Suddenly they're in a palace courtyard; suddenly it is snowing; suddenly there is a prison wall; suddenly it's spring.

While we were filming, I noted how much the project benefited from its long gestation period. Never has a production unfolded with so few hindrances. The solutions lined up and

"The two guards with the fiery helmets sing the chorus." Preparations and scene. ▷

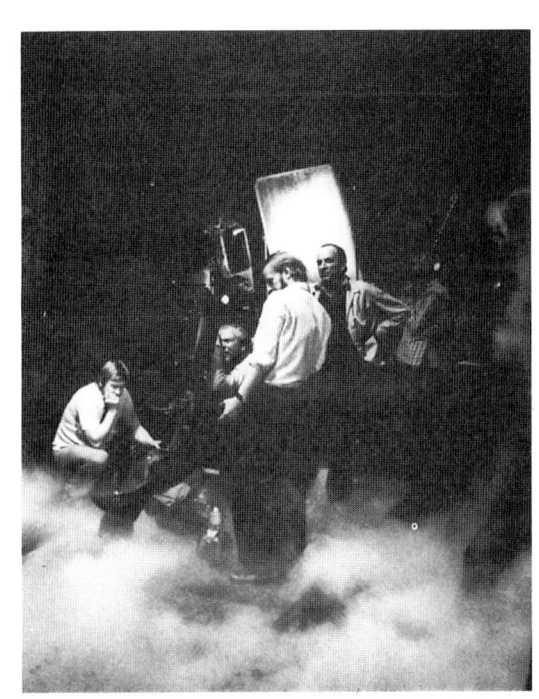

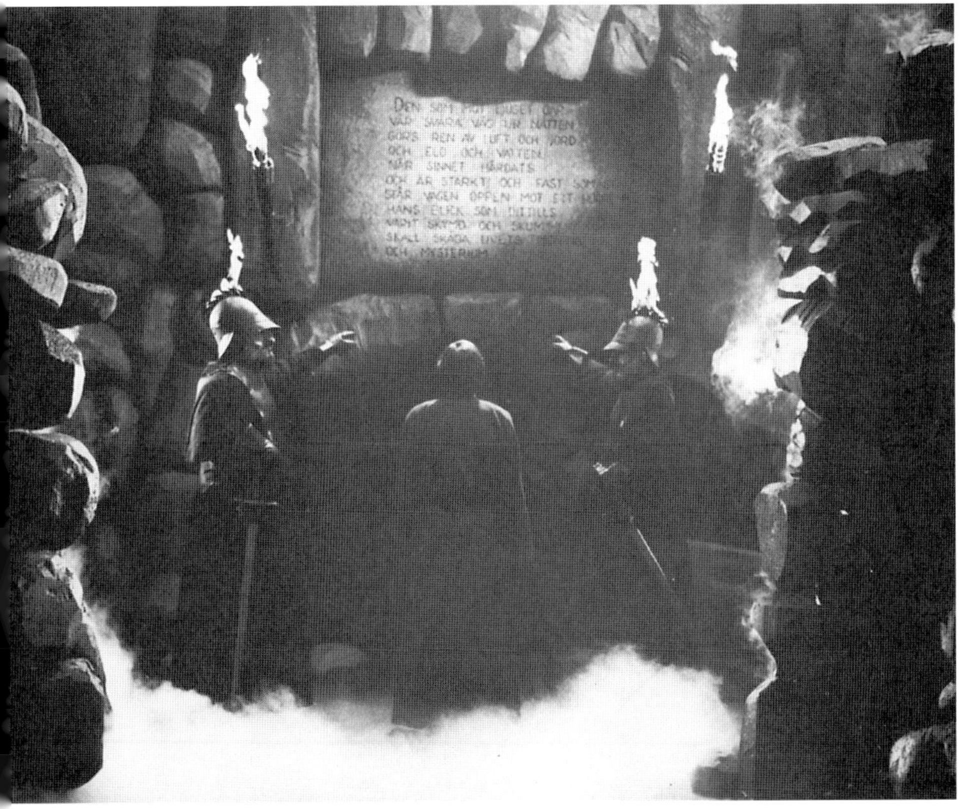
GÖRS REN AV LUFT OCH JORD
OCH ELD OCH VATTEN
NÄR SINNET HÄRDATS
OCH MYSTERIUM

announced themselves one by one. In no case was there even a shadow of forced efforts, nor did any idea arise merely to give me a chance to prove my cleverness as a director. It was a highly creative time, carried along, day and night, by Mozart's music.

In the introduction to Tamino's and Pamina's three trials lies one of the most central scenes of the drama. It was Käbi Laretei's piano teacher, Andrea Vogler-Corelli, who drew my attention to its indisputable significance. In *The Magic Lantern* I wrote:

> Daniel Sebastian was born by cesarean on September 7, 1962. Käbi and Andrea Vogler worked at the piano without stopping until the last minute. The evening following his birth, when Käbi had fallen asleep after nine months of suffering, Andrea took the score of *The Magic Flute* down from the bookshelf. I told her about my dream of directing it, and Andrea opened it to the part where the two guards with the fiery helmets sing the chorus. She pointed out how remarkable it was that Mozart, a Catholic, had chosen a chorus inspired by Bach for his message and that of Schikaneder. She showed me the score and said: "This must be the keel of the boat. *The Magic Flute* is difficult to steer. Without a keel, it doesn't work at all. The Bach chorus is the keel."

The film was edited on Fårö. When the work print was ready with a complete sound track, we held our own world premiere in my film studio. Invited to the premiere were all those involved in the film, plus neighbors, children, and grandchildren. It was a hot evening in August with a luminous moon shining on the ocean. We drank champagne, and outside we lit colorful lanterns and sent up a small fireworks.

◁ *With Pamina (Irma Urrila) and Papageno (Håkan Hagegård).*

THERE ARE TWO godfathers to *Fanny and Alexander*. One of them is E. T. A. Hoffmann.

Toward the end of the 1970s, I was supposed to direct *Tales of Hoffmann* at the Opera House in Munich. I began to fantasize about the real Hoffmann, who sat in Luther's wine cellar, sick and nearly dying. I wrote in my notes: "Death is everpresent. The barcarole [a Venetian boat song], the sweetness of death. The Venice scene stinks of decay, raw lust, and heavy perfumes. In the Antonia scene, the mother is intensely frightening. The room is peopled with shadows, dancing, and mouths gaping. The mirror in the mirror aria is small and gleams like a murder weapon."

In a short story written by Hoffmann there is a gigantic, magical room. It was that magical room I wanted to re-create on stage. The drama would be played out with that room set in the foreground and the orchestra in the background.

There is also an illustration from E. T. A. Hoffmann's stories that had haunted me time and time again, a picture from *The Nutcracker*. Two children are quivering close together in the twilight of Christmas Eve, waiting impatiently for the candles on the tree to be lighted and the doors to the living room to be opened.

It is that scene that gave me the idea of beginning *Fanny and Alexander* with a Christmas celebration.

The second godfather is Dickens: the bishop and his home, the Jew in his boutique of fantasies, the children as victims; the contrast between flourishing outside life and a closed

Fanny and Alexander: *with Sven Nykvist and Ewa Fröling.* ▷

world in black and white. [All of these elements are in Berg-man's film *Fanny and Alexander*.]

One could say that it all began during the fall of 1978. I was living in Munich and felt ill at ease. I was still enmeshed in the tax imbroglio, and I didn't know how or when it would end. On September 27, I wrote in my workbook:

> There is no longer any distinction between my anxiety and the reality that causes it. And yet I think I know what kind of film I want to make next. It is far different from anything I have ever done.
>
> Anton is eleven years old and Maria is twelve. They act as observers of the reality I wish to depict. The time is the beginning of the First World War; the place is a small town, exceedingly quiet and well-kept. There is a university, a theater, and a hotel some distance away. Life is peaceful.
>
> Anton and Maria's mother is director of a theater. When their father died, she took over the management of his theater and now runs it with authority and shrewdness. They live on a quiet street. In the back of the theater lives a Jew, Isak, who owns a toy store. It contains some other interesting and exciting objects as well. A frequent Sunday visitor is an old lady who used to be a missionary in China. She performs Chinese shadow plays. There is also an uncle who is a little crazy but is harmless and who takes certain liberties. The house is well-to-do and extremely bourgeois. The grandmother is an almost mystical figure who lives in the apartment below. She is fabulously wealthy and was in her past a royal mistress and a great actress. Now she has retired, but sometimes she will appear in an occasional part. In

either case, it is a world completely dominated by women, from the cook who has been around for a hundred years to the little nanny who is cheerful, freckled, and limps because one leg is shorter than the other, and who smells deliciously of sweat.

The theater is both a playground for the children and a haven. Sometimes they are allowed to participate in a play, which they find enormously exciting. The children sleep in the same room, and they have many things to keep themselves occupied — their own puppet theater, their own movie projector, toy trains, dollhouses. They are inseparable.

Maria is the one who takes the most initiative. Anton is rather anxious. Their upbringing is strict, and severe punishment for even the most trivial offenses is not out of the question. The church bells measure the passage of time; the small bell at a nearby castle announces when it is morning and when it is evening. The Vicar is always a welcome guest even at the theater. One might suspect that Mother has a special relationship with the vicar. However, this is difficult to know right away.

Then Mother decides to marry the vicar. Mother cannot continue to manage her theater; she must become a wife and mother. It is already apparent that her belly is swelling. Maria does not like the vicar; Anton does not like him either. Mother transfers the ownership of the theater to her actors; crying bitterly, she bids her people farewell and moves into the vicarage with Maria and Anton, who are raging with anger.

Mother is a good wife to the clergyman. She plays her part irreproachably: she gives birth to a child and

Three generations: Gunn Wållgren, Ewa Fröling, and Bertil Guve. ▷

invites the parishioners in for coffee after the morning service. The church bells ring, and Maria and
Anton brood, thinking of revenge. They are no longer
allowed to sleep together in the same room, and the
cheerful Maj, the nanny, who has become pregnant,
is fired and replaced by the vicar's sister, who is a
dragon.

With my divining rod, I searched the ground for a source
and came upon a vein of water. When I began to drill, it
gushed out like a geyser. My notes continue:

Through my playing, I want to master my anxiety,
relieve tension, and triumph over my deterioration.
I want to depict, finally, the joy that I carry within me
in spite of everything, and which I so seldom and so
feebly have given attention to in my work. To be able
to express the power of action, decisiveness, the vitality, and the kindness. Yes, for once, that would not
be a bad idea.

From the very beginning one can see that with *Fanny and
Alexander* I have landed in the world of my childhood. Here
is the university town and Grandmother's house with the old
cook; here is the Jew who lived out back; and here is the
school. I am already in the place and beginning to roam
around in the familiar environment. My childhood has of
course always been my main supplier, without my ever having
bothered to find out where the deliveries were coming from.
On November 10, I write in my workbook:

I often think of Ingrid Bergman. I would like to write
something for her that would not be too demanding,

and I see a summer porch in rain. She is alone, waiting for her children and grandchildren. It is afternoon. The whole film is set on a veranda. The film will last only as long as the rain. Nature is showing her fairest face; everything is enveloped in this soft unceasing rain. When the film opens, she is speaking on the telephone. Her family is out on an excursion around the lake. She talks with an old friend of hers, who is much older than she. A deep trust exists between the two. She writes a letter. She finds some object. She remembers a theater performance — her big break-through. She sees her reflection in the window-panes — and can catch a glimpse of herself as a young woman.

The reason she has stayed at home is that she has sprained her ankle — it is only a slight sprain; mostly it feels good to be alone. Toward the end of the film, she sees the family returning from their trip; the rain is still falling, but it is now a peaceful, quiet drip.

Everything should happen in a major key.

The porch in summer — everything is enveloped in a soft chiaroscuro. In this piece there are no hard edges; everything must be as soft as the rain. A neighbor's child comes and asks for the other children. She has brought wild strawberries, and she is given a treat. She is wet from the rain and smells sweet. It is a kind life, a good, simple, incredible life. When she sees the child's hands, the most unusual thoughts come to her, thoughts that she has never had before. The cat purrs, stretched out on the sofa; the clock ticks; the smell of summer pervades over all. She stands in the doorway to the porch and looks out over the meadow with the oak tree, the meadow that leads down to the old

Cinematography in Fanny and Alexander. ▷

bridge and the bay. To her, everything looks both old and familiar and yet new and unexpected. It is strange how longing emanates from sudden solitude.

This looks like a different film, independent of the first, but the material came to good use in *Fanny and Alexander*. The decision to depict a life, luminous and happy, was there from the moment I found life truly difficult to bear.

It was the same with *Smiles of a Summer Night*, which also burst forth during a time of uncertainty. I think it may be because the creative juices flow faster when the soul is threatened. Sometimes such a state brings luck and insight in its wake, as in *Smiles of a Summer Night*, *Fanny and Alexander*, and *Persona*. Sometimes, as in *The Serpent's Egg*, all goes awry.

I conceived *Fanny and Alexander* during the fall of 1978, a time when everything around me left me in darkest despair. But I wrote the screenplay during the spring of 1979, and by that time many things had eased up. *Autumn Sonata* had a successful premiere, and the whole tax business had dissolved into thin air. I found myself liberated suddenly. I think that *Fanny and Alexander* benefited from my relief. To know that I had what I had.

Harmony is not a feeling that is totally unusual or foreign to me. If I am just allowed to live quietly and create in a calm environment without being tormented, where I can have a clear perspective of my existence, where it is possible for me to be kind and not need anything or have to keep lots of appointments, then I can function at my best. Such an existence reminds me of the good-natured passive life of my childhood.

On April 12, 1979, we arrived on Fårö. "It feels like coming home. Everything else is a dream, an unreality." A few days later I began to write *Fanny and Alexander*. Wednesday,

With Gunn Wållgren and Erland Josephson. Preparation and scene. ▷

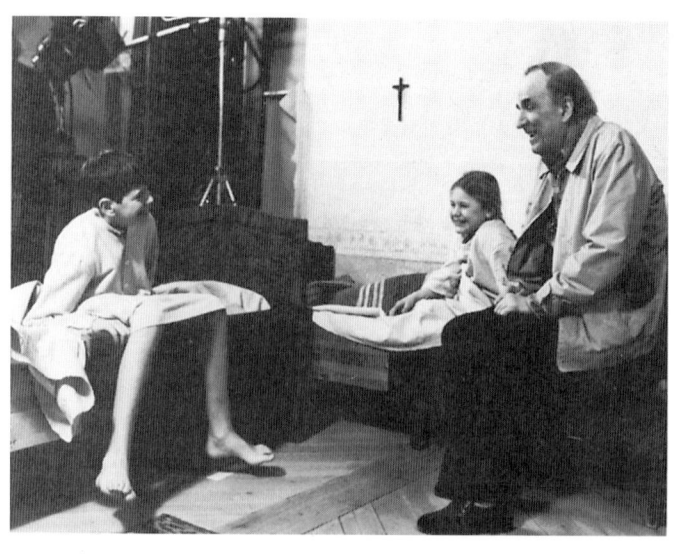

April 18 I wrote: "I don't know much about this film. Yet it tempts me more than any other. It is enigmatic and demands reflection, but the most important thing of course is that the desire is there."

On April 23 I note: "Today I wrote the first six pages of *Fanny and Alexander*. I actually enjoyed doing it. Now I am going to write about the theater, the apartment, and the grandmother."

Wednesday, May 2:

> I must get away from rushing and straining. I have the entire summer in front of me to do this, more than four months. On the other hand, I should not stay away from my desk too long. But no, it's all right to walk around a bit! Let the scenes settle themselves down as they please. Let them become what they will. Then they will be on their best behavior!

Tuesday, June 5:

> It is dangerous to invoke the infernal powers. In Isak's house lives an idiot with the face of an angel, a thin, fragile body, and colorless eyes that see all. He is able to do evil. He is like a membrane for wishes that quivers with the slightest touch.
>
> It is Alexander's experience of the Secret that makes him what he is. The conversation with his dead father. God showing himself to him. His meeting with the dangerous Ismael, who sends the burning woman to annihilate the bishop.

The manuscript was finished on July 8, not quite three months after I began it. There followed a year of preparation for filming, a long and surprisingly pleasant time.

◁ *Being serious and having fun with the children.*

Then, I suddenly stood there and had to materialize my film.

On September 9, 1980, before going out, I wrote: "Not an especially good night. At least my worry and tension have left me. And that feels good. Hot and hazy weather. Everyone is bursting with a pulsating eagerness."

This is how it always is when you are making films. All it takes is a couple of days for me to get the feeling that I am in the midst of something that has always existed. It becomes like a way of breathing. I described it this way when I summed up the first week: "The first week of filming went better in every way than anyone had expected. Besides, it was much more fun to work than I had remembered. I think it also has to do with working in my own language. It's been a long time since I have done so. The children are also very good, at ease and funny. Of course, adversity lurks around every corner. Sometimes, a terrible anxiety cuts right through me."

Nobody can say that the adversity was content with just lurking. Sven Nykvist and I were nearly crushed one day when we were pacing back and forth in the Film Institute's large studio. A crossbeam weighing about a ton thundered down to the floor so close to us that we felt the wind whistle past our ears. Our chief electrician fell down into the orchestra pit at the South Theater, and he broke both his legs. Cecilia Drott, who was going to take care of the wigs and masks and who, for a long time, was one of my close associates, displaced a vertebra and was forbidden by her physician to work. She was replaced by two people from the Royal Dramatic Theater who, though very skilled, had never worked on a movie. The man who was supposed to head the costume shop, creating all the imposingly detailed period costumes, died just a few weeks before we began filming.

Around Christmas time the whole cast and crew came

Mirrored with Jan Malmsjö and Sven Nykvist. In rehearsal with Hamlet and the ghost (Per Mattsson, Allan Edwall). ▷

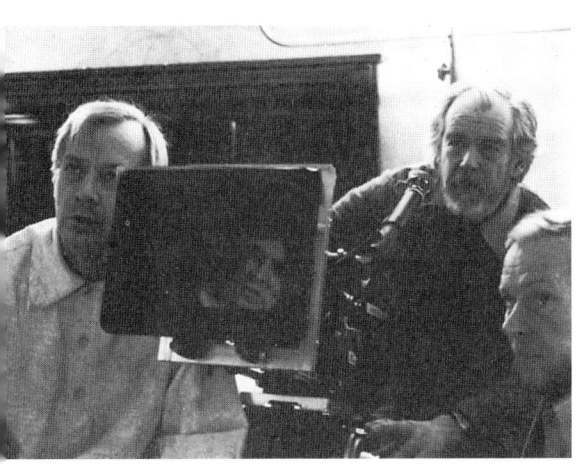

down with a terrible flu. We had to stop working for three weeks. I was bedridden, my teeth chattering. Sven Nykvist was replaced for a few weeks by Tony Forsberg, an underrated but first-class photographer. Young Bertil Guve, who played Alexander, damaged his knee while playing ice hockey. And so it went.

And yet I don't remember during the actual filming ever feeling hit by any serious dissension.

At the same time I felt that my strength was waning. Every day was a great strain to get through, in spite of my circumstances being inordinately agreeable: I had returned to my own language. I was working with hand-picked actors and a good crew in complete harmony, a perfect organization. And yet, a strong fear haunted me daily: Would I manage to get through another day? Would I find the strength? For two hundred and fifty days of filming?

Then I began to catch a glimpse of what I needed to do.

A few weeks after we finished shooting the film, the time came to sift through the enormous amount of footage, more than twenty-five hours of film.

I wrote down my first reaction to this on Wednesday, March 31: "At last I am reviewing the rushes. The first day we sat through four hours of material. The result was indeed a mixed bag. At times I was rather shocked by what I saw. What I had thought worked well, turned out to be bad, uneven, deplorable. Other things, I suppose, were passable. But nothing, except Gunn Wållgren, was really good."

The next day: "Hardly any sleep, worrying over what I saw yesterday. We continued today starting with the rushes of the early morning Christmas mass up to the porch scene with Gunn and Pernilla. It was considerably more fun today. But I still see the curious mistakes. I am worried about the size and shape of the film."

When we had gone through all the rushes once, we began again from the beginning: "Having had enough time to calm down, I can now view the images as a future continuum. My impression is therefore more positive."

After a week, the mood was better, but I was beginning to worry about the extent of the material. "Am watching the rushes. All is going rather smoothly, actually. The weaknesses are obvious, but nothing is irreparable." The next day: "We watched new material, the last hours. I'm worried about the length. The whole ending is clearly problematic. Must be resolved."

In looking over my diary, I sense that people must have become tired of me! I rushed ahead furiously, like a savage beast, nagging everyone over the littlest detail and demanding to know why something turned out *that* way, and what is *this*, and what is *that*. But the trouble that was now beginning to develop had to do with creating two versions. *Fanny and Alexander* was to be produced two ways: one version intended for television, to be shown in five episodes (not necessarily of equal length); the other for theatrical release, to be of "normal length" — which was vague — and to run for more than two and a half hours.

The long version was more important. That is the film I stand totally behind today. Theatrical distribution was necessary, but it was not a priority. For practical and technical reasons, we finished the five-act television production first. Once edited, we had a film that ran more than five hours.

In August 1981 my editor, Sylvia Ingemarsson, came to Fårö. The idea was that we would quickly, in a few days, design the theater version that I already had planned out in my head. I knew rather clearly what I wanted to cut, and my goal was to end up with a two-and-a-half-hour film.

We worked at a rapid pace. When we had finished, I

The grand finale. ▷

discovered to my horror that I had a film almost four hours long. What a shock! I had always given myself credit for having an excellent sense of time and timing.

There was nothing to do but start over from the beginning. It was extraordinarily troublesome, since I now had to cut into the vital parts of the film.

I knew that with each cut I reduced the quality of my work. We finally ended up in a compromise: the film was three hours and eight minutes long.

Watching it today, I see that the long version could have been trimmed down half an hour to forty minutes without anyone noticing it. As it was, the work was heavily edited down to the five different episodes for television. But from that point down to the reduced theatrical version was a long step.

The basic chords in *Fanny and Alexander* are summed up exhaustively in *The Magic Lantern:*

> To be honest, it is with delight and curiosity that I think back on my childhood. My imagination and senses gained nourishment, and I cannot remember ever being bored. Rather the days and hours exploded with these strange wonders, unexpected sights, and magical moments. I can still roam through the landscape of my childhood and re-create the lighting, smells, people, places, moments, gestures, intonations, and objects. Seldom do these memories have any particular meaning; they are like bits of film, short or long, with no point, shot at random.
>
> This is the prerogative of childhood: to move in complete freedom between magic and oatmeal porridge, between boundless terror and a joy that threatens to burst within you. There were no limits except

forbidden things and rules, which were like shadows, mostly unfathomable. I know, for instance, that I could not grasp the concept of time: You must learn to be punctual; you have been given a watch, you must learn how to tell time. Yet time did not exist. I was late for school; I was late for meals. Unconcerned, I roamed around in the park by the hospital, looking around and dreaming; time ceased to exist; then something reminded me that I was hungry, and the trouble began.

It was difficult for me to differentiate between what existed in my imagination and what was real. If I made the effort, perhaps I could make the reality remain real, but then, for instance, there were always the ghosts and the visions. What was I supposed to do with them? And the fairy tales, were they real or not?

Filmography

Two film titles are given when different titles were used for the American and British releases. The American title appears first, followed by a slash. In a few instances, when the film was never formally released in the United States, the first title is apparently more common in both territories and the second (preceded by an "or") is an American alternative.

1944
TORMENT/FRENZY (Hets)

Production/distribution: Svensk Filmindustri. Director: Alf Sjöberg. Producers: Harald Molander, Victor Sjöström (artistic consultant). Screenplay: Ingmar Bergman and Alf Sjöberg. Assistant to the director: Ingmar Bergman. Cinematography: Martin Bodin. Music: Hilding Rosenberg. Art direction: Arne Åkermark. Editing: Oscar Rosander. Premiere: October 2, 1944, at Röda Kvarn. Length: 101 minutes. With Stig Järrel (Caligula), Alf Kjellin (Jan-Erik Widgren), Mai Zetterling (Bertha Olsson), Olof Winnerstrand (headmaster), Gösta Cederlund ("Pippi"), Stig Olin (Sandman), Jan Molander (Pettersson), Olav Riégo (Widgren, an executive), Märta Arbin (Mrs. Widgren), Hugo Björne (physician), Anders Nyström (Bror Widgren), Nils Dahlgren (commissioner), Gunnar Björnstrand (young teacher), Carl-Olof Alm, Curt Edgård, Sten Gester, Palle Granditsky, Birger Malmsten, and Arne Ragneborn (students).

1945
CRISIS (Kris)

Production/distribution: Svensk Filmindustri. Director: Ingmar Bergman. Screenplay: Ingmar Bergman, adapted from the play *Moderdyret* (*A Mother's Heart*) by Leck Fischer. Producer: Harald Molander, Victor Sjöström (artistic consultant). Cinematography: Gösta Roosling. Music: Erland von Koch. Art direction: Arne

Åkermark. Editor: Oscar Rosander. Premiere: February 25, 1946, at Spegeln. Length: 93 minutes. With Dagny Lind (Ingeborg), Marianne Löfgren (Jenny), Inga Landgré (Nelly), Stig Olin (Jack), Allan Bohlin (Ulf), Ernst Eklund (Uncle Edvard), Signe Wirff (Aunt Jessie), Svea Holst (Malin), Arne Lindblad (mayor), Julia Caesar (mayor's wife), Dagmar Olsson (singer at the ball), Anna-Lisa Baude (customer in the millinery), Karl Erik Flens (Nelly's escort to the ball), Wiktor Andersson, Gus Dahlström, John Melin, Holger Höglund, Sture Ericson, and Ulf Johanson (musicians).

1946
IT RAINS ON OUR LOVE or MAN WITH AN UMBRELLA (Det regnar på vår kärlek)

Production: Sveriges Folkbiografer. Distribution: Nordisk Tonefilm. Director: Ingmar Bergman. Producer: Lorens Marmstedt. Screenplay: Ingmar Bergman and Herbert Grevenius, adapted from the play Bra mennesker (Good People) by Oscar Braathen. Cinematography: Hilding Bladh, Göran Strindberg. Music: Erland von Koch. Art direction: P. A. Lundgren. Editing: Tage Holmberg. Premiere: November 9, 1946, at Astoria. Length: 95 minutes. With Barbro Kollberg (Maggi), Birger Malmsten (David), Gösta Cederlund (man with umbrella), Ludde Gentzel (Håkansson), Douglas Håge (Andersson), Hjördis Petterson (Mrs. Andersson), Julia Caesar (Hanna Ledin), Gunnar Björnstrand (Mr. Purman), Magnus Kesster (Folke Törnberg), Sif Ruud (Gerti Törnberg), Åke Fridell (pastor), Benkt-Åke Benktsson (prosecuting attorney), Erik Rosén (judge), Sture Ericson ("Boot Strap"), Ulf Johanson ("Steel Whisk"), Torsten Hillberg (vicar), Erland Josephson (public servant).

1947
WOMAN WITHOUT A FACE (Kvinna utan ansikte)

Production/distribution: Svensk Filmindustri. Director: Gustaf Molander. Producers: Harald Molander, Victor Sjöström (artistic consultant). Screenplay: Ingmar Bergman and Gustaf Molander, based on an idea by Bergman. Cinematography: Åke Dahlqvist. Music: Erik Nordgren and Julius Jacobsen. Art direction: Arne Åkermark and Nils Svenwall. Editing: Oscar Rosander. Premiere: September 16, 1947, at Röda Kvarn. Length: 102 minutes. With Alf Kjellin (Martin Grandé), Gunn Wållgren (Rut Kohler), Anita Björk (Frida Grandé), Stig Olin (Ragnar Ekberg), Olof Winnerstrand (executive Grandé), Marianne Löfgren (Charlotte), Georg Funkquist (Victor), Åke Grönberg (Sam Svensson), Linnéa Hillberg (Mrs. Grandé), Calle Reinholdz and Karl Erik Flens (chimney sweeps), Sif Ruud (Magda Svensson), Ella Lindblom (Marie), Artur Rolén ("Flotten"), Wiktor Andersson (night guard), Björn Montin (Pil), Carl-Axel Elfving (mailman), Carin Swensson (Magda's girlfriend), Arne Lindblad (hotel manager), Lasse Sarri (bellboy), David Eriksson (porter), Torsten Hillberg (police detective), Ernst Brunman (cabdriver).

1947
A SHIP BOUND FOR INDIA or THE LAND OF DESIRE (Skepp till Indialand)

Production: Sveriges Folkbiografer. Distribution: Nordisk Tonefilm. Director: Ingmar Bergman. Screenplay: Ingmar Bergman, based on the play by Martin Söderhjelm. Producer: Lorens Marmstedt. Cinematography: Göran Strindberg. Music: Erland von Koch. Art direction: P. A. Lundgren. Editing: Tage Holmberg. Premiere: September 22, 1947 at Royal. Length: 98 minutes. With Holger Löwenadler (Captain Alexander Blom), Birger Malmsten (Johannes Blom), Gertrud Fridh (Sally), Anna Lindahl (Alice Blom), Lasse Krantz (Hans), Jan Molander (Bertil), Erik Hell (Pekka), Naemi Briese (Selma), Hjördis Petterson (Sofie), Åke Fridell (cabaret manager), Peter Lindgren (foreign crew member), Gustaf Hiort af Ornäs and Torsten Bergström (Blom's friends), Ingrid Borthen (girl on the street), Gunnar Nielsen (young man), Amy Aaröe (young girl).

1947
NIGHT IS MY FUTURE/MUSIC IN DARKNESS
(Musik i mörker)

Production/distribution: Terrafilm. Director: Ingmar Bergman. Producer: Lorens Marmstedt. Screenplay: Dagmar Edqvist, based on her novel. Cinematography: Göran Strindberg. Music: Erland von Koch. Art direction: P. A. Lundgren. Editing: Lennart Wallén. Premiere: January 17, 1948, at Royal. Length: 87 minutes. With Mai Zetterling (Ingrid), Birger Malmsten (Bengt Vyldeke), Bengt Eklund (Ebbe), Olof Winnerstrand (vicar), Naima Wifstrand (Mrs. Schröder), Åke Claesson (Mr. Schröder), Bibi Skoglund (Agneta), Hilda Borgström (Lovisa), Douglas Håge (Kruge), Gunnar Björnstrand (Klasson), Segol Mann (Anton Nord), Bengt Logardt (Einar Born), Marianne Gyllenhammar (Blanche), John Elfström (Otto Klemens), Rune Andreasson (Evert), Barbro Flodquist (Hjördis), Ulla Andreasson (Sylvia), Sven Lindberg (Hedström), Svea Holst (postal worker), Georg Skarstedt (Jönsson), Reinhold Svensson (intoxicated man in pub), Mona Geijer-Falkner (woman by trash can), Arne Lindblad (restaurant chef).

1948
PORT OF CALL (Hamnstad)

Production/distribution: Svensk Filmindustri. Director: Ingmar Bergman. Producer: Harald Molander. Screenplay: Ingmar Bergman and Olle Länsberg, based on Länsberg's story *The Gold and the Walls*. Cinematography: Gunnar Fischer. Music: Erland von Koch. Art direction: Nils Svenwall. Editing: Oscar Rosander. Premiere: October 18, 1948, at Skandia. Length: 100 minutes. With Nine-Christine Jönsson (Berit), Bengt Eklund (Gösta), Berta Hall (Berit's mother), Erik Hell (Berit's father), Mimi Nelson (Gertrud), Birgitta Valberg (social worker Vilander), Hans Stråat (engineer Vilander), Nils Dahlgren (Gertrud's father), Harry Ahlin ("Skåningen"), Nils Hallberg (Gustav), Sven-Eric Gamble ("Eken"), Sif Ruud (Mrs. Krona), Kolbjörn Knudsen (sailor), Yngve Nordwall

With Göran Strindberg, cinematographer for the first films. ▷

(supervisor), Bengt Blomgren (Gunnar), Hanny Schedin (Gunnar's mother), Helge Karlsson (Gunnar's father), Stig Olin (Thomas), Else-Merete Heiberg (reform school girl), Britta Billsten (prostitute), Sture Ericson (police commissioner).

1948
EVA

Production/distribution: Svensk Filmindustri. Director: Gustaf Molander. Producer: Harald Molander. Screenplay: Ingmar Bergman and Gustaf Molander, based on Bergman's short film *The Trumpet Player and Our Lord*. Cinematography: Åke Dahlqvist. Music: Erik Nordgren. Art direction: Nils Svenwall. Editing: Oscar Rosander. Premiere: December 12, 1948, at Röda Kvarn. Length: 98 minutes. With Birger Malmsten (Bo), Eva Stiberg (Eva), Eva Dahlbeck (Susanne), Stig Olin (Göran), Åke Claesson (Fredriksson), Wanda Rothgardt (Mrs. Fredriksson), Inga Landgré (Frida), Hilda Borgström (Maria), Lasse Sarri (Bo at age 12), Olof Sandborg (Berglund), Carl Ström (Johansson), Sture Ericson (Josef), Erland Josephson (Karl), Hans Dahlin (Olle), Hanny Schedin (midwife), Yvonne Eriksson (Lena), Monica Wienzierl (Frida at age 7), Anne Karlsson (Marthe).

1948/49
THE DEVIL'S WANTON/PRISON (Fängelse)

Production/distribution: Terrafilm. Director, screenplay: Ingmar Bergman. Producer: Lorens Marmstedt. Cinematography: Göran Strindberg. Music: Erland von Koch. Art direction: P. A. Lundgren. Editing: Lennart Wallén. Premiere: March 19, 1949, at Astoria. Length: 79 minutes. With Doris Svedlund (Birgitta Carolina), Birger Malmsten (Thomas), Eva Henning (Sofi), Hasse Ekman (Martin Grandé), Stig Olin (Peter), Irma Christenson (Linnéa), Anders Henrikson (Paul), Marianne Löfgren (Mrs. Bohlin), Kenne Fant (Arne), Inger Juel (Greta), Curt Masreliez (Alf), Torsten Lilliecrona (cinematographer), Segol Mann (main electrician), Börje Mellvig (police commissioner), Åke Engfeldt (policeman), Bibi Lindqvist (Anna), Arne Ragneborn (Anna's fiancé).

Martin Grandé, a film director, is visited on the set by an old teacher, Paul, who presents him with an idea for a film about hell on earth. Martin relates this idea to the writer Thomas and his wife, Sofi. Thomas says that he has already found the female lead: he has just auditioned Birgitta Carolina, a prostitute.

After this prologue, six months pass. Birgitta Carolina gives birth to a child and is persuaded by her protector, Peter, and her sister, Linnéa, to get rid of it. Thomas and Sofi drink and argue. Sofi hits him on the head with a bottle. The police look for Birgitta Carolina and bring her in. At the police station she meets Thomas, who believes that he has killed his wife. Birgitta Carolina is let go after Peter intervenes on her behalf. Thomas discovers that Sofi is not dead but that she has left him.

Later Thomas encounters Birgitta Carolina again. They take a room at a pension where Thomas stayed as a child. Using an old-fashioned movie projector, he shows a silent film farce on the wall of their attic room. Birgitta Carolina dreams. Thomas makes her tell him about the child she gave away. Peter reads in the newspaper that a dead infant has been found. He locates Sofi and tells her where Thomas is. Thomas tells Sofi that he loves Birgitta Carolina and wants to help her. Birgitta Carolina goes back to live with Peter and Linnéa. She turns Thomas away. A customer rapes her. Peter finds her lying in the cellar with a knife in her hand. Birgitta Carolina dies.

Thomas returns to Sofi. Martin (the director) again meets with his old teacher. The film idea does not really hold water. It would end with a question, and there is nobody to whom one might ask this question.

1949
THREE STRANGE LOVES/THIRST (Törst)

Production/distribution: Svensk Filmindustri. Director: Ingmar Bergman. Producer: Helge Hagerman. Screenplay: Herbert Grevenius, based on a collection of short stories by Birgit Tengroth. Cinematography: Gunnar Fischer. Music: Erik Nordgren. Art

direction: Nils Svenwall. Editing: Oscar Rosander. Premiere: October 17, 1949, at Spegeln. Length: 83 minutes. With Eva Henning (Rut), Birger Malmsten (Bertil), Birgit Tengroth (Viola), Mimi Nelson (Valborg), Hasse Ekman (Dr. Rosengren), Bengt Eklund (Raoul), Gaby Stenberg (Astrid), Naima Wifstrand (Miss Henriksson), Sven-Eric Gamble (glass worker), Gunnar Nielsen (physician's assistant), Estrid Hesse (patient), Helge Hagerman and Calle Flygare (clergymen), Monica Wienzierl (little girl on train), Verner Arpe (German conductor), Else-Merete Heiberg (Norwegian woman on train), Sif Ruud (talkative widow in graveyard).

1949
TO JOY (Till glädje)

Production/distribution: Svensk Filmindustri. Director, screenplay: Ingmar Bergman. Producer: Allan Ekelund. Cinematography: Gunnar Fischer. Art direction: Nils Svenwall. Editing: Oscar Rosander. Premiere: February 20, 1950, at Spegeln. Length: 98 minutes. With Stig Olin (Stig), Maj-Britt Nilsson (Marta), Victor Sjöström (Sönderby), Birger Malmsten (Marcel), John Ekman (Mikael Bro), Margit Carlqvist (Nelly Bro), Sif Ruud (Stina), Rune Stylander (Persson), Erland Josephson (Bertil), Georg Skarstedt (Anker), Berit Holmström (young Lisa), Björn Montin (Lasse), Svea Holst (nurse), Ernst Brunman (caretaker of Concert House), Maud Hyttenberg (saleswoman in toy store).

1950
WHILE THE CITY SLEEPS (Medan staden sover)

Production/distribution: Svensk Filmindustri. Director: Lars-Eric Kjellgren. Producer: Helge Hagerman. Screenplay: Lars-Eric Kjellgren and Per Anders Fogelström, after an idea by Ingmar Bergman based on Fogelstrom's *Ligister* (*Gang Members*). Cinematography: Martin Bodin. Music: Stig Rybrant. Art direction: Nils Svenwall. Editing: Oscar Rosander. Premiere: September 8, 1950, at Skandia. Length: 102 minutes. With Sven-Eric Gamble (Jompa), Inga Landgré (Iris), Adolf Jahr (Iris's father), John Elfström

◁ *With Hasse Ekman during the filming of* Three Strange Loves.

(Jompa's father), Märta Dorff (Iris's mother), Elof Ahrle (the boss), Ulf Palme (Kalle Lund), Hilding Gavle (fence), Barbro Hiort af Ornäs (Rut), Rolf Bergström (Gunnar), Ilse-Nore Tromm (Jompa's mother), Ulla Smidje (Asta), Ebba Flygare (wife of fence), Carl Ström (concierge), Mona Geijer-Falkner (manager), Alf Östlund (Andersson), Hans Sundberg (Knatten), Lennart Lundh (Slampen), Arne Ragneborn (Sune), Hans Dahlberg (Lång-Sam), Åke Hylén (Pekå), Börje Mellvig (prosecuting attorney), Olav Riégo (judge), Arthur Fischer (policeman), Harriet Andersson (Lucia), Henrik Schildt (party guest), Julius Jacobsen (piano player at restaurant), Gunnar Hellström (young man at restaurant).

1950
ILLICIT INTERLUDE/SUMMER INTERLUDE
(Sommarlek)

Production/distribution: Svensk Filmindustri. Director: Ingmar Bergman. Producer: Allan Ekelund. Screenplay: Ingmar Bergman and Herbert Grevenius, based on *Mari*, a story by Bergman. Cinematography: Gunnar Fischer. Music: Erik Nordgren, Bengt Wallerström, and Eskil Eckert-Lundin. Art direction: Nils Svenwall. Editing: Oscar Rosander. Premiere: October 1, 1951, at Röda Kvarn. Length: 96 minutes. With Maj-Britt Nilsson (Marie), Birger Malmsten (Henrik), Alf Kjellin (David), Annalisa Ericson (Kaj), Georg Funkquist (Uncle Erland), Stig Olin (ballet master), Renée Björling (Aunt Elisabeth), Mimi Pollak (petite woman), John Botvid (Karl), Gunnar Olsson (pastor), Douglas Håge (Nisse with the nose), Julia Caesar (Maja), Carl Ström (Sandell), Torsten Lilliecrona (Light-Pelle), Olav Riégo (physician), Ernst Brunman (skipper), Fylgia Zadig (nurse), Sten Mattsson (deckhand), Carl-Axel Elfving (flower deliveryman).

1950
THIS CAN'T HAPPEN HERE or HIGH TENSION
(Sånt händer inte här)

Production/distribution: Svensk Filmindustri. Director: Ingmar Bergman. Producer: Helge Hagerman. Screenplay: Herbert Grevenius, based on the novel *During Twelve Hours* by Peter Valentin (Waldemar Brøgger). Cinematography: Gunnar Fischer. Music: Erik Nordgren. Art direction: Nils Svenwall. Editing: Lennart Wallén. Premiere: October 23, 1950, at Röda Kvarn. Length: 84 minutes. With Signe Hasso (Vera), Alf Kjellin (Almkvist), Ulf Palme (Atkä Natas), Gösta Cederlund (physician), Yngve Nordwall (Lindell), Stig Olin (young man), Ragnar Klange (Filip Rundblom), Hannu Kompus (pastor), Sylvia Tael (Vanja), Els Vaarman (refugee woman), Edmar Kuus (Leino), Rudolf Lipp ("The Shadow"), Lillie Wästfeldt (Mrs. Rundblom), Segol Mann, Willy Koblanck, Gregor Dahlmann, Gösta Holmström, and Ivan Bousé (agents), Hugo Bolander (hotel manager), Helena Kuus (woman at wedding), Alexander von Baumgarten (sea captain), Eddy Andersson (ship's engineer), Fritjof Hellberg (first mate), Mona Åstrand (young girl), Mona Geijer-Falkner (woman in apartment building), Erik Forslund (concierge), Georg Skarstedt (worker with hangover), Tor Borong (caretaker), Magnus Kesster (neighbor in Ålsten), Maud Hyttenberg (graduate), Helga Brofeldt (shocked old woman), Sven Axel Carlsson (youngster).

1950
DIVORCED (Frånskild)

Production/distribution: Svensk Filmindustri. Director: Gustaf Molander. Producer: Allan Ekelund. Screenplay: Ingmar Bergman and Herbert Grevenius. Cinematography: Åke Dahlqvist. Music: Erik Nordgren and Bengt Wallerström. Art direction: Nils Svenwall. Editing: Oscar Rosander. Premiere: December 26, 1951, at Röda Kvarn. Length: 103 minutes. With Inga Tidblad (Gertrud Holmgren), Alf Kjellin (Dr. Bertil Nordelius), Doris Svedlund

(Marianne Berg), Hjördis Petterson (Mrs. Nordelius), Håkan Westergren (P. A. Beckman, manager), Irma Christenson (Dr. Cecilia Lindeman), Holger Löwenadler (Tore Holmgren, engineer), Marianne Löfgren ("The Boss, Mrs. Ingeborg") Stig Olin (Hans), Elsa Prawitz (Elsie), Birgitta Valberg (Eva Möller, attorney), Sif Ruud (Rut Boman), Carl Ström (Öhman), Ragnar Arvedson (department head), Ingrid Borthen (his wife), Yvonne Lombard (beautiful young wife), Einar Axelsson (businessman), Rune Halvarson (advertising executive), Rudolf Wendbladh (banker), Guje Lagerwall, Nils Ohlin, and Nils Jacobsson (dinner guests), Hanny Schedin (Mrs. Nilsson), Harriet Andersson (prospective employee), Christian Bratt (tennis player).

1952
SECRETS OF WOMEN/WAITING WOMEN
(Kvinnors väntan)

Production/distribution: Svensk Filmindustri. Director, screenplay: Ingmar Bergman. Producer: Allan Ekelund. Cinematographer: Gunnar Fischer. Music: Erik Nordgren. Art direction: Nils Svenwall. Editing: Oscar Rosander. Premiere: November 3, 1952, at Röda Kvarn. Length: 107 minutes. With Anita Björk (Rakel), Maj-Britt Nilsson (Marta), Eva Dahlbeck (Karin), Gunnar Björnstrand (Fredrik Lobelius), Birger Malmsten (Martin Lobelius), Jarl Kulle (Kaj), Karl-Arne Holmsten (Eugen Lobelius), Gerd Andersson (Maj), Björn Bjelfvenstam (Henrik Lobelius), Aino Taube (Annette), Håkan Westergren (Paul Lobelius), Kjell Nordenskiöld (Bob), Carl Ström (anesthesiologist), Märta Arbin (nurse Rut), Torsten Lilliecrona (maitre d' at nightclub), Victor Violacci (patron), Naima Wifstrand (old Mrs. Lobelius), Wiktor Andersson (trash collector), Douglas Håge (concierge), Lil Yunkers (emcee), Lena Brogren (practical nurse).

With Maj-Britt Nilsson in Waiting Women. *Behind the camera: Gunnar Fischer.* ▷

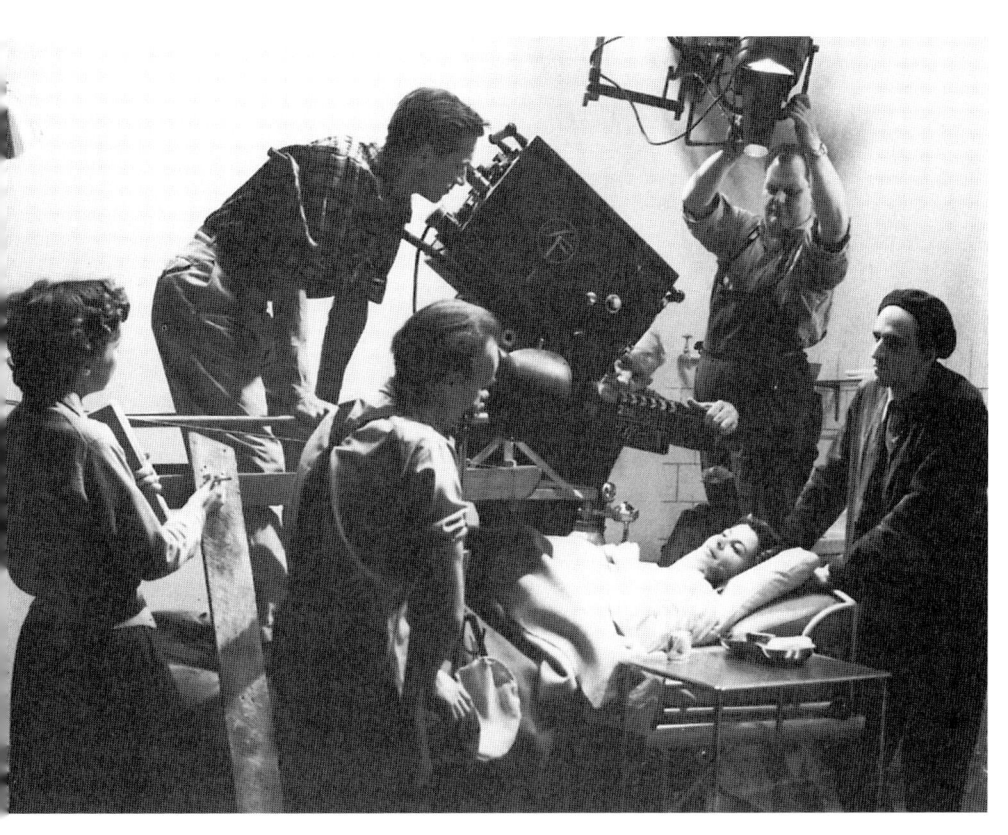

1952
MONIKA/SUMMER WITH MONIKA (Sommaren
med Monika)

Production/distribution: Svensk Filmindustri. Director: Ingmar Bergman. Producer: Allan Ekelund. Screenplay: Ingmar Bergman and Per Anders Fogelström, based on Fogelström's novel. Cinematography: Gunnar Fischer. Music: Erik Nordgren, Eskil Eckert-Lundin and Walle Söderlund. Art direction: P. A. Lundgren. Editing: Tage Holmberg, Gösta Lewin. Premiere: February 9, 1953, at Spegeln. Length: 96 minutes. With Harriet Andersson (Monika), Lars Ekborg (Harry), John Harryson (Lelle), Georg Skarstedt (Harry's father), Dagmar Ebbesen (Harry's aunt), Åke Fridell (Monika's father), Naemi Briese (Monika's mother), Åke Grönberg (foreman), Gösta Eriksson (Forsberg, an executive), Gösta Gustafsson (Forsberg's accountant), Sigge Fürst (foreman at porcelain warehouse), Gösta Prüzelius (salesman at Forsberg's), Arthur Fischer (head of vegetable warehouse), Torsten Lilliecrona (driver at vegetable warehouse), Bengt Eklund (foreman at vegetable warehouse), Gustaf Färingborg (assistant at vegetable warehouse), Ivar Wahlgren (homeowner), Renée Björling (his wife), Catrin Westerlund (their daughter), Wiktor Andersson and Birger Sahlberg (beer drinkers), Hanny Schedin (Mrs. Boman in Apartment 12), Anders Andelius and Gordon Löwenadler (Monika's suitors), Nils Hultgren (vicar), Nils Whitén, Tor Borong, and Einar Söderbäck (ragmen), Bengt Brunskog (Sicke), Magnus Kesster and Carl-Axel Elfving (workers), Astrid Bodin & Mona Geijer-Falkner (wives in windows), Ernst Brunman (tobacco store owner).

1953
THE NAKED NIGHT/SAWDUST AND TINSEL
(Gycklarnas afton)

Production: Sandrewproduktion. Distribution: Sandrew-Bauman. Director, screenplay: Ingmar Bergman. Producer: Rune Waldekranz. Cinematography: Hilding Bladh, Sven Nykvist. Music: Karl-

Birger Blomdahl. Art direction: Bibi Lindström. Editing: Carl-Olov Skeppstedt. Premiere: September 14, 1953, at Grand. Length: 93 minutes. With Harriet Andersson (Anne), Åke Grönberg (Albert Johansson), Hasse Ekman (Frans), Anders Ek (Frost), Gudrun Brost (Alma), Annika Tretow (Agda), Gunnar Björnstrand (Sjuberg, theater manager), Erik Strandmark (Jens), Kiki (dwarf), Åke Fridell (officer), Majken Torkeli (Mrs. Ekberg), Vanje Hedberg (her son), Curt Löwgren (Blom), Conrad Gyllenhammar (Fager), Mona Sylwan (Mrs. Fager), Hanny Schedin (Aunt Asta), Michael Fant (pretty Anton), Naemi Briese (Mrs. Meijer), Lissi Alandh, Karl-Axel Forssberg, Olav Riégo, John Starck, Erna Groth, and Agda Helin (actors), Julie Bernby (tightrope walker), Göran Lundquist and Mats Hådell (Agda's boys).

The threadbare Circus Alberti is on its way to yet another small town. It is dawn. The owner of the circus, Albert Johansson, sits next to the coachman, together with Jens, one of the clowns. The latter tells the story of how Alma, the wife of the white circus clown Frost, went swimming in the nude one summer day in front of several artillery men.

Albert wants to arrange a parade to draw people to the circus. He and Anne, his circus rider and mistress, go to visit Sjuberg, manager of the city theater, in order to beg him to lend them costumes.

Sjuberg is patronizing but finally agrees to let them borrow the clothes if they will invite the theater's ensemble to the gala performance at the circus. Anne meets Frans, the leading actor at the theater. The parade through town is stopped by city officials. Albert looks up his wife and family, whom he had deserted. He finds that his wife, Agda, has settled down into a financially secure, idyllic situation and suggests they become a family again. But Agda has had enough of circus life and humiliation.

Anne, wildly jealous, goes back to the theater, where Frans takes advantage of her situation. When Albert realizes that he has been betrayed, he gets drunk with the clown Frost. The evening's gala performance ends up with Albert and Frans fighting. After losing the fight, Albert, bruised and bloody, locks himself in his trailer with a revolver. He attempts suicide but fails. Instead the old, sick circus bear absorbs the brunt of his wrath. The circus hits the road again. Anne meets Albert, and the two walk behind the circus trailers, heading for the next stop. The circus rolls onward. On and on forever.

1953
A LESSON IN LOVE (En lektion i kärlek)

Production/distribution: Svensk Filmindustri. Director, screenplay: Ingmar Bergman. Producer: Allan Ekelund. Cinematography: Martin Bodin. Music: Dag Wirén. Art direction: P. A. Lundgren. Editing: Oscar Rosander. Premiere: October 4, 1954, at Röda Kvarn. Length: 96 minutes. With Eva Dahlbeck (Marianne Erneman), Gunnar Björnstrand (Dr. David Erneman), Yvonne Lombard (Suzanne), Harriet Andersson (Nix), Åke Grönberg (Carl-Adam), Olof Winnerstrand (Professor Henrik Erneman), Renée Björling (Svea Erneman), Birgitte Reimer (Lise), John Elfström (Sam), Dagmar Ebbesen (nurse), Helge Hagerman (traveling sales-man), Sigge Fürst (pastor), Gösta Prüzelius (train conductor), Carl Ström (Uncle Axel), Torsten Lilliecrona (porter), Arne Lindblad (hotel manager), Yvonne Brosset (dancer).

1954/55
DREAMS/JOURNEY INTO AUTUMN (Kvinnodröm)

Production: Sandrewproduktion. Distribution: Sandrew-Bauman. Director, screenplay: Ingmar Bergman. Producer: Rune Waldekranz. Cinematography: Hilding Bladh. Music: Stuart Görling. Art direction: Gittan Gustafsson. Editing: Carl-Olov Skeppstedt. Premiere: August 22, 1955, at Grand. Length: 87 minutes. With Eva Dahlbeck (Susanne), Harriet Andersson (Doris), Gunnar Björnstrand (consul), Ulf Palme (Lobelius, chief manager), Inga Landgré (Mrs. Lobelius), Sven Lindberg (Palle), Naima Wifstrand (Mrs. Arén), Benkt-Åke Benktsson (Magnus, an executive), Git Gay (lady in women's boutique), Ludde Gentzel (photographer Sundström), Kerstin Hedeby (Marianne), Jessie Flaws (makeup artist), Marianne Nielsen (Fanny), Bengt Schött (fashion designer in photo studio), Axel Düberg (photographer in Stockholm), Gunhild Kjellqvist (dark-haired girl in boutique), Renée Björling (wife of Professor Berger), Tord Stål (Mr. Barse), Richard Mattsson (Månsson), Inga Gill (saleswoman in bakery), Per-Erik Åström (chauffeur), Carl-Gustaf Lindstedt (porter), Asta Beckman (waitress).

1955
SMILES OF A SUMMER NIGHT (Sommarnattens leende)

Production/distribution: Svensk Filmindustri. Director, screenplay: Ingmar Bergman. Producer: Allan Ekelund. Cinematography: Gunnar Fischer. Music: Erik Nordgren. Art direction: P. A. Lundgren. Editing: Oscar Rosander. Premiere: December 26, 1955, at Röda Kvarn. Length: 108 minutes. With Eva Dahlbeck (Desirée Armfeldt), Gunnar Björnstrand (Fredrik Egerman), Ulla Jacobsson (Anne Egerman), Harriet Andersson (Petra), Margit Carlqvist (Charlotte Malcolm), Åke Fridell (coachman Frid), Björn Bjelfvenstam (Henrik Egerman), Naima Wifstrand (old Mrs. Armfeldt), Jullan Kindahl (cook), Gull Natorp (Malla), Birgitta Valberg and Bibi Andersson (actresses), Anders Wulff (Fredrik), Jarl Kulle (Count Carl Magnus Malcolm), Gunnar Nielsen (Niklas), Gösta Prüzelius (valet), Svea Holst (wardrobe manager), Hans Strååt (photographer Almgren), Lisa Lundholm (Mrs. Almgren), Lena Söderblom and Mona Malm (lady's maids), Josef Norman (elderly dinner guest), Arne Lindblad (actor), Börje Mellvig (assessor), Ulf Johanson (assistant at legal firm), Yngve Nordwall (Ferdinand), Sten Gester and Mille Schmidt (valets).

In a small town at the turn of the century, an actress, Desirée Armfeldt, is guest-starring in a play at the local theater. A lawyer, Fredrik Egerman, once Desirée's lover, is taking a nap after dinner with his young wife, Anne. In his sleep, he mumbles Desirée's name.

During the evening's performance Anne begins to cry; Fredrik takes her home. There he surprises his grown son, Henrik, a theology student, with the maid, Petra.

Fredrik and his young wife have a platonic marriage. After saying good night to her, he returns to the theater and goes to Desirée's dressing room. He seeks advice from his former lover and brings her to her lodgings. He finds out that she has a small son, named Fredrik. Dressed in a borrowed dressing gown, he is surprised by a knock on the door. Count Malcolm, the owner of the dressing gown, enters. Fredrik and his clothes are thrown out.

Desirée visits her old mother's castle to tell her that she has ended her relationship with Count Malcolm. She asks her mother to arrange a party with Fredrik Egerman and his wife, the count and his wife, and Henrik (Fredrik's son) as guests.

The guests arrive. Frid, the coachman, shows the maid Petra a secret button in Henrik's bedroom. If the button is pressed, a bed from the adjoining bedroom, occupied by Fredrik and Anne, slides into the room.

Desirée and Countess Charlotte are busy with their intrigues. During dinner Henrik indulges in an angry outburst toward his father (Fredrik). Henrik and Anne leave the table. Henrik tries to hang himself in his room but falls against the button that Frid showed Petra. Into the room pivots the bed with the sleeping Anne. Henrik kisses her awake. Frid tells Petra about the three smiles of the summer night. They help Henrik and Anne flee.

Desirée tells Count Malcolm that she has seen Countess Charlotte and Fredrik in the castle's garden pavilion. Malcolm rushes over there, throws his wife out, and challenges his rival to Russian roulette. The two women wait in the park. A shot is heard. The count appears at the door of the pavilion, laughing. He had loaded his gun with soot. Desirée consoles the blackened Fredrik. Over by the haystack Frid promises to marry Petra. The summer night smiles.

1956

LAST COUPLE OUT (Sista Paret Ut)

Production/distribution: Svensk Filmindustri. Director: Alf Sjöberg. Producer: Allan Ekelund. Screenplay: Ingmar Bergman. Cinematography: Martin Bodin. Music: Erik Nordgren, Charles Redland, Bengt Hallberg, and Julius Jacobsen. Art direction: Harald Garmland. Editing: Oscar Rosander. Premiere: November 12, 1956, at Röda Kvarn and Fontänen. Length: 103 minutes. With Olof Widgren (attorney Hans Dahlin), Eva Dahlbeck (Susanne Dahlin), Björn Bjelfvenstam (Bo Dahlin), Johnny Johansson (Sven Dahlin), Märta Arbin (grandmother), Jullan Kindahl (Alma), Jarl Kulle (Dr. Farell), Nancy Dalunde (Mrs. Farell), Bibi Andersson (Kerstin), Harriet Andersson (Anita), Aino Taube (Kerstin's mother), Jan-Olof Strandberg (Claes Berg), Hugo Björne (lector), Göran Lundquist ("Knatten"), Kerstin Hörnblad, Mona Malm, Olle Davide, Claes-Håkan Westergren, Lena Söderblom, and Kristina Adolphson (students), Svenerik Perzon (newspaper vendor).

1956

THE SEVENTH SEAL (Det sjunde inseglet)

Production/distribution: Svensk Filmindustri. Director, screenplay: Ingmar Bergman, based on his play *Wood Painting*. Producer: Allan Ekelund. Cinematography: Gunnar Fischer. Music: Erik Nordgren. Art Direction: P. A. Lundgren. Editing: Lennart Wallén. Premiere: February 16, 1957, at Röda Kvarn. Length: 96 minutes. With Max von Sydow (Antonius Block), Gunnar Björnstrand (Jöns), Nils Poppe (Jof), Bibi Andersson (Mia), Bengt Ekerot (Death), Åke Fridell (Plog), Inga Gill (Lisa), Erik Strandmark (Skat), Bertil Anderberg (Raval), Gunnel Lindblom (speechless woman), Inga Landgré (Block's wife), Anders Ek (monk), Maud Hansson (witch), Gunnar Olsson (church painter), Lars Lind (young monk), Benkt-Åke Benktsson (innkeeper), Gudrun Brost (woman at the inn), Ulf Johanson (leader of the soldiers).

On a beach, the knight, Antonius, meets Death. They play chess; at stake is the knight's life.

The clown Jof awakens and sees the Holy Virgin in a vision. He arouses his wife, Mia, and tells her. Antonius and his squire, Jöns, arrive at a church. Jöns speaks to a church painter who is painting the Dance of Death and tells him about the plague. In an abandoned house Jöns surprises a grave robber whom he recognizes as Raval, the initiator of the crusade from which Antonius and Jöns have just returned. On stage, in front of an audience, Jof and Mia perform. They are interrupted by a procession of flagellants. The clown Skat courts the blacksmith's wife, Lisa.

Plog, the blacksmith, who is looking for Lisa at the inn, attacks the innocent Jof, who is saved by Jöns. When Jof returns to his wagon, Maria offers the knight and Jöns wild strawberries and milk.

The knight encounters Death again. Their chess game continues. Jof and Mia accompany the knight. In the woods Plog finds his wife, Lisa, who is now repentant. Skat pretends to be dead and climbs a tree, but Death cuts it down. In the woods a young woman is burned as a witch responsible for the plague. Raval dies, the victim of pestilence.

Jof watches as the knight and Death continue their chess game. When the knight returns home, his wife is alone in the fortress. She serves the morning meal, and Death knocks on the portal for the last chess move. Morning dawns over Jof and Mia and their son. Jof has another vision: Death dancing off, followed by the Knight and his retinue.

1957
WILD STRAWBERRIES (Smultronstället)

Production/distribution: Svensk Filmindustri. Director, screenplay: Ingmar Bergman. Producer: Allan Ekelund. Cinematography: Gunnar Fischer. Music: Erik Nordgren and Göte Lovén. Art direction: Gittan Gustafsson. Editing: Oscar Rosander. Premiere: December 26, 1957, at Röda Kvarn and Fontänen. Length: 91 minutes. With Victor Sjöström (Isak Borg), Bibi Andersson (Sara),

◁ *On the set of* Wild Strawberries *with Victor Sjöström and Gösta Ekman, a young assistant director.*

Ingrid Thulin (Marianne), Gunnar Björnstrand (Evald), Folke Sundquist (Anders), Björn Bjelfvenstam (Viktor), Naima Wifstrand (Isak's mother), Jullan Kindahl (Agda), Gunnar Sjöberg (engineer Alman), Gunnel Broström (Mrs. Alman), Gertrud Fridh (Isak's wife), Åke Fridell (her lover), Max von Sydow (Åkerman), Sif Ruud (the aunt), Yngve Nordwall (Uncle Aron), Per Sjöstrand (Sigfrid), Gio Petré (Sigbritt), Gunnel Lindblom (Charlotta), Maud Hansson (Angelica), Lena Bergman (Kristina), Per Skogsberg (Hagbart), Göran Lundquist (Benjamin), Eva Norée (Anna), Monica Ehrling (Birgitta), Ann-Mari Wiman (Eva Åkerman), Vendela Rudbäck (Elisabeth), Helge Wulff (promotor).

Professor Isak Borg is to receive an honorary degree at Lund University on his fiftieth anniversary as a professor. During the night he dreams that he finds himself in an unknown, empty city. A coffin falls off a wagon. A hand reaches out from the coffin and grabs hold of him. He sees himself lying in the coffin.

Instead of flying from Stockholm to Lund, Borg decides to drive there. He is accompanied by his daughter-in-law, Marianne. During the trip Marianne tells him about her marriage with Evald and comments on the icy relationship between her father-in-law and her husband. Isak stops the car by a forest. He tells her that he and his siblings used to stay there every summer, a long, long time ago. Marianne wants to go for a swim and sets out for the lake. Isak gets lost in his memories. He sees his brother Sigfrid kiss Sara, who was Isak's beloved.

He is awakened by a young girl looking for a ride. Her name is also Sara. She and her companions, Anders and Viktor, are given a ride. They come close to colliding with another car, which veers into a ditch. The driver and his wife are given a ride by Borg. Between the new passengers, Mr. and Mrs. Alman, a marital fight breaks out. It reaches such violence that Marianne asks them to get out of the car. After lunch Isak Borg visits his old mother.

Continuing on the drive, he dreams again: he loses Sara to Sigfrid. He is called in for an academic examination by Mr. Alman, who accuses him of emotional frigidity. In a forest he sees his dead wife meet her lover. Marianne tells Isak that she is pregnant and that the reason for her marital crisis is that Evald does not want this new responsibility. Borg is awarded his honorary degree. When he goes to bed, the young people to whom he gave a lift stand outside his window, congratulating him. He speaks with Evald and Marianne. He remembers his childhood again. He and Sara arrive at a place where the wild strawberries grow. On the other side of the bay he sees his father and mother. They wave to him.

1957
BRINK OF LIFE/SO CLOSE TO LIFE (Nära livet)

Production/distribution: Nordisk Tonefilm. Director: Ingmar Bergman. Producer: Gösta Hammarbäck. Screenplay: Ulla Isaksson, based on her short stories *The Friendly and Dignified* and *The Immovable*. Cinematography: Max Wilén. Art direction: Bibi Lindström. Editing: Carl-Olov Skeppstedt. Premiere: March 31, 1958, at Röda Kvarn and Fontänen. Length: 84 minutes. With Ingrid Thulin (Cecilia Ellius), Eva Dahlbeck (Stina Andersson), Bibi Andersson (Hjördis Petterson), Barbro Hiort af Ornäs (nurse Brita), Max von Sydow (Harry Andersson), Erland Josephson (Anders Ellius), Anne-Marie Gyllenspetz (social worker), Gunnar Sjöberg (Dr. Nordlander), Margaretha Krook (Dr. Larsson), Lars Lind (Dr. Thylenius), Sissi Kaiser (nurse Mari), Inga Gill (new mother), Kristina Adolphson (practical nurse), Maud Elfsiö (student nurse), Monica Ekberg (Hjördis's girlfriend), Gun Jönsson (night nurse), Gunnar Nielsen (doctor), Inga Landgré (Greta Ellius).

1958
THE MAGICIAN/THE FACE (Ansiktet)

Production/distribution: Svensk Filmindustri. Director, screenplay: Ingmar Bergman. Producer: Allan Ekelund. Cinematography: Gunnar Fischer. Music: Erik Nordgren. Art direction: P. A. Lundgren. Editing: Oscar Rosander. Premiere: December 26, 1958, at Röda Kvarn and Fontänen. Length: 100 minutes. With Max von

Sydow (Albert Emanuel Vogler), Ingrid Thulin (Manda Vogler/ Aman), Åke Fridell (Tubal), Naima Wifstrand (Vogler's grand- mother), Lars Ekborg (Simson), Gunnar Björnstrand (health offi- cial Vergérus), Erland Josephson (consul Egerman), Gertrud Fridh (Ottilia Egerman), Toivo Pawlo (police chief Starbeck), Ulla Sjöblom (Henrietta Starbeck), Bengt Ekerot (Johan Spegel), Sif Ruud (Sofia Garp), Bibi Andersson (Sara), Birgitta Pettersson (Sanna), Oscar Ljung (Antonsson), Axel Düberg (Rustan), Tor Borong, Arne Mårtensson, Harry Schein, and Frithiof Bjärne (cus- toms officers).

In a covered wagon (Doctor Vogler's Magnetic Health Theater) travel Vogler, a magician specializing in magnetism, his wife, Manda, disguised as young Mr. Aman, his grandmother, and his assistant, Tubal. On the coachman's box sits Simson. They are on their way to Stockholm. The year is 1846. In a dark forest they pick up Johan Spegel, an alcoholic and an obviously faded actor.

The troupe is escorted from one of Stockholm's customs points to consul Egerman's house. The consul and his wife have guests: police chief Starbeck and health official Vergérus. Tubal speaks on behalf of the group. The magician Vogler is speechless; Mr. Aman answers questions for him. Vergérus sees Vogler as a charlatan, who must be unmasked scientifically at the following day's perform- ance. Grandmother, Tubal, and Simson consort with the Egermans' servants in the kitchen. Tubal disappears with the cook Sofia, Simson with the maid Sara. A ghostly apparition is seen by the valet Rustan and the coachman Antonsson; he steals their alcohol. The ghost is Spegel, not yet dead.

While Vogler and Manda/Aman are preparing for their perform- ance, Mrs. Egerman enters the room. She asks Vogler to come to her bedroom. Now Spegel shows himself to Vogler and dies in the magician's coffin. Vergérus discovers that Mr. Aman is Manda. He offers her his protection. Vogler enters and attacks Vergérus. Then he removes his mask. Unmasked, the married couple (Mr. and Mrs.

◁ *With Sif Ruud, Åke Fridell, and Bibi Andersson in* The Magician.

Vogler) lie in bed and speak of the golden times that once were theirs.

It is time for the performance. The police chief's wife is hypnotized by Vogler, and she bursts out with insults toward her husband. The coachman Antonsson is draped in invisible chains. Once liberated, he knocks Vogler to the ground. Vergérus establishes that Vogler is dead. He intends to perform an autopsy on the body in the attic. The grandmother finds the coachman Antonsson. He has hanged himself.

Vergérus performs the autopsy, alone in the attic. In a mirror he sees Vogler without his mask. Terror grips Vergérus. He rushes down the stairs. It turns out that Vergérus has performed the autopsy on the dead actor Spegel. He says that he has experienced a terribly bad performance.

The group is ready to leave. Tubal stays with the cook Sofia. The grandmother declares that her traveling days are over. But the maid Sara follows Simson. Policemen come over. Vogler and Manda are brought back to Egerman's house, where the police chief declares that His Majesty the King wishes to see their performance. In triumph Vogler and Manda, Simson, and Sara set out for the castle.

1959
THE VIRGIN SPRING (Jungfrukällan)

Production/distribution: Svensk Filmindustri. Director: Ingmar Bergman. Screenplay: Ulla Isaksson, based on the ballad *Töre's Daughter in Wänge*. Cinematography: Sven Nykvist. Music: Erik Nordgren. Art direction: P. A. Lundgren. Editing: Oscar Rosander. Premiere: February 8, 1960, at Röda Kvarn. Length: 89 minutes. With Max von Sydow (Töre), Birgitta Valberg (Märeta), Gunnel Lindblom (Ingeri), Birgitta Pettersson (Karin), Axel Düberg (the skinny one), Tor Isedal (the one without a tongue), Allan Edwall (beggar), Ove Porath (boy), Axel Slangus (bridge guard), Gudrun Brost (Frida), Oscar Ljung (Simon), Tor Borong and Leif Forstenberg (farmhands).

1959/60
THE DEVIL'S EYE (Djävulens öga)
Production/distribution: Svensk Filmindustri. Director, screenplay: Ingmar Bergman, based on the radio play *Don Juan Returns* by Oluf Bang. Producer: Allan Ekelund. Cinematography: Gunnar Fischer. Music: Erik Nordgren. Art direction: P. A. Lundgren. Editing: Oscar Rosander. Premiere: October 17, 1960, at Röda Kvarn and Fontänen. Length: 87 minutes. With Jarl Kulle (Don Juan), Bibi Andersson (Britt-Marie), Stig Järrel (Satan), Nils Poppe (vicar), Gertrud Fridh (Mrs. Renata), Sture Lagerwall (Pablo), Gunnar Björnstrand (actor), Georg Funkquist (Count Armand de Rochefoucauld), Gunnar Sjöberg (Marquis Giuseppe Maria de Macopanza), Axel Düberg (Jonas), Torsten Winge (the old one), Kristina Adolphson (veiled woman), Allan Edwall (the demon who whispers in the ear), Ragnar Arvedson (guard demon), Börje Lundh (hairdresser), Lenn Hjortzberg (enema doctor), John Melin (beauty doctor), Sten Torsten Thuul (tailor), Arne Lindblad (his assistant), Svend Bunch (transformation expert), Tom Olsson (masseur), Inga Gill (parlormaid).

1960
THROUGH A GLASS DARKLY (Såsom i en spegel)
Production/distribution: Svensk Filmindustri. Director, screenplay: Ingmar Bergman. Producer: Allan Ekelund. Cinematography: Sven Nykvist. Music: Erik Nordgren. Art direction: P. A. Lundgren. Editing: Ulla Ryghe. Premiere: October 16, 1961, at Röda Kvarn and Fontänen. Length: 89 minutes. With Harriet Andersson (Karin), Max von Sydow (Martin), Gunnar Björnstrand (David), Lars Passgård (Fredrik, called Minus).

Four people come out of the ocean after a swim. David, a widower, is a writer. His daughter, Karin, has been in and out of the hospital for schizophrenia. She is married to Martin, a physician. Minus is Karin's seventeen-year-old brother.

David and Martin cast fishing nets; the sister and brother go to fetch milk. During dinner David says that he will soon be returning to Switzerland, where he has just been. Brother and sister perform a play that Minus has written. It concerns a writer who can experience love only when he is writing about it.

Toward dawn David is sitting in his room, working on his latest novel. Karin is awake. In the attic she has an experience with her split world. Then she falls asleep in her father's room. While David and Minus bring in the nets, Karin awakens and reads in her father's diary that he believes her illness is incurable.

David and Martin leave the island together to run an errand. Karin has told Martin about the diary, and Martin accuses David of emotional coldness. David confesses that he attempted suicide while in Switzerland. Karin tells Minus about her two worlds. Minus finds her later in an old wreck down by the seashore. When David and Martin return, Minus tells them about Karin's confused condition. Martin orders a helicopter. They pack. Karin disappears into the attic again. There she engages in a conversation with the world that exists only behind the wallpaper. She is given a calming injection and says there is a spider who visits her: "I have seen God." Karin is taken away in the helicopter. David and Minus are alone on the island. They speak about God's love. Minus whispers, "Daddy spoke to me."

1961
THE PLEASURE GARDEN (Lustgården)

Production/distribution: Svensk Filmindustri. Director: Alf Kjellin. Producer: Allan Ekelund. Screenplay: "Buntel Eriksson" (Ingmar Bergman and Erland Josephson). Cinematography: Gunnar Fischer (color). Music: Erik Nordgren. Art direction: P. A. Lundgren. Editing: Ulla Ryghe. Premiere: December 26, 1961, at Röda Kvarn and Fanfaren. Length: 93 minutes. With Sickan Carlsson (Fanny), Gunnar Björnstrand (David), Bibi Andersson (Anna), Per Myrberg (Emil), Kristina Adolphson (Astrid), Stig Järrel (Lundberg), Hjördis Petterson (Ellen), Gösta Cederlund (Liljedahl), Torsten Winge (Wibom), Lasse Krantz (restaurant manager), Fillie

Lyckow (Berta), Jan Tiselius (Ossian), Stefan Hübinette (volunteer), Sven Nilsson (bishop), Rolf Nystedt (mayor), Sten Hedlund (principal), Stina Ståhle (his wife), Lars Westlund (postmaster), Ivar Uhlin (Dr. Brusén), Birger Sahlberg (policeman).

1961/62
WINTER LIGHT (Nattvardsgästerna)

Production/distribution: Svensk Filmindustri. Director, screenplay: Ingmar Bergman. Producer: Allan Ekelund. Cinematography: Sven Nykvist. Art direction: P. A. Lundgren. Editing: Ulla Ryghe. Premiere: February 11, 1963, at Röda Kvarn and Fontänen. Length: 81 minutes. With Gunnar Björnstrand (Tomas Ericsson), Ingrid Thulin (Märta Lundberg), Max von Sydow (Jonas Persson), Gunnel Lindblom (Karin Persson), Allan Edwall (Algot Frövik), Olof Thunberg (Fredrik Blom), Elsa Ebbesen (widow), Kolbjörn Knudsen (Aronsson), Tor Borong (Johan Åkerblom), Bertha Sånnell (Hanna Appelblad), Eddie Axberg (Johan Strand), Lars-Owe Carlberg (police superintendent), Johan Olafs (man), Ingmari Hjort (Persson's daughter), Stefan Larsson (Persson's son), Lars-Olof Andersson and Christer Öhman (boys).

Pastor Tomas Ericsson performs morning service in Mitsunda Church. Among the communicants are Märta Lundberg, a teacher at the grammar school; Jonas Persson, a fisherman; and his wife, Karin.

Tomas has a cold. After the service Jonas and Karin visit him in the vestry. Karin tells him about her husband's anxiety. They decide that Tomas should have a private conversation with Jonas later. Märta Lundberg enters and asks Tomas if he has read her letter. She wants to help him, but he rebuffs her. When she has left, he reads the letter. The fisherman Jonas returns. Tomas speaks to him about his own relation to God, trying to console Jonas. A little while later a woman brings word that Jonas has shot himself.

Tomas goes to the site of the suicide with Märta. Then they continue on to the school where she lives and works. Again Tomas

rejects her concern and her love. They go to the fisherman's home. Tomas offers the widow comfort and support but feels that he stands outside the circle of the bereaved family. On the way back Tomas tells Märta that he became a clergyman to please his parents.

They arrive at Frostnäs for the second service of the day. The church caretaker, Algot Frövik, speaks to Tomas about his suffering. The organist, Blom, tells Märta about Tomas's dead wife. When the church bells call the congregation to the church, only four people come. Despite that, Tomas decides to hold the service.

1962
THE SILENCE (Tystnaden)

Production/distribution: Svensk Filmindustri. Director, screenplay: Ingmar Bergman. Producer: Allan Ekelund. Cinematography: Sven Nykvist. Music: Ivan Renliden. Art direction: P. A. Lundgren. Editing: Ulla Ryghe. Premiere: September 23, 1963, at Röda Kvarn and Fontänen. Length: 95 minutes. With Ingrid Thulin (Ester), Gunnel Lindblom (Anna), Jörgen Lindström (Johan), Håkan Jahnberg (room service waiter), Birger Malmsten (bar waiter), "Eduardinis" (performing dwarfs), Eduardo Gutierrez (the dwarfs' impressario), Lissi Alandh (woman in variety theater), Leif Forstenberg (man in variety theater), Nils Waldt (cashier), Birger Lensander (caretaker), Eskil Kalling (bar owner), K. A. Bergman (newspaper vendor), Olof Widgren (the old one).

Traveling home from their vacation, two sisters, Anna and Ester, and Anna's son, Johan, are forced to stop at a hotel in Timoka, a foreign city in a foreign country, because Ester is gravely ill. The hotel is large, but there are few guests. Among them is a troupe of dwarfs performing at a nearby cabaret. The language of the country is one that not even Ester, who is a translator, understands.

Johan goes exploring in the twilight-gray hotel corridors — the baroque-style hotel was built at the turn of the century. Anna goes out and walks through the warm streets. She makes eye contact with a waiter in a bar. At a variety show she sees a couple in the

◁ *With Jörgen Lindström and Märklin miniature train for* The Silence.

audience making love. The sight arouses her, and she returns to the bar and the waiter.

The bedridden Ester is alone. An old waiter assists her. When Anna returns, Ester senses that something has happened and confronts her sister. Anna leaves to keep her date with the waiter. Johan tells Ester that he has seen his mother enter a room with a stranger. Ester looks for and finds Anna, but her sister turns away from her toward her silent lover.

Ester breaks down. That same day Anna continues on her journey with Johan, leaving Ester to fend for herself. On a piece of paper, Ester has written a few words to Johan in the foreign language.

1963

ALL THESE WOMEN/NOW ABOUT THESE WOMEN (För att inte tala om alla dessa kvinnor)

Production/distribution: Svensk Filmindustri. Director: Ingmar Bergman. Producer: Allan Ekelund. Screenplay: Ingmar Bergman and Erland Josephson. Cinematography: Sven Nykvist (color). Music: Erik Nordgren. Art direction: P. A. Lundgren. Editing: Ulla Ryghe. Premiere: June 15, 1964, at Röda Kvarn. Length: 80 minutes. With Jarl Kulle (Cornelius), Bibi Andersson (Humlan), Harriet Andersson (Isolde), Eva Dahlbeck (Adelaide), Karin Kavli (Madame Tussaud), Gertrud Fridh (Traviata), Mona Malm (Cecilia), Barbro Hiort af Ornäs (Beatrice), Allan Edwall (Jillker), Georg Funkquist (Tristan), Carl Billquist (young man), Jan Blomberg (British radio reporter), Göran Graffman (French radio reporter), Gösta Prüzelius (Swedish radio reporter), Jan-Olof Strandberg (German radio reporter), Ulf Johanson, Axel Düberg, and Lars-Eric Liedholm (men dressed in black), Lars-Owe Carlberg (chauffeur), Doris Funcke and Yvonne Igell (waitresses).

1963/65
DANIEL

An episode in the collective film *Stimulantia*. Production/distribution: Svensk Filmindustri. Director, screenplay, cinematography: Ingmar Bergman. Editing: Ulla Ryghe. Premiere: March 28, 1967, at Spegeln. With Daniel Sebastian Bergman and Käbi Laretei.

1965
PERSONA

Production/distribution: Svensk Filmindustri. Director, screenplay: Ingmar Bergman. Producer: Lars-Owe Carlberg. Cinematography: Sven Nykvist. Music: Lars Johan Werle. Art direction: Bibi Lindström. Editing: Ulla Ryghe. Premiere: October 18, 1966, at Spegeln. Length: 85 minutes. With Bibi Andersson (Alma), Liv Ullmann (Elisabet Vogler), Margaretha Krook (physician), Gunnar Björnstrand (Mr. Vogler), Jörgen Lindström (boy).

After a performance, the actress Elisabet Vogler totally stops communicating with anyone. She is in a hospital. She is not ill but has chosen to enter an existence of complete silence. Together with her nurse, Alma, she goes to stay on an island. The two women confront each other in different situations and grow closer and closer. Their interaction becomes a game of identities. They slide toward — and into — each other.

1966
HOUR OF THE WOLF (Vargtimmen)

Production/distribution: Svensk Filmindustri. Director, screenplay: Ingmar Bergman. Producer: Lars-Owe Carlberg. Cinematography: Sven Nykvist. Music: Lars Johan Werle. Art direction: Marik Vos-Lundh. Editing: Ulla Ryghe. Premiere: February 19, 1968, at Röda Kvarn. Length: 90 minutes. With Liv Ullmann (Alma), Max von Sydow (Johan), Erland Josephson (Baron von Merkens), Gertrud Fridh (Corinne von Merkens), Gudrun Brost (old Mrs. von

Merkens), Bertil Anderberg (Ernst von Merkens), Georg Rydeberg (archivist Lindhorst), Ulf Johanson (curator Heerbrand), Naima Wifstrand (woman with hat), Ingrid Thulin (Veronica Vogler), Lenn Hjortzberg (orchestra conductor Kreisler), Agda Helin (maid), Mikael Rundquist (boy in dream sequence), Mona Seilitz (corpse in morgue), Folke Sundquist (Tamino in *The Magic Flute*).

The artist Johan Borg and his wife, Alma, live on a rocky island. Johan suffers from nightmares, which he depicts on the pages of his sketch pad.

A very old woman comes to visit Alma and urges her to read Johan's diary. Alma reads it and discovers that Johan has met a woman from his past, Veronica Vogler, on the island. Alma also finds out that they have been invited to Baron von Merken's castle. At the castle Alma sees people who look just like the demons Johan has drawn in his sketch pad. During the evening the archivist Lindhorst shows one of the guests at the castle a scene from Mozart's *The Magic Flute* with the marionette theater.

On the way home, Alma tells Johan that she has read his diary. He answers by confessing that he has killed a boy on a cliff ridge, the boy having enticed and provoked him. Johan gets a message that he may meet with Veronica Vogler. He returns to the castle where the demons have gathered to revile him. Veronica is lying dead in a coffin in one of the rooms. He caresses her body and she comes alive. With the demons as scornful witnesses, she offers him her love. Johan runs off, chased by the demons. Alma, whom Johan has wounded with a pistol shot, is looking for Johan. She finds only the satchel in which he keeps his diary.

1967
SHAME/THE SHAME (Skammen)

Production: Svensk Filmindustri, Cinematograph. Distribution: Svensk Filmindustri. Director, screenplay: Ingmar Bergman. Producer: Lars-Owe Carlberg. Cinematography: Sven Nykvist. Art direction: P. A. Lundgren. Editing: Ulla Ryghe. Premiere:

With Liv Ullmann and Max von Sydow in Shame. ▷

420

September 29, 1968, at Spegeln. Length: 103 minutes. With Liv
Ullmann (Eva Rosenberg), Max von Sydow (Jan Rosenberg),
Gunnar Björnstrand (Colonel Jacobi), Birgitta Valberg (Mrs.
Jacobi), Sigge Fürst (Filip), Hans Alfredson (Lobelius), Willy Peters (elderly
officer), Per Berglund (soldier), Vilgot Sjöman (interviewer),
Ingvar Kjellson (Oswald), Rune Lindström (fat man), Frank Sund-
strom (interrogator), Frej Lindqvist (stooping man), Ulf Johanson
(physician), Björn Thambert (Johan), Gösta Prüzelius (vicar), Karl-
Axel Forssberg (secretary), Bengt Eklund (guard), Åke Jornfalk
(man on death row), Jan Bergman (Jacobi's chauffeur), Stig Lindberg (physician's assistant).

Eva and Jan are musicians. They have retired to an island after
disbanding their orchestra. War rages on the mainland.

They go into town to sell berries, and on the way they meet Filip,
a fisherman, and the mayor, Colonel Jacobi. Invading troops have
landed, and a resistance on the island is being organized. Eva and
Jan visit their friend, the antique store owner Lobelius. When they
return home, Eva tells Jan of her desire to have a child. The war
comes closer; bombs are falling. Jan and Eva try to escape but are
taken prisoners. Jan is questioned by the enemy. He is deathly
afraid.

The island's defense drives off the invaders. Suspected collaborators are brought to a school building and interrogated. Colonel
Jacobi frees Jan and Eva. Jacobi seeks Eva's love, then gives her
his life savings. He is arrested as a collaborator with the enemy.
Jan takes possession of Eva's money and refuses to help Colonel
Jacobi. Having been given the order by the fisherman Filip, he
executes the colonel.

Filip's men search in vain for the money Eva received from
Jacobi. Then they burn down Jan and Eva's house. In a greenhouse
the couple encounter a young deserter, intending to escape from
the island. Jan shoots him, and using Jacobi's money, he buys fares
for himself and Eva on a refugee boat. Far out to sea the boat gets
stuck in a wide-reaching cluster of drifting soldiers' corpses.

1967
THE RITUAL/THE RITE (Riten)

Production: Cinematograph. Director, screenplay: Ingmar Bergman. Producer: Lars-Owe Carlberg. Cinematography: Sven Nykvist. Art direction, costumes: Mago (Max Goldstein). Editing: Siv Kanälv. Premiere: March 25, 1969, on TV. Length: 72 minutes. With Ingrid Thulin (Thea Winkelmann), Anders Ek (Sebastian Fischer), Gunnar Björnstrand (Hans Winkelmann), Erik Hell (Judge Ernst Abrahamsson), Ingmar Bergman (clergyman).

Three internationally famous performance artists — Hans Winkelmann, Thea Winkelmann, and Sebastian Fischer — have had one of their stage numbers censored and reported. They are called for an inquiry by the investigatory judge Ernst Abrahamsson. Thea Winkelmann had been married to another member of the company, who was killed during a violent argument with Winkelmann. Thea has since married Hans Winkelmann.

In the examination room the judge first meets with all three of them, then speaks with them one by one. Between these scenes, the artists are together, two at a time — Sebastian and Thea, Thea and Hans, and Hans and Sebastian. In the last scene the three perform the staged ritual for the judge, who suffers a heart attack.

1968
THE PASSION OF ANNA/A PASSION (En passion)

Production: Svensk Filmindustri, Cinematograph. Distribution: Svensk Filmindustri. Director, screenplay: Ingmar Bergman. Producer: Lars-Owe Carlberg. Cinematography: Sven Nykvist (color). Art direction: P. A. Lundgren. Editing: Siv Kanalv. Premiere: November 10, 1969, at Spegeln. Length: 101 minutes. With Max von Sydow (Andreas Winkelman), Liv Ullmann (Anna Fromm), Bibi Andersson (Eva Vergérus), Erland Josephson (Elis Vergérus), Erik Hell (Johan Andersson), Sigge Fürst (Verner), Svea Holst (his wife), Annika Kronberg (Katarina), Hjördis Petterson (Johan's sister), Lars-Owe Carlberg and Brian Wikström (policemen), Barbro Hiort af Ornäs, Malin Ek, Britta Brunius, Brita Öberg, and Marianne Karlbeck (women in dream sequence).

Andreas Winkelman is repairing the roof of his house. He lives alone on an island. Three mock suns can be seen in the sky.

Andreas meets Johan, a poor recluse. Anna Fromm, another islander, comes to use Andreas's telephone. Anna forgets her purse at his house. He reads a letter that reveals that Anna's husband wants to leave her. Anna Fromm is living at the house of Elis Vergérus, a successful architect, and his wife, Eva. During a dinner party, Andreas gets to know them. Elis's hobby is to collect photographs of people. Elis says that Eva was the mistress of Anna's husband. Anna tries to convince everyone of her perfect marriage. When Elis is away on business, Eva comes to Andreas and stays with him all night. Andreas finds out that Anna's husband and son have been killed in a traffic accident when Anna was driving.

A farmer on the island finds a number of his sheep fatally wounded. Suspicion falls on Johan, the recluse. Elis helps Andreas with his business and discovers why he has turned his back on society.

Anna and Andreas begin to live together. Anna tells him about her marriage and the accident. She tries to get Andreas to admit to his relationship with Eva. The police find Johan. He has hanged himself.

Violence breaks out in Andreas and Anna's relationship. A fire engine drives past. Somebody has set fire to a cattle shed. Anna picks up Andreas by the fire. In the car he asks her to give him back his solitude. Their relationship has been based on lies. Andreas gets out of the car. He doesn't know which direction to take and collapses on the road.

1969
THE FÅRÖ DOCUMENT 1969
(Fårödokument 1969)

Production: Cinematograph. Director: Ingmar Bergman. Producer: Lars-Owe Carlberg. Cinematography: Sven Nykvist. Editing: Siv Lundgren-Kanälv. Premiere: January 1, 1970, on TV. Length: 78 minutes. With Ingmar Bergman as the reporter, and actual inhabitants of Fårö.

1969/70
THE RESERVATION (Reservatet)

Director: Jan Molander. Screenplay: Ingmar Bergman. Producers: Bernt Callenbo and Hans Sackemark. Editing: Inger Burman (color). Art direction: Bo Lindgren and Henny Noremark. Premiere: October 28, 1970, on TV. Length: 95 minutes. With Gunnel Lindblom (Anna), Per Myrberg (Andreas), Erland Josephson (Elis), Georg Funkquist (the father), Toivo Pawlo (Albert), Elna Gistedt (Berta), Erik Hell (director general), Göran Graffman (Bauer), Börje Ahlstedt (Feldt), Sif Ruud (Miss Prakt), Barbro Larsson (Karin), Helena Brodin (Nurse Ester), Olof Bergström (Dr. Farman), Gun Arvidsson (Magda Farman), Catherine Berg (Elis's wife), Claes Thelander (Fredrik Sernelius), Irma Christenson (Inger Sernelius), Leif Liljeroth (Sten Ahlman), Gun Andersson (Petra Ahlman), Per Sjöstrand (Count Albrekt), Margaretha Byström (Karin Albrekt).

1970
THE TOUCH (Beröringen)

Production: Cinematograph, ABC Pictures (New York). Distribution: Svensk Filmindustri. Director, screenplay: Ingmar Bergman. Producer: Lars-Owe Carlberg. Cinematography: Sven Nykvist (color). Music: Carl Michael Bellman, William Byrd, Peter Covent. Art direction: P. A. Lundgren. Editing: Siv Lundgren. Premiere: August 30, 1971, at Spegeln. Length: 115 minutes. With Elliott Gould

(David Kovac), Bibi Andersson (Karin Vergérus), Max von Sydow (Andreas Vergérus), Sheila Reid (Sara, David's sister), Barbro Hiort af Ornäs (Karin's mother), Åke Lindström (Dr. Holm), Mimmo Wåhlander (nurse), Elsa Ebbesen (head of hospital kitchen), Staffan Hallerstam (Anders Vergérus), Maria Nolgård (Agnes Vergérus), Karin Nilsson (Vergérus's neighbor), Erik Nyhlén (archaeologist), Margaretha Byström (Andreas Vergérus's secretary), Alan Simon (curator at museum), Per Sjöstrand (curator), Aino Taube (woman on staircase), Ann-Christin Lobråten (museum worker), Carol Zavis (flight attendant), Dennis Gotobed (British civil servant), Bengt Ottekil (bellhop).

1971
CRIES AND WHISPERS (Viskningar och rop)

Production: Cinematograph, the Film Institute, Liv Ullmann, Ingrid Thulin, Harriet Andersson, Sven Nykvist. Distribution: Svensk Filmindustri. Director, screenplay: Ingmar Bergman. Producer: Lars-Owe Carlberg. Cinematography: Sven Nykvist (color). Art direction: Marika Vos. Editing: Siv Lundgren. Premiere: March 5, 1973, at Spegeln. Length: 91 minutes. With Harriet Andersson (Agnes), Kari Sylwan (Anna), Ingrid Thulin (Karin), Liv Ullmann (Maria/Maria's mother), Anders Ek (Pastor Isak), Inga Gill (the storyteller), Erland Josephson (David, a physician), Henning Moritzen (Joakim, a cabinet member and Maria's husband), Georg Årlin (Fredrik, a diplomat and Karin's husband), Linn Ullmann (Maria's daughter), Greta and Karin Johansson (mortician's helpers), Rosanna Mariano (young Agnes), Malin Gjörup (Anna's daughter), Lena Bergman (young Maria), Ingrid von Rosen, Ann-Christin Lobråten, Börje Lundh, and Lars-Owe Carlberg (audience members at picture exhibit), Monika Priede (young Karin).

With the ringing of bells and red colors, with cries and whispers, the day dawns in a residential park. By Agnes's sickbed, her sister Maria has kept vigil all night. Agnes awakens. She writes in her diary. Anna, the servant, serves coffee. The third sister, Karin,

◁ *Thinking about color with Sven Nykvist during the filming of* Cries and Whispers.

enters the room. The physician, David, makes a house call. He tells Karin that the end is near. When David is ready to go, Maria calls for him. They fall into each other's arms.

Flashback: Anna's daughter has taken ill, and Maria has called the doctor. After his examination of the child, Maria invites David to stay for a meal. Her husband, Joakim, is staying in town, and Agnes and Karin are in Italy. The guest room is readied for David; Maria comes to him. In the morning she tells her husband that she called the doctor. When she later knocks on the door to his office, she finds him with a knife in his chest. He begs her to help him.

In the present, it is now evening. Agnes calls for Anna, who comes to her bed and crawls in with her. Agnes is in pain. Anna consoles her. During the night Anna awakens the sisters. Agnes has taken a turn for the worse. The sisters wash her and change her nightgown. She falls asleep while Maria reads to her from *The Pickwick Papers*. Agnes's death struggle ensues. Anna stays close to her. In the adjacent room her sisters Karin and Maria wait. A priest comes to pray for Agnes's soul.

Flashback: Karin and her husband, Fredrik, are staying temporarily at the manor (where they are now). They sit at the dinner table, silent. Karin breaks a wine glass. Karin gets ready for bed. Alone, she wounds herself by putting a sliver of glass — to damage and be damaged — inside her vagina. She walks into the bedroom to her husband.

In the present, Maria is caressing her sister Karin's cheek. Reluctantly Karin lets her do it. Then she accuses Maria of being false.

In the dark house Anna hears screams. She goes in to Agnes, who says, "I'm dead but I can't leave you." In icy terror, her two sisters reject her. Anna stays with the crying Agnes.

After the funeral Karin and Maria get ready to leave. Anna remains, now alone in the house. She reads in Agnes's diary about her gratefulness toward life.

1972
SCENES FROM A MARRIAGE
(Scener ur ett äktenskap)

Production: Cinematograph. Director, screenplay: Ingmar Bergman. Producer: Lars-Owe Carlberg. Cinematography: Sven Nykvist (color). Art direction: Björn Thulin. Editing: Siv Lundgren. Part l: "Innocence and Panic" — premiere April 11, 1973, on TV. Part 2: "The Art of Sweeping Things under the Carpet" — premiere April 18, 1973, on TV. Part 3: "Paula" — premiere April 25, 1973, on TV. Part 4: "The Valley of Tears" — premiere May 2, 1973, on TV. Part 5: "The Illiterates" — premiere May 9, 1973, on TV. Part 6: "In the Middle of the Night in a Dark House Somewhere in the World" — premiere May 16, 1973, on TV. Length: Around 49 minutes per episode. A theatrical version was created for the United States and other parts of the world in 1974; length, 155 minutes. With Liv Ullmann (Marianne), Erland Josephson (Johan), Bibi Andersson (Katarina), Jan Malmsjö (Peter), Anita Wall (Mrs. Palm), Rosanna Mariano and Lena Bergman (the children Eva and Karin), Gunnel Lindblom (Eva), Barbro Hiort af Ornäs (Mrs. Jacobi), Wenche Foss (mother), Bertil Norström (Arne).

1974
THE MAGIC FLUTE (Tröllflojten)

Director, screenplay: Ingmar Bergman, based on Wolfgang Amadeus Mozart's opera *Die Zauberflöte* with a libretto by Emanuel Schikaneder. Producer: Måns Reuterswärd. Cinematography: Sven Nykvist (color). Music: The Radio Choir, Swedish Radio's Symphony Orchestra, and conductor Eric Ericson. Art direction: Henny Noremark. Editing: Siv Lundgren. Premiere: January 1, 1975, on TV; shown at Röda Kvarn movie theater October 4, 1975. Length: 135 minutes. With Josef Köstlinger (Tamino), Irma Urrila (Pamina), Håkan Hagegård (Papageno), Elisabeth Erikson (Papagena), Britt-Marie Aruhn (first woman), Kirsten Vaupel (second woman), Birgitta Smiding (third woman), Ulrik Cold (Sarastro), Birgit

Nordin (queen of the night), Ragnar Ulfung (Monostatos), Erik Saedén (speaker), Gösta Prüzelius (first priest), Ulf Johanson (second priest), Hans Johansson and Jerker Arvidson (guards in the House of Trials), Urban Malmberg, Ansgar Krook, and Erland von Heijne (boys), Lisbeth Zachrisson, Nina Harte, Helena Högberg, Elina Lehto, Lena Wennergren, Jane Darling, and Sonja Karlsson (maidens), Einar Larsson, Siegfried Svensson, Sixten Fark, Sven-Eric Jacobsson, Folke Johnsson, Gösta Bäckelin, Arne Hendriksen, Hans Kyhle, and Carl Henric Qvarfordt (priests).

1975
FACE TO FACE (Ansikte mot ansikte)
Production: Cinematograph. Director, screenplay: Ingmar Bergman. Producer: Lars-Owe Carlberg. Cinematography: Sven Nykvist (color). Music: Wolfgang Amadeus Mozart. Art direction: Anne Hagegård, Peter Kropénin. Editing: Siv Lundgren. Part 1: "The Departure" — premiere April 28, 1976, on TV. Part 2: "The Border" — premiere May 5, 1976, on TV. Part 3: "The Twilight Land" — premiere May 12, 1976, on TV. Part 4: "The Return" — premiere May 19, 1976, on TV. Length: 50 minutes per episode. A theatrical version was created for the United States and other parts of the world; length, 135 minutes. With Liv Ullmann (Dr. Jenny Isaksson), Erland Josephson (Dr. Tomas Jacobi), Aino Taube (grandmother), Gunnar Björnstrand (grandfather), Sif Ruud (Elisabeth Wankel), Sven Lindberg (Erik, Jenny's husband), Tore Segelcke (woman), Kari Sylwan (Maria), Ulf Johanson (Helmuth Wankel), Gösta Ekman (Mikael Stromberg), Kristina Adolphson (nurse Veronica), Marianne Aminoff (Jenny's mother), Gösta Prüzelius (Jenny's father), Birger Malmsten and Göran Stangertz (rapists), Rebecca Pawlo and Lena Olin (saleswomen).

Jenny is a psychologist, married to a gifted colleague, and the mother of a teenage daughter. Her husband is at a convention in Chicago and her daughter at horseback-riding camp. Jenny herself

◁ *With Tamino (Josef Köstlinger) in* The Magic Flute.

is going to stay with her grandparents in their old apartment and looks forward to a calm, peaceful work period.

The first night at her grandparents' she is awakened by a stranger, a woman, who takes shape in the room and tries to tell her something.

The following day Jenny speaks to a colleague, Dr. Wankel, about Maria, a case at the psychiatric clinic. Jenny has a violent confrontation with Maria. She then goes to a party given by Dr. Wankel's wife. There she meets Dr. Tomas Jacobi, a relative of her patient Maria. They have dinner together and then go to Tomas's house. In the morning she is awakened by a phone call and is asked to return to her empty house.

There she finds Maria and two men. One of these men tries to rape Jenny. Thoroughly shaken, she calls Tomas Jacobi. They meet for a concert the same night and return to his house. Jenny takes a sleeping pill, and when they go to bed, Jenny tells Tomas about the attempted rape. She begins to laugh. The laughter transforms itself into convulsive sobs. Tomas drives her to her grandparents' apartment.

When her grandmother awakens her, she finds she has slept more than twenty-four hours. It is Saturday morning, and her old grandparents are going to stay with friends for the weekend. Jenny falls asleep again and is awakened Sunday morning by the church bells ringing. She calls Tomas, and when she hangs up, the strange woman appears in her room again. Frightened, Jenny dictates a letter to her husband on a tape recorder. Then she swallows all her sleeping pills.

Jenny is reborn forty-three hours later in a tempest of cramps and screams in an intensive care ward. When she dozes off again, she moves around in her dreams. She awakens, finding Tomas by her side. She dreams about her dead parents. When she awakens the next time, her husband, Erik, is with her. He has come directly from the airport. They talk, exhausted by the emotional upheaval and sorrow. Jenny sinks back into her dreams.

Jenny tells Tomas about her childhood. She loses consciousness

again and enters new dreams. She attends her own funeral. Tomas
says good-bye. Jenny is visited by her daughter, Anna. She tells
her daughter that she has tried to take her own life. They speak
to each other but lack real communication.

The same day Jenny returns to her grandparents' apartment.
She watches the intimacy between these two old people in their
slow movement toward death. During a walk she encounters the
woman again. This time she helps her cross the street.

1976
THE SERPENT'S EGG
(Ormens ägg; Das Schlangenei)

Production: Rialto Film (Berlin), Dino De Laurentiis Corp. (Los
Angeles). Distribution: Fox-Stockholm. Director, screenplay:
Ingmar Bergman. Producer: Dino De Laurentiis. Cinematography:
Sven Nykvist (color). Music: Rolf Wilhelm. Art direction: Rolf
Zehetbauer. Editing: Petra von Oelffen. Premiere: October 28, 1977,
at Röda Kvarn. Length: 119 minutes. With Liv Ullmann (Manuela
Rosenberg), David Carradine (Abel Rosenberg), Gert Fröbe (police
commissioner Bauer), Heinz Bennent (Hans Vergérus), James
Whitmore (priest), Glynn Turman (Monroe), Georg Hartmann
(Hollinger), Edith Heerdegen (Mrs. Holle), Kyra Mladeck (Miss
Dorst), Fritz Strassner (Dr. Soltermann), Hans Quest (Dr.
Silbermann), Wolfgang Weiser (civil servant), Paula Braend (Mrs.
Hemse), Walter Schmidinger (Solomon), Lisi Mangold (Mikaela),
Grischa Huber (Stella), Paul Bürks (cabaret comedian), Isolde
Barth, Rosemarie Heinikel, Andrea L'Arronge, and Beverly
McNeely (girls in uniform), Toni Berger (Mr. Rosenberg), Erna
Brunell (Mrs. Rosenberg), Hans Eichler (Max), Harry Kalenberg
(court physician), Gaby Dohm (woman with baby), Christian Berkel
(student), Paul Burian (guinea pig), Charles Regnier (physician),
Günter Meisner (prisoner), Heide Picha (wife), Günter Malzacher
(husband), Hubert Mittendorf (consoler), Hertha von Walther
(woman in street), Ellen Umlauf (hostess), Renate Grosser and

Hildegard Busse (prostitutes), Richard Bohne (policeman), Emil
Feist ("the greedy one"), Heino Hallhuber ("the bride"), Irene
Steinbeiser ("the groom").

Berlin, November 1923. Abel Rosenberg arrives at a pension in
the evening and discovers that his brother, Max, has shot himself.
Abel, Max, and Max's wife, Manuela, have been performing as a
trapeze trio in the circus.

The following day Abel is interrogated about Max's suicide by
police commissioner Bauer. In the evening Abel goes to the cabaret
where Manuela performs and tells her what has happened to Max.
He meets Hans Vergérus, a scientist whom he knew when they
both were young. Abel takes Manuela home. Manuela insists that
she has an office job, but Abel discovers that her workplace is a
bordello. Bauer brings Abel to the morgue to identify a woman.
Abel becomes extremely upset but is let go when Manuela arrives.
Abel and Manuela spend their first night together in an apartment
that Vergérus has found for them.

They begin working at a clinic that is run by Vergérus, Abel in
the archives, Manuela in the laundry. The files in the archives
contain reports of Vergérus's experiments with human beings. Abel
finds Manuela dead in their bed. In rage and sorrow he crushes a
mirror and discovers a hidden camera behind it. When Bauer arrives
with his men, Vergérus takes his life by swallowing poison.

Abel awakens in prison. Bauer offers him safe passage to Switzerland
and the circus he worked for earlier. On his way to the
railway station, Abel escapes the guards. He is swallowed up by the
crowds of people.

1977

AUTUMN SONATA (Höstsonaten; Herbstsonate)

Production: Personafilm (Munich). Distribution: Svensk Filmindustri.
Director, screenplay: Ingmar Bergman. Producer: Katinka
Faragó. Cinematography: Sven Nykvist (color). Art direction: Anna
Asp. Editing: Sylvia Ingemarsson. Premiere: October 8, 1978, at

Spegeln. Length: 93 minutes. With Ingrid Bergman (Charlotte), Liv Ullmann (Eva), Lena Nyman (Helena), Halvar Björk (Viktor), Marianne Aminoff (Charlotte's secretary), Erland Josephson (Josef), Arne Bang-Hansen (Uncle Otto), Gunnar Björnstrand (Paul), Georg Løkeberg (Leonardo), Mimi Pollak (piano teacher), Linn Ullmann (young Eva).

Charlotte is an internationally renowned pianist. She has two daughters: Eva and Helena. Helena has been severely handicapped for many years. Eva, the older of the two daughters, has lost her only child in a drowning accident. She is married to Viktor, the pastor at a small country church.

Charlotte is experiencing great sorrow because her friend Leonardo, also a musician, has died after a long illness. Eva, who has not seen her mother in almost seven years, writes to her when she hears about Leonardo's death and asks her to come for a visit at the parsonage.

Charlotte arrives. She immediately becomes very upset upon discovering that Helena, whom she believed to be in an institution, is in fact being cared for by Viktor and Eva. She overcomes this deep shock only with difficulty. During their polite talk, Charlotte and Eva feel memories and humiliations reawaken. The dam bursts during a late night conversation between mother and daughter. When things calm down, Charlotte hastily leaves her two daughters to return to her music and her solitude. In the parsonage Eva and Viktor continue to nurse their quiet marriage.

1977/79
THE FÅRÖ DOCUMENT 1979
(Fårödokument 1979)

Production: Cinematograph, Swedish Radio-TV Channel 2 1977/79. Director: Ingmar Bergman. Producer: Lars-Owe Carlberg. Cinematography: Arne Carlsson (color). Music: Svante Pettersson, Sigvard Huldt, Dag and Lena, Ingmar Nordströms, Strix Q, Rock de Luxe, Ola and the Janglers. Editing: Sylvia Ingemarsson. Premiere: December 24, 1979, on TV. Length: 103 minutes. With the inhabitants of Fårö Island.

1979/80

FROM THE LIFE OF THE MARIONETTES (Ur Marionetternas liv; Aus dem Leben der Marionetten)

Production: Personafilm (Munich). Distribution: Sandrews. Director, screenplay: Ingmar Bergman. Producers: Horst Wendlandt and Ingmar Bergman. Cinematography: Sven Nykvist (black and white/color). Music: Rolf Wilhelm. Art direction: Rolf Zehetbauer. Editing: Petra von Oelffen. Premiere: January 24, 1981, at Grand. Length: 104 minutes. With Robert Aztorn (Peter Egerman), Christine Buchegger (Katarina Egerman), Martin Benrath (Mogens Jensen), Rita Russek (Ka), Lola Muethel (Cordelia Egerman), Walter Schmidinger (Tim), Heinz Bennent (Arthur Brenner), Ruth Olafs (nurse), Karl Heinz Pelser (interrogator), Gaby Dohm (secretary), Toni Berger (guard).

Peter and Katarina Egerman seem to be a well-adjusted married couple; he is a businessman, she a fashion executive. But on a deeper level they do not communicate. For a couple of years now, Peter has had a recurring dream of killing his wife.

He tells his psychiatrist, Mogens, about this obsession. Mogens, who has a sexual relationship with Katarina, does nothing. Peter makes a halfhearted suicide attempt. He goes to a porno club where a prostitute ignites his desire to kill. In a moment of psychological short-circuiting, Peter chooses a substitute victim.

In brief interviews after the catastrophe, those who knew Peter offer their explanations for what happened. Peter now lives in a clinic where he has imprisoned himself in silence.

1981/82

FANNY AND ALEXANDER (Fanny och Alexander)

Production: Cinematograph for the Film Institute, Swedish TV Channel 1, Gaumont (Paris), Personafilm (Munich), Tobis

With the children in Fanny and Alexander. ▷

Filmkunst (Berlin). Distribution: Sandrews. Director, screenplay: Ingmar Bergman. Producer: Jörn Donner. Cinematography: Sven Nykvist (color). Art direction: Anna Asp. Editing: Sylvia Ingemarsson. Premieres: December 17, 1982, at Astoria, length, 197 minutes; and December 17, 1983, at Grand 2, length, 312 minutes. With Pernilla Allwin (Fanny Ekdahl), Bertil Guve (Alexander), Börje Ahlstedt (Carl Ekdahl), Harriet Andersson (Justina, the kitchen maid), Pernilla Östergren (Maj, the nanny), Mats Bergman (Aron), Gunnar Björnstrand (Filip Landahl), Allan Edwall (Oscar Ekdahl), Stina Ekblad (Ismael), Ewa Fröling (Emilie Ekdahl), Erland Josephson (Isak Jacobi), Jarl Kulle (Gustav Adolf Ekdahl), Käbi Laretei (Aunt Anna), Mona Malm (Alma Ekdahl), Jan Malmsjö (Bishop Edvard Vergérus), Christina Schollin (Lydia Ekdahl), Gunn Wållgren (Helena Ekdahl), Kerstin Tidelius (Henrietta Vergérus), Anna Bergman (Hanna Schwartz), Sonya Hedenbratt (Aunt Emma), Svea Holst-Widén (Ester), Majlis Granlund (Vega), Maria Granlund (Petra), Emilie Werkö (Jenny), Christian Almgren (Putte), Angelica Wallgren (Eva), Siv Ericks (Alida), Inga Alenius (Lisen), Kristina Adolphson (Siri), Eva von Hanno (Berta).

It is Christmas in the home of the Ekdahl family. The year is 1907 in a Swedish city with a cathedral and a university.

The head of the family is Helena Ekdahl. She was once an actress at the theater still run by the family. Her son Oscar is now head of the theater; his brother Gustav Adolf owns a restaurant, and his brother Carl is a professor with debts. Fanny and Alexander are the children of Oscar and Emilie Ekdahl. Oscar takes ill while rehearsing his part as the ghost in *Hamlet*. He dies surrounded by his family. The city's bishop, Edvard Vergérus, officiates at the funeral and consoles the young widow, Emilie. This association eventually leads to marriage. In the bishop's home, life is ascetic to the extreme.

Alexander hates his stepfather and revolts. The bishop responds with his idea of love and authority: strict discipline and harsh punishment. When the rest of the Ekdahl family becomes aware of the suffering of Emilie and her children, they seek the assistance of the Jewish antique dealer Isak Jacobi in order to rescue the children from Vergérus's clutches. Vergérus's response consists of retaliations against his wife, who is pregnant. In Jacobi's antique store Alexander meets Ismael, who is kept locked up. Together they wish for the death of the bishop. He dies in flames.

Again Christmas is celebrated in the home of the Ekdahl family. Emilie has returned. She has had her baby. Another infant is christened along with hers. The father to that baby is Gustav Adolf; the mother is the young nanny, Maj. In the quiet after the celebration party, Emilie awakens Helena Ekdahl's theater ambitions with a newly published copy of Strindberg's *A Dream Play*.

1983
AFTER THE REHEARSAL (Efter repetitionen)

Production: Personafilm (Munich). Director, screenplay: Ingmar Bergman. Producer: Jörn Donner. Cinematography: Sven Nykvist (color). Art direction: Anna Asp. Editing: Sylvia Ingemarsson. Premiere: April 9, 1984, on TV. Length: 70 minutes. With Erland Josephson (Henrik Vogler), Lena Olin (Anna), Ingrid Thulin (Rakel).

1985
THE BLESSED ONES (De två saliga)

Director: Ingmar Bergman. Screenplay: Ulla Isaksson, based on her novel. Producers: Pia Ehrnvall and Katinka Faragó. Cinematography: Per Norén (color). Art direction: Birgitta Bensén. Premiere: February 19, 1986, on TV. Length: 81 minutes. With Harriet Andersson (Viveka Burman), Per Myrberg (Sune Burman), Christina Schollin (Annika), Lasse Pöysti (Dr. Dettow), Irma Christenson (Mrs. Storm), Björn Gustafson (neighbor), Majlis Granlund (cleaning woman at school), Kristina Adolphson (nurse in psychiatric ward), Margreth Weivers, Bertil Norström, Johan Rabaeus, Lennart Tollén, and Lars-Owe Carlberg.

1986
DOCUMENTARY OF FANNY AND ALEXANDER
(Dokument Fanny och Alexander)
Production: Cinematograph, the Film Institute. Director, screenplay: Ingmar Bergman. Cinematography: Arne Carlsson (color). Editing: Sylvia Ingemarsson. Premiere: August 18, 1986, on TV. Length: 110 minutes.

1986
KARIN'S FACE (Karins ansikte)
Production: Cinematograph. Director, screenplay: Ingmar Bergman. Music: Käbi Laretei. Premiere: September 29, 1986, on TV. Length: 14 minutes.

1991
THE BEST INTENTIONS (Den goda viljan)
Production: Swedish TV Channel 1 Drama in association with ZDF, Channel 4, Raidus, La Sept, DR, YLE 2, NRK, RUV. Distribution: Svensk Filmindustri. Director: Bille August. Screenplay: Ingmar Bergman. Producer: Ingrid Dahlberg. Cinematography: Sven Nykvist (color). Music: Stefan Nilsson. Art direction: Anna Asp. Editing: Janus Billeskov Jansen. Premiere: June 4, 1992, at Riviera. Length: 181 minutes. With Samuel Fröler (Henrik Bergman), Pernilla August (Anna Bergman), Max von Sydow (Johan Åkerblom), Ghita Nørby (Karin Åkerblom), Lennart Hjulström (executive Nordenson), Mona Malm (Alma Bergman), Lena Endre (Frida Strandberg), Keve Hjelm (Fredrik Bergman), Björn Kjellman (Ernst Åkerblom), Börje Ahlstedt (Carl Åkerblom), Hans Alfredson (pastor Gransjö), Lena T. Hansson (Magda Säll), Anita Björk (Queen Victoria), Elias Ringquist (Petrus Farg), Ernst Günther (Freddy Paulin), Marie Göranzon (Elin Nordenson), Bjorn Granath (Oscar Åkerblom), Gunilla Nyroos (Svea Åkerblom), Michael Segerström (Gustav Åkerblom).

Earlier shown on TV as a miniseries in four chapters: December 25, 1991, December 26, 1991, December 29, 1991, and December 30, 1991. Total length: approximately 340 minutes.

1991/1992
SUNDAY'S CHILDREN (Söndagsbarn)

Production: Sandrew Film & Theater in association with the Film Institute, Sweetland Films, Swedish TV Channel 1 Drama, Metronome Productions, Finland's Filmstiftelse, Iceland's Film Fund, Norsk Film with support of Nordisk Film & TV Fund, Eurimages/Europarådet. Distribution: Sandrews. Director: Daniel Bergman. Screenplay: Ingmar Bergman. Producer: Katinka Faragò. Cinematography: Tony Fosberg. Music: Johann Sebastian Bach, Rune Gustafsson, Zoltán Kodály. Art direction: Sven Wichmann. Editing: Darek Hodor. Premiere: August 28, 1992, at Olympa and Biopalatset 3. Length: 121 minutes. With Thommy Berggren (father), Henrik Linnros (Pu), Lena Endre (mother), Jakob Leygraf (Dag), Anna Linnros (Lillian), Malin Ek (Märta), Marie Richardson (Marianne), Irma Christenson (Aunt Emma), Birgitta Valberg (Grandma), Börje Ahlstedt (Uncle Carl), Maria Bolme (Maj), Majlis Granlund/Birgitta Ulfsson (Lalla), Carl Magnus Dellow (jeweler), Melinda Kinnaman (woman), Per Myrberg (Ingmar), Helena Brodin (nurse Edit), Halvar Björk (Ericsson), Gunnel Gustafsson (Mrs. Berglund), Kurt Sävström (church elder), Lis Nilheim (pastor's wife), Hans Strömblad (Konrad), Bertil Norström (pastor), Suzanne Ernrup (Helga Smed), Lars Rockström (Smed, the smith), Josefin Andersson (young woman).

*

In 1951 Ingmar Bergman wrote and directed nine commercials for AB Sunlight for the soap Bris (Sweden's first deodorant soap). Bibi Andersson appeared in one of these.

*

Ingmar Bergman directed a number of theatrical productions for television: Hjalmar Bergman's *Sleeman's Coming* (1957), *The Venetian* (1958), Olle Hedberg's *Rabies* (1958), August Strindberg's *Storm Weather* (1960) and *A Dream Play* (1963), as well as Molière's *School for Wives* (1983).

Images was originally planned in an interview format with Lasse Bergström. The project was conceived in the summer of 1987, during the final editing of Bergman's book, *The Magic Lantern*. Conversations with Ingmar Bergman commenced on Fårö Island on September 28, 1988, and concluded in Stockholm on February 1, 1990. The basis for the book was the edited transcript, approximately sixty hours of conversation, from which the interviewer had deleted his questions. The text was then revised by Bergman and finally finished on June 11, 1990. Lars Åhlander selected the accompanying photographs. The filmography was compiled by Bertil Wredlund. For those films examined in detail in the book, the data were supplemented with brief descriptions of the plots, provided from material available in *Swedish Filmography*.

◁ *Lasse Bergström and Ingmar Bergman, Fårö, May 1990.*

Photo Credits

Per B. Adolphson, Thomas Bergman, Inga Lill Bergström, John Bryson, Arne Carlsson, Cinematograph, Bo-Erik Gyberg, Harry Kampf, K. G. Kristoffersson, Lars Looschen, Vicke Malmström, Pressens Bild, Sandrew Film & Theater, Anders Svahn, Svensk Filmindustri, Swedish Film Institute, Swedish National Museum, Swedish Photo Service, Swedish Radio, Bo A. Vibenius, Max Wilén, Christian Wirsén.